Clinical Approaches to
Working with Young Offenders

Wiley Series in

Clinical Approaches to Criminal Behaviour

Clinical Approaches to Violence
Edited by Kevin Howells *and* Clive R. Hollin

Clinical Approaches to Sex Offenders and Their Victims
Edited by Clive R. Hollin *and* Kevin Howells

Clinical Approaches to the Mentally Disordered Offender
Edited by Kevin Howells *and* Clive R. Hollin

Clinical Approaches to Working with Young Offenders
Edited by Clive R. Hollin *and* Kevin Howells

Clinical Approaches to Working with Young Offenders

Edited by

CLIVE R. HOLLIN
School of Psychology
University of Birmingham
and
Glenthorne Youth Treatment Centre
Birmingham, UK

and

KEVIN HOWELLS
Psychology Department
Edith Cowan University
Perth, Australia

JOHN WILEY & SONS
Chichester · New York · Brisbane · Toronto · Singapore

Other Wiley Editorial Offices

John Wiley & Sons, Inc., 605 Third Avenue,
New York, NY 10158–0012, USA

Jacaranda Wiley Ltd, 33 Park Road, Milton,
Queensland 4064, Australia

John Wiley & Sons (Canada) Ltd, 22 Worcester Road,
Rexdale, Ontario M9W 1L1, Canada

John Wiley & Sons (Asia) Pte Ltd, 2 Clementi Loop #02-01,
Jin Xing Distripark, Singapore 0512

Library of Congress Cataloging-in-Publication Data
Clinical approaches to working with young offenders/edited by Clive
  R. Hollin and Kevin Howells.
      p. cm.— (Wiley series in clinical approaches to criminal
  behaviour)
    Includes bibliographical references and index.
    ISBN 0-471-95348-2
    1. Juvenile delinquents—Mental health. 2. Juvenile delinquents–
  Mental health services. I. Hollin, Clive R. II. Howells, Kevin.
  III. Series.
  RJ506.J88C555   1995
  364.3′6—dc20   95-24739
                                                               CIP

British Library Cataloguing in Publication Data

A catalogue record for this book is available from the British Library

ISBN 0-471-95348-2

Typeset in 10/12pt Times by Mathematical Composition Setters Ltd
Printed and bound in Great Britain by Bookcraft (Bath) Ltd
This book is printed on acid-free paper responsibly manufactured from sustainable forestation,
for which at least two trees are planted for each one used for paper production.

Contents

List of Contributors

DON ANDREWS, Department of Psychology, Carleton University, Ottawa, Canada K15 5B6.

JUDITH V. BECKER, Department of Psychology, University of Arizona, Tucson, Arizona 85721, USA.

WILLIAM S. DAVIDSON II, Department of Psychology, Michigan State University, East Lansin, Michigan 48824, USA.

KEVIN EPPS, Youth Treatment Service, Glenthorne Centre, Kingsbury Road, Erdington, Birmingham B24 9SA, UK.

DAVID FARRINGTON, Institute of Criminology, University of Cambridge, 7 West Road, Cambridge CB3 9DT, UK.

JOHN C. GIBBS, Department of Psychology, Ohio State University, 142 Townshend Mall, 1885 Neil Avenue Mall, Columbus, Ohio 43210–1222, USA.

BARRY GLICK, New York State Division for Youth, New York, USA.

ARNOLD P. GOLDSTEIN, School of Education, Syracuse University, 805 S. Crouse Avenue, Syracuse, New York 13244–2280, USA.

CLIVE R. HOLLIN, School of Psychology, University of Birmingham, Edgbaston, Birmingham B15 2TT, UK & Youth Treatment Service, Birmingham, UK.

KEVIN HOWELLS, Department of Psychology, Edith Cowan University, Joondalup Campus, Joondalup, Western Australia 6027, Australia.

JOHN A. HUNTER, Department of Psychology, University of Arizona, Tucson, Arizona 85721, USA.

BRADLEY R. JOHNSON, Department of Psychology, University of Arizona, Tucson, Arizona 85721, USA.

RAYMOND E. LEGLER, Department of Psychology, Michigan State University, East Lansing, Michigan 48824, USA.

FRIEDRICH LÖSEL, Institut für Psychologie I der Universität Erlangen-Nürnberg, Bismarkstrasse 1, D-91054 Erlangen, Germany.

MARY MCMURRAN, Psychology Department, Arnold Lodge, Cordelia Close, Leicester LE5 0LE. UK.

MICHAEL A. MILAN, Department of Psychology, Georgia State University, Atlanta, Georgia 30303–3083, USA.

BARBARA A. SCHILLO, Department of Psychology, Michigan State University, East Lansing, Michigan 48824, USA.

LORETTA A. SERNA, College of Education, University of New Mexico, Albuquerque, New Mexico 87121–1261, USA.

JAN B. SHELDON, University of Kansas, Kansas, USA.

JAMES A. SHERMAN, University of Kansas, Kansas, USA.

TIMOTHY W. SPETH, Department of Psychology, Michigan State University, East Lansing, Michigan 48824, USA.

About the Editors

Clive R. Hollin is Senior Lecturer in Psychology at the University of Birmingham and Director of Rehabilitation in the Youth Treatment Service. However, he will presently move to the split post of Consultant Forensic Psychologist at Rampton Hospital and Senior Lecturer in Psychology at the University of Leicester.

Kevin Howells is Associate Professor of Psychology at Edith Cowan University, Perth, Australia.

Series Preface

This series around the theme of *Clinical Approaches to Criminal Behaviour* has its origin in a sequence of conferences we organized between 1984 and 1988. Our intention, both then and now, was to make some progress towards re-establishing an approach to changing criminal behaviour which has become unfashionable, unpopular and much maligned in recent years. It should be made absolutely clear that in the present context the term 'clinical' is not intended to imply a medical model, in which criminal behaviour is viewed as pathological, but to define an approach in which the focus is on the individual and on psychological methods of producing change. Having said that, we are not blind to the crucial importance of economic, political and social factors in crime and criminological theory. We agree that change is necessary at all levels to reduce crime, and have no wish to be seen as placing the spotlight of blame and responsibility exclusively on the offender to the exclusion of environmental factors. (As behaviourists, admittedly of differing persuasions within that broad church of theoretical opinion, how could we say otherwise?) However, we would also maintain that it is important not to lose sight of the individual, and it is here that the clinical approach comes into its own. The series is intended to serve two functions: to inform clinicians of developments in the clinical approach to criminal behaviour in its many forms, and to convince others that the clinical approach has a role to play in changing criminal behaviour. There is no reason why social reform and clinical change should be incompatible: others have written on the former approach, we now seek to re-assert the latter.

CLIVE R. HOLLIN
KEVIN HOWELLS

Preface

This is the fourth, and probably the penultimate, volume in the Wiley Series in *Clinical Approaches to Criminal Behaviour*. In our Preface to Volume 3, published in 1993, we reflected on the four sources of criticism—our personal opinion, informal feedback from colleagues, sales figures and published reviews—that we use to judge the success or otherwise of the books in the series. Two years on we can still reflect with overall satisfaction that the series continues to achieve the aims set out in the Series Preface.

The feedback via colleagues and sales continues to reinforce our editing behaviour. Several chapters from the earlier books are now regularly cited in the literature, and we know from both personal contact and correspondence that students and teachers, at many levels, find the books a valuable resource. The sales have been remarkably steady, with the paperback editions of Volumes 1 and 2 proving popular. This suggests that we are achieving our original goal of stimulating debate and interest in what we call a clinical approach to criminal behaviour.

Also, accepting that one cannot please all the reviewers all of the time, the reviews have been broadly encouraging. Certainly, the books have attracted reviews in a range of journals from a variety of disciplines. While it is always interesting to read the reviews for their, not always constructive, criticisms, it is also amusing to see how different professions react to what they clearly see as an invasion of their territory. In a recent review of Volume 3, a reviewer from one of the helping professions asked in the most sniffy fashion how the author of one of the chapters on victimization, an academic criminologist, could possibly know the first thing about the suffering of real victims. The wonderful irony to such a precious and patronizing view of the world is that the reviewer was quite wrong: the author in question came from the same profession as the reviewer! While diverting at one level, it is sad that some commentators are more interested in scoring points than in offering comments that are genuinely constructive and informative.

On which note we come to Volume 4. Previous volumes in the Clinical Approaches Series have attracted contributions from scholars of the highest calibre and we think the same is true here. The contributors to this current volume very much represent the state of the art in the field of working with young offenders. It is important, in our view, that efforts at working with offenders are placed in a philosophical and empirical context. The scholars contributing the opening three chapters perform that task. Chapter 1 by Don Andrews argues the case for the place of a *psychological* approach to understanding criminal conduct. Further, he suggests such an approach should be based on evidence, not on dogma, rhetoric or capricious whim. Chapter 2, by David Farrington, shows just how much empirical, substantial evidence is available on factors that play a decisive role in the development of delinquency, while in Chapter 3, Friedrich Lösel takes a similar empirical stance in considering the possibilities of success in working with young offenders. In a cogent review of the evidence from the meta-analyses, Lösel suggests that while we should not be over-enthusiastic, there is clear evidence that effective work to reduce reoffending is a real possibility.

Alongside these conceptual and empirical considerations, practitioners must be aware of the context in which their work takes place. In Chapter 4 Michael Milan offers a comprehensive summary of the issues associated with working in institutions. William S. Davidson II and his colleagues, in Chapter 5, consider the role of initiatives designed to divert young offenders away from the criminal justice system.

For practitioners the style and content of the clinical work with young offenders are fundamentally important. We have selected contributions here to cover three important developments in working with young offenders. In Chapter 6 John Gibbs addresses sociomoral treatment, Arnie Goldstein and Barry Glick discuss aggression replacement training in Chapter 7, and in Chapter 8 Loretta Serna and her colleagues review family work. All three chapters show how practice is evolving as empirical research accrues and theoretical understanding grows.

In the final three chapters to complement discussion of working specifically with young offenders, we consider the issues when the focus is on working with adolescent offences. Judith Becker and her colleagues consider adolescent sex offenders in Chapter 9, Clive Hollin and Kevin Epps discuss adolescent firesetters in Chapter 10, and in Chapter 11 Mary McMurran looks at adolescent substance misuse. Of course, the division between offenders and offences is not real, and these chapters show how an integrated approach must be taken. However, it is apparent that a scientist-practitioner stance can play real dividends in working constructively with even the most demanding of young people who commit serious crimes.

In our opinion the quality of the books in this series has gone from strength to strength. We think that this book will enhance the series still further and we are grateful to all contributors for the excellence of their work. The force of this book, we believe, is that there are grounds for optimism in working with young offenders but clearly much remains to be done. We hope that this book will contribute to the collective efforts of all those who work with young offenders.

CLIVE R. HOLLIN
KEVIN HOWELLS

Young Offenders: A Clinical Approach

CLIVE R. HOLLIN
School of Psychology, The University of Birmingham, UK

KEVIN HOWELLS
Department of Psychology, Edith Cowan University, Australia

In 1974 Robert Martinson published an article entitled 'What works? Questions and answers about prison reform' that has become one of the most widely cited pieces in support of the doctrine that nothing works in efforts to rehabilitate offenders. However, as Cullen and Gendreau (1989) note in their discussion of the effectiveness of rehabilitation programmes with offenders, the view that 'nothing works' owes more to rhetoric than to scientific evidence.

Martinson's 1974 paper, based on a much larger research effort (Lipton, Martinson & Wilks, 1975), was concerned with the evaluation of 231 outcome studies, conducted between 1945 and 1967, of treatment programmes with offenders. Martinson concluded that most of these programmes had little or no effect on recidivism and that therefore there was little hope that the ideal of rehabilitation could be achieved. However, Martinson also noted a variety of procedural shortcomings in both the implementation of the rehabilitation programmes and the evaluative research that could account for the lack of success. In other words, there may be explanations for the null findings other than 'nothing works'.

With this in mind, Thornton (1987) reexamined the 231 studies used by Martinson, using three stringent criteria: (1) the use of recidivism as an outcome variable; (2) a research design involving either random allocation of offenders to treatment/control conditions, or matched treatment and control groups; (3) a level of methodological sophistication acceptable by the criteria defined by Lipton, Martinson and Wilks in their study. When subjected to this level of scrutiny, Thornton found that only 38 of the 231 studies satisfied all three criteria demanded of strong clinical evaluation studies. Of these 38 studies, 34 involved a

Clinical Approaches to Working with Young Offenders. Edited by C. R. Hollin and K. Howells.
© 1996 John Wiley & Sons Ltd.

comparison between a group of offenders treated using a psychological therapy, such as psychotherapy or counselling, and an untreated control group.

The first point made by Thornton is that the limited number of highly robust studies reduces the amount of reliable information from which conclusions about treatment effectiveness can be drawn. Secondly, the limited range of psychological therapies in these studies leaves open to speculation the effects of other interventions based on, say, education, skills training or behavioural principles. Finally, of the 34 robust studies, Thornton found that 16 showed a significant advantage following treatment; 17 showed no difference in outcome between treatment and control groups; and only one study reported a worse outcome for the treatment group. Thornton concludes that: 'Either the catalogue of studies on which Martinson based his assertions may properly be read as indicating that psychological therapy can have positive effects on recidivism, or it can be read as indicating that no conclusion can safely be drawn. The one interpretation that is not acceptable is that it has been shown that "Nothing Works"' (Thornton, 1987, p. 188).

Thornton's conclusions bear out the reservations expressed by Martinson in 1974 about the outright rejection of rehabilitation programmes for offenders. Yet further, a second paper by Martinson, published in 1979, explicitly said that some treatment programmes can and do have a beneficial effect on recidivism rates.

A major difficulty in establishing the overall message from a body of research lies in trying to compare the findings of studies that have used different designs, different statistical tests, and even different definitions of 'success'. Yet further, different studies examine different variables such as style of intervention, types of measures, type of setting, and so on. In some areas of research there are literally hundreds of outcome studies, making it impossible to draw meaningful conclusions about what works, for whom, and under what conditions, simply by pooling all the available results.

This inability to draw meaningful conclusions from the outcome literature proved to be a problem in any area of research (in many disciplines) for which there was a large and diverse body of experimental evidence. However, the development of the statistical technique of meta-analysis has gone some way towards solving this problem.

As Izzo and Ross (1990) explain, meta-analysis is 'a technique that enables a reviewer to objectively and statistically analyse the findings of many individual studies by regarding the findings of each study as data points ... The procedure of meta-analysis involves collecting relevant studies, using the summary statistics from each study as units of analysis, and then analysing the aggregated data in a quantitative manner using statistical tests' (p. 135). When applied to treatment outcome studies, meta-analysis provides a means by which to produce a detailed picture of what works.

There have been several meta-analyses in the field of offender rehabilitation (Andrews *et al.*, 1990; Izzo & Ross, 1990; Lipsey, 1992). In a typical meta-analytic study, Garrett (1985) included 111 studies reported between 1960 and 1983, involving a total of 13 055 young offenders (mainly male) of average age 15.8 years. The first step in the meta-analysis is to calculate the effect size, that is, the extent to which the treatment groups differ from the control groups following the treatment. A positive effect size shows an advantage to the treatment group; a negative effect size shows a disadvantage following treatment. Garrett reported an effect size of +0.37 across *all* the studies on *all* measures, which is relatively modest, but nonetheless evidence for a positive advantage resulting from treatment.

Garrett subdivided the treatment studies into several groups: these included psychodynamic, behavioural (including contingency management and cognitive-behaviour modification), and life skills (including academic and vocational training). Garrett then calculated the effect sizes for the different types of intervention with regard to recidivism. She found that the contingency management programmes had an effect size of +0.25 and the cognitive-behavioural programmes an effect size of +0.24. In other words, both styles of behavioural approach had modest but positive effects on later offending.

In considering the findings of the meta-analytical studies it is important to make the distinction between clinical and criminogenic outcomes: it is, for example, quite possible for rehabilitation programmes to produce good outcomes in terms of, say, improved psychological adjustment or improved social skills, but to have little or no effect on recidivism and further acts of delinquency (Hollin & Henderson, 1984). As a generalization, programmes aimed at producing psychological or behavioural changes do tend to produce favourable outcomes (Lipsey & Wilson, 1993). However, in offender rehabilitation, the crucial issue lies in what is known of interventions that have the most criminogenic success. Hollin (1994) has suggested that a distillation of the meta-analysis literature yields the following seven broad conclusions.

First, indiscriminate targeting of treatment programmes is counterproductive in reducing recidivism: important predictors of success are that medium- to high-risk offenders should be selected, and programmes should focus on criminogenic areas. Second, the type of treatment programme is important in that structured treatments, such as behavioural and skill-orientated programmes, are more effective than less structured and focused approaches such as counselling. Third, the most successful studies, while behavioural in orientation, include a cognitive component to focus on the attitudes, values and beliefs that support and maintain delinquent behaviour. Fourth, with respect to the type and style of service, some therapeutic approaches are not suitable for general use with offenders. Specifically, Andrews *et al.* (1990) argue that 'traditional psychodynamic and nondirective client-centred therapies are to be avoided within general samples of offenders' (p. 376). Fifth, treatment programmes conducted in the community have stronger effects on delinquency than residential programmes. While residential programmes can be effective, they should be structurally linked with community-based interventions. Sixth, the most effective programmes have high 'treatment integrity' in that they are conducted by trained staff and the treatment initiators are involved in all the operational phases of the treatment programme. In other words, there is effective management of the process of treatment. Finally, effective programmes also include an element of family work (Roberts & Camasso, 1991).

Regarding size of effect, Lipsey (1992) states that treatment programmes can produce reductions in recidivism of 20% or more with treated juveniles compared with control juveniles. It is therefore difficult to resist the conclusion that it is simply untrue that 'nothing works' when it comes to treatment with offenders: intervention, particularly cognitive-behavioural intervention, can have an impact on a range of target behaviours, including criminal behaviours. The 'failures' of the type discussed previously can be accounted for in terms of the above conclusions: that is, the use of non-directive therapeutic approaches not directed specifically at offending behaviour, and treatment programmes with low-risk offender populations.

If, as we believe, rehabilitation for young offenders is back on the agenda it is clear that two basic arguments must be won. The first, rehearsed here by Don Andrews, is that there must be a place for the psychology of criminal conduct. Without this acknowledgement, future efforts to advance the rehabilitative ideal will be sorely hampered. The second, implicit throughout this book, is awareness of the vast amount of knowledge already to hand about the role of social and individual factors in delinquency. Armed with this body of knowledge, we are in a strong position to answer the question of 'what works' when working with young offenders. The challenge for the future is to persuade others of the benefits to all concerned of effective work with young offenders.

REFERENCES

Andrews, D. A., Zinger, I., Hoge, R. D., Bonta, J., Gendreau, P. & Cullen, F. T. (1990). Does correctional treatment work? A clinically relevant and psychologically informed meta-analysis. *Criminology*, **28**, 369–404.

Cullen, F. T. & Gendreau, P. (1989). The effectiveness of correctional rehabilitation: Reconsidering the 'nothing works' debate. In L. Goodstein & D. L. MacKenzie (eds), *The American Prison: Issues in Research and Policy*. NY: Plenum Press.

Garrett, C. J. (1985). Effects of residential treatment on adjudicated delinquents: A meta-analysis. *Journal of Research on Crime and Delinquency*, **22**, 287–308.

Hollin, C. R. (1994). Designing effective rehabilitation programmes for young offenders. *Psychology, Crime and Law*, **1**, 193–9.

Hollin, C. R. & Henderson, M. (1984). Social skills training with young offenders: False expectations and the 'failure of treatment'. *Behavioural Psychotherapy*, **12**, 331–41.

Izzo, R. L. & Ross, R. R. (1990). Meta-analysis of rehabilitation programs for juvenile delinquents: A brief report. *Criminal Justice and Behavior*, **17**, 134–42.

Lipsey, M. W. (1992). Juvenile delinquency treatment: A meta-analytic inquiry into the variability of effects. In T. D. Cook, H. Cooper, D. S. Cordray, H. Hartmann, L. V. Hedges, R. J. Light, T. A. Louis & F. Mosteller (eds), *Meta-analysis for Explanation: A Casebook*. New York: Russell Sage Foundation.

Lipsey, M. W. & Wilson, D. B. (1993). The efficacy of psychological, educational, and behavioral treatment: Confirmation from meta-analysis. *American Psychologist*, **48**, 1181–209.

Lipton, D. N., Martinson, R. & Wilks, D. (1975). *The Effectiveness of Correctional Treatment*. New York: Praeger.

Martinson, R. (1974). What works? Questions and answers about prison reform. *The Public Interest*, **35**, 22–54.

Martinson, R. (1979). New findings, new views: A note of caution regarding sentencing reform. *Hofstra Law Review*, **7**, 243–58.

Roberts, A. R. & Camasso, M. J. (1991). The effect of juvenile offender treatment programs on recidivism: A meta-analysis of 46 studies. *Notre Dame Journal of Law, Ethics and Public Policy*, **5**, 421–41.

Thornton, D. M. (1987). Treatment effects on recidivism: A reappraisal of the 'nothing works' doctrine. In B. J. McGurk, D. M. Thornton & M. Williams (eds), *Applying Psychology to Imprisonment: Theory & Practice*. London: HMSO.

Part 1

The Research Base for Working with Young Offenders

1

The Psychology of Criminal Conduct and Evidence-Based Assessment and Intervention*

D. A. ANDREWS
Department of Psychology, Carleton University, Ottawa, Canada

There now is a human science of criminal conduct. There are theories of criminal conduct that are empirically defensible and that may be helpful in designing and delivering effective service. The literature is reasonably strong and supports vigorous pursuit of ethical, decent, humane and cost-efficient approaches to prevention and rehabilitative programming for higher-risk cases under a variety of conditions of just sanctioning. The active and effective human service agency may contribute to a still more powerful knowledge base by building assessment, reassessment and research into the agency.

A major issue, one on which research is really only beginning, is how to make use of what works. Research on the dissemination, implementation, and ongoing development of effective programming is a priority. (Andrews & Bonta, 1994, p. 236)

The general personality and social psychology of criminal conduct (or PCC: Psychology of Criminal Conduct) referred to above takes a basic scientific or rational empirical approach to understanding individual differences in criminal behaviour, both interindividual and intraindividual. PCC is truly interdisciplinary in that it is open to evidence regarding the covariates of crime regardless of the rhetorical association of any particular covariate with narrow disciplinary preferences for biological, personal, interpersonal, structural/cultural or politico-economic variables. The approach is as interested in the impact of broader social arrangements on criminal conduct as it is in the impact of the immediate situation of action.

---

* Portions of this paper draw upon a proposal for a national training center submitted to SSHRC by D. A. Andrews and Paul Gendreau.

Clinical Approaches to Working with Young Offenders. Edited by C. R. Hollin and K. Howells.
© 1996 John Wiley & Sons Ltd.

This general personality and social psychology of crime reflects a basic scientific approach in that it seeks an understanding of individual differences with the following features.

1. It is explanatory and conceptual in the sense of valuing logic, internal consistency and rational organization.
2. It is empirically defensible in that it yields (a) risk factors which in fact possess predictive validity, and (b) the ability (if not the will) to influence the probability of future criminal behaviour through deliberate intervention.
3. It has practical value in prevention, criminal justice processing and corrections.

Additionally, as part of a broad human psychology, the understanding is expected to reflect a respect for human diversity and an appreciation of the complexity of human experience, to be mindful of ethicality, legality and decency, and to display a serious commitment to giving the knowledge away regardless of the social location of the potential user.

For too many years (according to, for example, Andrews & Wormith, 1989a; Cullen & Gendreau 1989; Hirschi & Hindelang, 1977), the interdisciplinary field of criminal justice and criminology was not devoted to developing a rational and empirically defensible understanding of criminal behaviour and its processing. In fact, much of the mainstream was devoted to the promotion of anti-psychological and pro-sociological themes in combination with anti-empirical ideological slants (to both the left and the right politically). The situation became so serious that the dysjunction between the content of mainstream sociological textbooks and the content of the disciplinary and more truly interdisciplinary research journals reached levels described as an 'intellectual scandal' (Andrews & Bonta, 1994, p. 85) and as a 'professional embarrassment and disgrace' (Wright, 1993, p. 10).

Such descriptions of mainstream textbook sociological criminology, however, do not imply that, in social psychological terms, the situation was not an understandable reflection of broader social, political, professional and educational trends (see, for example: Andrews & Wormith, 1989a; Crews, 1986; Cullen & Gendreau, 1989; Currie, 1989; Laub & Sampson, 1991; Wright, 1993). In direct contrast, the denial and disrespect of evidence favourable to a PCC were core elements of the early sociologies of crime that continue to be replicated in some recent sociological and criminal justice textbooks (see Andrews & Wormith, 1989a; Laub & Sampson, 1991):

> From the beginning, the thrust of sociological theory has been to deny the relevance of individual differences to an exploration of delinquency, and the thrust of sociological criticism has been to discount research findings apparently to the contrary. 'Devastating' reviews of the research literature typically meet with uncritical acceptance or even applause, and 'new criminologies' are constructed in a research vacuum (Hirschi & Hindelang, 1977, pp. 571–572).

> Sociology possessed a conceptual scheme that explicitly denied the claims of all other disciplines potentially interested in crime (Gottfredson & Hirschi, 1990, p. 70).

For whatever combination of reasons (as reviewed by Andrews & Bonta, 1994), mainstream sociological textbook knowledge has been in a desperate shape for years, and thus it is little wonder that the contributions of social science to major social issues are often dismissed. It is also little wonder that the media, politicians, the public, and managers and practitioners within intervention agencies are confused, and many have escaped to simplistic variations on themes of official punishment as the dominant response to antisocial behaviour (Andrews et al., 1990b; Cullen et al., 1988; Gendreau, 1993; Gendreau & Ross, 1981). The fact is that the anti-empiricism and anti-psychological themes of mainstream textbook sociological criminology have reached deep into policy (see for example: Barr, 1992; Canada, 1987) and practice (for example see Parent the (1993) analysis of boot camps). The effect has been increased punishment, increased costs, decreased treatment and no apparent reduction in crime (Andrews, 1990; Cullen & Gilbert, 1982; Gendreau 1993; Leschied, Austin & Jaffe, 1988).

A recent survey of programmes for young offenders, for example, revealed that 50% or more of the promising features of interventions identified in the research literature (as will be reviewed), were represented in fewer than 10% of the programmes surveyed (Hoge, Leschied & Andrews, 1993). This finding parallels the finding of Miller and Hester (1986) that a list of empirically validated approaches to substance abuse treatment and a list of the most popular approaches to substance abuse treatment overlapped not at all.

In brief, the content of official textbooks and the specifics of dominant practices are out of touch with the research findings that reside in the systematic and quantitative general personality and social psychological research literature. In regard to the predictors of crime, the textbooks and practice reflect theories of personal distress (class-based anomie/strain in mainstream sociological criminology, anxiety/low self-esteem in clinical psychology/psychiatry, and variations on themes of victimization in pop psychology). Similarly, in regard to intervention, the textbooks and practice reflect an astonishing belief in the power of official punishment wherein rhetoric about stigma (labelling theory), fear of punishment (deterrence theory) and the purifying value of just pain (just desert) overrides evidence. Astonishment is reinforced when faith is expressed in some magical combination of official punishments that yields a special mix of stigma, fear and justice that, in an unspecified way, will result not only in reduced recidivism but in the prevention of the breakdown of the rule of law (as discussed by Andrews, 1990). In is incredible, for example, except within the intellectual tradition in which they work, that mainstream reviewers of the treatment literature (e.g. Whitehead & Lab, 1989) have found and reported that nearly 50% of the studies of correctional treatment services revealed reduced recidivism and yet concluded that correctional treatment services do not work but that a precise mix of 'stigma' and 'fear' through official punishment is promising. Such systematic disservice to social science and human service must be confronted and is being confronted by the research community within human science.

Adopting a rational empirical, interdisciplinary and meta-analytic perspective on individual differences in criminal conduct, certain findings in the areas of prediction and intervention become clear.

Prediction

First and foremost, lower class origins (as emphasized by sociological theory) and personal distress (as emphasized by both sociological and mental health perspectives) are weak correlates of criminal conduct. Second, personal attitudes, temperament, interpersonal association patterns, family process, and socio-economic achievement are much stronger correlates of antisocial conduct. Without here reviewing the outstanding meta-analyses of scholars such as Tittle, Villimez and Smith (1978) and the Loebers, I summarize the current state of knowledge through reference to findings reported by Andrews and Bonta (1994: based on the databank developed at UNB Saint John by Gendreau et al. (1992)).

This ongoing project involves a survey of all studies of the correlates of crime published in English since 1970. As of September 1992, approximately 1000 studies had been listed, 700 studies located, and 372 studies subjected to content and meta-analysis. This yielded over 1770 Pearson Product moment correlation coefficients, each of which reflected the covariation of some potential correlate of individual criminal conduct with some measure of criminal conduct.

Reflecting the general social psychological perspective, particular risk/need factors were assigned to six categories. These categories were: (1) lower class origins as assessed by parental educational and occupational indices and by neighbourhood characteristics; (2) personal distress indicators including 'psychological' measures of anxiety, depression and low self-esteem as well as more 'sociological' assessments of anomie, alienation and powerlessness; (3) personal educational/vocational/economic achievement; (4) parental psychological status and functioning as well as family cohesiveness and parenting practices; (5) antisocial temperament, personality and behavioural history; and (6) antisocial attitudes and antisocial associates.

The mean correlation coefficients for each of the six categories of risk/need factors were as follows (with number of coefficients in parentheses):

(1) Lower class origins   0.06   (97)
(2) Personal distress/psychopathology   0.08   (226)
(3) Personal educational/vocational achievement   0.12   (129)
(4) Parental/family factors   0.18   (334)
(5) Temperament/misconduct/personality   0.21   (621)
(6) Antisocial attitudes/associates   0.22   (168)

The rank ordering of the six sets of risk/need factors has proven to be very robust across various types of subjects (differentiated according to gender, age and race) and across methodological variables (such as self-report versus official measures of crime, and longitudinal versus cross-sectional designs).

Linda Simourd (Simourd & Andrews, 1994) has recently extended the above-noted findings by focusing exclusively upon studies that employed the same predictor variables for young men and women. She also distinguished between the more distal measures of parental problems and the less distal measures of parenting practices. In addition, she distinguished between distal personality measures such as emotional empathy and less distal personality measures such as low socialization/psychopathy. Her mean correlation coefficients, corrected for sample size, were as follows:

(1) Lower class origins   0.05 (38)
(2) Personal distress/psychopathology   0.07 (34)
(3) Family structure/parent problems   0.07 (28)
(4) Minor personality variables   0.12 (18)
(5) Poor parent–child relations   0.20 (82)
(6) Personal educational/vocational achievement   0.28 (68)
(7) Temperament/misconduct/personality   0.38 (90)
(8) Antisocial attitudes/associates   0.48 (106)

In summary, extant research findings reveal that lower class origins and personal distress are minor risk factors for criminality relative to indicators of antisocial propensity drawn from assessments of family, personality, attitudes, inter-personal association patterns, and personal difficulties in the area of school and work. These findings do not negate the possibility that broader social arrange-ments may influence the more immediate personal and interpersonal factors linked to crime. Rather, they underscore the need to document these links in empirically defensible ways.

Effects of Deliberate and Controlled Interventions

The inadequacy of the mainstream sociological and mental health approaches is also evident in the findings of the meta-analyses of the effects of correctional treatment. First consider the mainstream criminological and criminal justice perspective on intervention. Grounded in the psychologically naïve perspectives of labelling, deterrence and just desert, each makes much of protection of the public from crime but, in fact, has been associated with programmes that increased processing, increased costs, reduced treatment, and either had no effects on criminal recidivism or increased it (Andrews et al., 1990a: Lipsey, 1990). Conversely, the delivery of correctional treatment services has been associated with at least mild reductions in recidivism (an average effect of -0.07 in 30 tests of official punishment relative to an average effect of 0.15 for 124 tests of treatment services: Andrews et al., 1990a).

Consider next the mainstream mental health fascination with non-directive, evocative, relationship-dependent, highly verbal and office-based approaches to intervention relative to the general social psychological preference for concrete, community-based, behavioural and social learning approaches. Within the behavioural set, the mean correlation of treatment and reduced recidivism was 0.29 ($n = 41$) compared with 0.07 ($n = 113$) for the non-behavioural treatments. Considering individually risk, need and responsivity, the mean correlations of various types of treatment and reduced recidivism were as follows (Andrews et al. 1990a); independently, Lipsey (1990) has noted that the treatments he identified as most successful overlapped considerably with our set of clinically appropriate treatments: (1) official punishment: -0.07; (2) clinically/psychologically inappropriate treatment: -0.06; (3) unspecified treatment services: 0.15; (4) clinically/psychologically appropriate treatment: 0.30. With the databank now up to 295 tests, it is clear that clinically/psychologically appropriate treatment is the single strongest moderator of effect size, with a non-residential setting for treatment, small sample size, and involvement of the evaluator in the design/delivery of treatment each contributing incrementally to the magnitude of effect size. Within the family therapy subset, it is clear that a substantial proportion of the contribution of the methodological/study variables may be attributed to enhanced therapeutic integrity (Andrews et al. in press).

The meta-analyses have served not only to clarify prediction and intervention issues but also to clarify the role of study and methodological factors in the determination of effect size. Narrative reviews of mainstream criminological critiques of the psychology of crime have shown that appeals to well known methodological threats-to-validity had degenerated into nothing less than 'knowledge destruction', wherein the identification of any potential threat was sufficient to dismiss positive research findings (see Andrews & Wormith, 1989b; Gottfredson, 1979).

Tables 1.1 and 1.2 summarize some of these knowledge destruction techniques in the areas of prediction (Table 1.1) and treatment (Table 1.2). The meta-analyses, on the other hand, have served to demonstrate that the effects of methodological weaknesses may be inflative, deflative or null in regard to the magnitude of effect sizes. For example, in analyses of prediction studies it is now clear that extreme group studies indeed yield inflated validity estimates and that the effect of unreliability in the assessment of the predictor and/or criterion domains is to underestimate validity. In analyses of effects of deliberate intervention, enhanced effect sizes are found in small sample studies and in studies in which the evaluator was also involved in the design/delivery of the intervention. In addition to the possibility of experimenter bias, the meta-analyses also suggest that enhanced therapeutic integrity mediates the effects of the methodological variables on effect size. Most notably, the effects of the powerful predictor and intervention variables are very robust and survive controls for methodology. Notably, with the development of large meta-analytic databanks, the possibility exists for the development of empirically derived corrections for deviations from methodological ideals.

Meta-analysis itself is a proper focus of systematic empirical exploration. I agree with Hunter and Schmidt (1990) that traditional narrative reviews have seriously underestimated the depth and breadth of knowledge in the behavioural and social sciences. Without necessarily endorsing corrections that maximize effect size estimates through the simulation of hypothetical ideals, I envision further systematic research on the empirically demonstrable effects of a broad range of study artifacts and sampling-related issues.

An increased appreciation of methodological issues will be accompanied by an enhanced body of human science knowledge of great value to human service. Let us hope that the criminal justice, criminological and mental health establishments are full participants in these steps forward and are not on the fringe as basically

Table 1.1   A sample of mainstream criminological rhetoric that is unfavourable to individual differences research

People interested in profiles of offenders are not nice people
- '... rightly or wrongly, a belief in [differentiation] is used as an index of authoritarian personality". (Matza, 1964, p. 15).
- '... the "bogeyman theories" ... slur over the existence of upperworld criminals and zero in almost entirely on lawbreakers from the underclass". (Gibbons, 1986, p. 509).

Prediction is impossible empirically
- 'A reliance on differentiation, whether constitutional, personal, or sociocultural, as the key explanation of delinquency has pushed the standard-bearers of diverse theories to posit what have almost always turned out to be empirically undemonstrable differences'. (Matza, 1964).
- 'So-called delinquents, in this view, are not significantly different from non-delinquents—except that they have been processed by the juvenile justice system'. (Schur, 1973, p. 154).
- 'Thus, the enterprise is doomed to failure: inconsistent results abound...' (Taylor, Walton & Young, 1973, p. 58).
- '... false predictions [often] exceed correct predictions... when false predictions exceed [50%]—and some go as high as 99%—you are further ahead to simply flip a coin'. (Lab & Whitehead, 1990).

Prediction is possible. but 'so what'?
- 'Almost everything in the universe has been found to be associated in some direct or indirect manner with criminality'. (Sutherland & Cressey, 1970, p. 624: cited by Hirschi & Gottfredson, 1982, p. 12).
- '...(measures of antisocial personality) provide no information not obtainable simply by procuring a list of offenders'. (Tennenbaum, 1977).
- '...testing, testing', (p. 183), (according to Cohen, 1985), 'it is ritualistic', (p. 187).

Prediction is possible, but it 'really' reflects social class
- '[These] may, in fact, in certain circumstances [be class-based value differences]'. (Taylor, Walton & Young (1973) on differential reinforcement histories (p. 52), on personality (p. 57), and on parenting variables (p. 64) associated with delinquency).
- 'The extraordinarily high rates of violence and other kinds of criminality in the United States are clear indicators that the causes of crime lie, not in biology or faulty socialization, but in economic and social inequality, the lack of meaningful jobs for large segments of the population, and other rents and tears in the social fabric of American society'. (Gibbons, 1986, p. 510).
- 'laws reflect only the notions held by 'moral entrepreneurs'; some people's criminals may be other people's heroes; in actuality, [any act of robbery, rape, or theft] is not an event [but a] social process; [an interest in individual differences] runs the risk [of *degeneration* into] correctionalism. (Maclean, 1986, p. 4).

Prediction is theoretically naive
- '"Significant" correlations where they occur merely result in false imputations of causality' (Taylor, Walton & Young, 1973, p. 58).
- 'Biological or psychological factors undoubtedly play a role in generating delinquent conduct by some adolescents at some times. However, as general explanations they seem to lack empirical support'. (Johnson, 1979, p. 10).
- 'It seems the best conclusion to draw is that the differences that appear between criminals and noncriminals on personality tests do not seem to have any theoretical relevance to understanding the causes of criminal behaviour'. (Vold & Bernard, 1986, pp. 121—2).
- 'Some authors have tended to wish away the interaction between environmental forces and the biological and psychological'. (Barlow, 1986, p. 33).

Even though the class–crime link is weak, we know better
- The linkage of poverty and crime is inexorable, despite the inability of researchers to establish it at the individual level. (Short, 1991, p. 501).

Table 1.2   Errors in conceptualization and methodology and the misuse of those errors in treatment criticism

	Example of misuse
If the theory underlying treatment is flawed, the treatment should fail to reduce recidivism	If crime is only a reflection of social inequality, the finding that a change in personal attitudes was followed by reduced recidivism must be in error
If unreliability in the measurement of recidivism is a serious problem, treatment effects will be underestimated	The positive effect of treatment may be dismissed because of unreliability in the assessment of recidivism
If there are deviations from the ideals of the experimental design, treatment effects will be overestimated, underestimated or unaffected depending upon the details of the deviations	Any deviation from experimental ideals allows us to reject findings favourable to treatment
If the positive effects of certain approaches to treatment are limited to certain types of offenders (for example, the higher risk, the more psychologically mature or the more motivated), the studies have yielded important information on 'who responds to what'	If a treatment does not work for everyone under all conditions, treatment does not work

negative forces. It is difficult to find hope within criminal law and criminal justice because there the rhetoric of deterrence, incapacitation, accountability and the cultural and spiritual value of 'just pain' continues. Still, John Braithwaite (1993) and Lawrence Sherman (1993) are beginning to state the complexity of punishment and recognize the importance of individual differences. There is much hope within mainstream criminology as the class-based perspectives of anomie/strain and labelling are being reformulated into general social psychological perspectives (see, for example, Agnew (1992)) and the behavioural reformulations of differential association theory (for example, Akers, 1973) are gaining the recognition they deserve. Within mainstream mental health, the research programme at Oak Ridge facility for mentally disordered offenders is convincingly documenting the value of a general personality and social psychological approach and, of course, the 'what works' group in the United Kingdom have kept human service and rational empiricism alive (McGuire, 1995; McIvor, 1990).

It is time to turn our attention to dissemination, implementation, and the development of agency-based competence for routine human service research and evaluation, and to build a human service culture supportive of evidence-based intervention (Andrews & Bonta, 1994; Backer et al., 1986; Fixsen & Blase, 1993). The evidence-based strength of the existing PCC may not be great by absolute standards, but it is very promising relative to its competitors.

REFERENCES

Agnew, R. (1992). Foundation for a general strain theory of crime and delinquency. *Criminology*, **30**, 47–87.

Akers, R. L. (1973). *Deviant Behavior: A Social Learning Approach*. Belmont, CA: Wadsworth.

Andrews, D. A. (1989). Recidivism is predictable and can be influenced: Using risk assessments to reduce recidivism. *Forum on Corrections Research*, **1**(2), 11–18.

Andrews, D. A. (1990). Some criminological sources of antirehabilitation bias in the Report of the Canadian Sentencing Commission. *Canadian Journal of Criminology*, **32**, 511–524.

Andrews, D. A. & Wormith, J. S. (1989a). Personality and crime: Knowledge destruction and construction in criminology. *Justice Quarterly*, **6**, 289–309.

Andrews, D. A. & Wormith, J. S. (1989b). Rejoinder—Personality and crime: Toward knowledge construction. *Justice Quarterly*, **6**, 325–32.

Andrews, D. A., Bonta, J. & Hoge, R. D. (1990). Classification for effective rehabilitation: Rediscovering psychology. *Criminal Justice and Behavior*, **17**, 19–52.

Andrews, D. A., Leschied, A. & Hoge, R. D. (1992). *Review of the Profile, Classification and Treatment Literature with Young Offenders: A Social-Psychological Approach*. Toronto: Ministry of Community and Social Services.

Andrews, D. A., Zinger, I., Hoge, R. D., Bonta, J., Gendreau, P. & Cullen, F. T. (1990a). Does correctional treatment work? A clinically relevant and psychologically informed meta-analysis. *Criminology*, **28**, 369–404.

Andrews, D. A., Zinger, I., Hoge, R. D., Bonta, J., Gendreau, P. & Cullen, F. T. (1990b). A human science approach or more punishment and pessimism—rejoinder. *Criminology*, **28**, 419–429.

Andrews, D. A. & Bonta, J. (1994). *Psychology of Criminal Conduct*. Cincinnati, OH: Anderson.

Andrews, D. A., Gordon, D. A., Hill, J., Kurkowski, K. & Hoge, R. D. (in press). Program integrity, methodology, and treatment characteristics: A meta-analysis of effects of family intervention with young offenders. *Criminal Justice and Behavior*.

Backer, T. E., Liberman, R. P. & Kuehnel, T. G. (1986). Dissemination and adoption of innovative psychosocial interventions. *Journal of Consulting and Clinical Psychology*, **54**, 111–118.

Barlow, H. D. (1986). *Introduction to Criminology*. Boston, MA: Little, Brown.

Barr, W. P. (1992). A memorandum from the US. Attorney General to the President of the United States of America re recommendations for state criminal justice systems. Reproduced in: *Combating Violent Crime: 24 Recommendations to Strengthen Criminal justice. A Report of the US Department of Justice*. Washington, DC.

Braithwaite, J. (1993). Beyond positivism: Learning from contextual integrated strategies. *Journal of Research in Crime and Delinquency*, **30**, 383–399.

Canada (1987). *Sentencing Reform: A Canadian Approach* (Report of the Canadian Sentencing Commission). Ottawa: Supply and Services Canada.

Cohen, S. (1985). *Visions of Social Control*. Cambridge: Polity Press.

Cullen, F. T. & Gendreau, P. (1989). The effectiveness of correctional rehabilitation. In L. Goodstein & D. L. MacKenzie (eds) *The American Prison: Issues in Research Policy*. New York: Plenum.

Cullen, F. T. & Gilbert, K. E. (1982). *Reaffirming Rehabilitation*. Cincinnati, OH: Anderson.

Cullen, F. T., Cullen, J. B. & Woznick, J. F. (1988). Is rehabilitation dead? The myth of the punitive public. *Journal of Criminal Justice*, **16**, 303–317.

Currie, E. (1989). Confronting crime: Looking toward the twenty-first century. *Justice Quarterly*, **6**, 5–25.

Crews, F. (1986). In the big house of theory. *The New York Review of Books*, **29**, May: 36, 41.

Fixsen, D. L. & Blase, K. A. (1993). Creating new realities: Program development and dissemination. *Journal of Applied Behavior Analysis*, **26**, 597–615.

Gendreau, P. (1993). Does 'punishing smarter' work? An assessment of the new generation of alternative sanctions. Discussion paper for Corrections Research, Ministry Secretariat, Solicitor General of Canada, February.

Gendreau, P. & Ross, R. R. (1981). Correctional potency: Treatment and deterrence on trial. In R. Roesch & R. R. Corrado (eds), *Evaluation and Criminal Justice Policy*. Beverly Hills, CA: Sage.

Gendreau, P., Andrews, D. A., Goggin, C. & Chanteloupe, F. (1992). The development of clinical and policy guidelines for the prediction of criminal behavior in criminal justice settings. An unpublished paper submitted to Corrections Research, Ministry Secretariat, Solicitor General of Canada.

Gibbons, D. C. (1986). Breaking out of prisons. *Crime and Delinquency*, **32**, 503–14.

Gottfredson, M. R. (1979). Treatment destruction techniques. *Journal of Research in Crime and Delinquency*, **16**, 39–54.

Gottfredson, M. R. & Hirschi, T. (1990). *A General Theory of Crime*. Stanford, CA: Stanford University Press.

Hirschi, T. & Hindelang, M. J. (1977). Intelligence and delinquency: A revisionist review. *American Sociological Review*. **42**, 571–87.

Hoge, R. D., Leschied, A. W. & Andrews, D. A. (1993). The repeat offender project: A survey of programs for young offenders. An unpublished report to the Ontario Ministry of Community and Social Services.

Hunter, J. E. and Schmidt, F. L. (1990). *Methods of Meta-analysis: Correcting Error and Bias in Research Findings*. London: Sage.

Johnson, R. E. (1979). *Juvenile Delinquency and its Origins: An Integrative Theoretical Approach*. Cambridge: Cambridge University Press.

Lab, S. P. & Whitehead, J. T. (1988). An analysis of juvenile correctional treatment. *Crime and Delinquency*, **34**, 60–85.

Lab, S. P. & Whitehead, J. T. (1990). From 'Nothing Works' to 'The Appropriate Works': The latest stop on the search for the secular grail. *Criminology*, **28**, 405–17.

Laub, J. H. & Sampson, R. J. (1991). The Sutherland–Glueck debate: On the sociology of criminological knowledge. *American Journal of Sociology*, **96**, 1402–1410.

Leschied, A. W., Austin, G. W. & Jaffe, P. G. (1988). Impact of the Young Offenders Act on recidivism rates of special need youth: Clinical and policy implications. *Canadian Journal of Behavioural Science*, **20**, 322–331.

Lipsey, M. W. (1990). Juvenile delinquency treatment: A meta-analytic inquiry into the variability of effects. Paper prepared for the Research Synthesis Committee of the Russell Sage Foundation.

Loeber, R. & Stouthamer-Loeber, M. (1987). Prediction. In H. C. Quay (ed.), *Handbook of Juvenile Delinquency* New York: Wiley.

Maclean, B. D. (1986). Critical criminology and some limitations of traditional inquiry. In B. D. Maclean (ed.), *The Political Economy of Crime*. Scarborough: Prentice-Hall.

Matza, D. (1964). *Delinquency and Drift*. (2nd edn). New York: Wiley.

McGuire, J. (ed.) (1995). *What Works: Reducing Reoffending*. Chichester: Wiley.

McIvor, G. (1990). *Sanctions for Serious or Persistent Offenders: A Review of the Literature*. Glasgow, UK: Social Work Research Centre, University of Stirling.

Miller, W. B. & Hester, R. K. (1986). The effectiveness of alcoholism treatment: What research reveals. In W. R. Miller & N. Heather (eds), *Treating Addictive Behaviors: Process of Change*. New York: Plenum.

Offord, D. R. (1992). *Epidemiology of antisocial behaviour in adolescents: Implications for policy, research and treatment*. Paper presented at The Roots of Violence, Midland, Ontario, June 1992.

Parent, D. G. (1993). *Boot Camps Revisited: A Time for Clear Thinking*. Paper presented at Correctional Options Program Orientation Meeting, Baltimore, MD, June 1993.

Schur, E. M. (1973). *Radical Nonintervention: Rethinking the Delinquency Problem.* Englewood Cliffs, NJ: Prentice-Hall.

Sherman, L. W. (1993). Defiance, deterrence, and irrelevance: A theory of criminal sanction. *Journal of Research in Crime and Delinquency*, **30**, 445–73.

Short, J. F. Jr. (1991). Poverty, ethnicity, and crime: Change and continuity in US cities. *Journal of Research in Crime and Delinquency*, **28**: 501–18.

Simourd, D., Bonta, J., Andrews, D. A. & Hoge, R. D. (1991). The assessment of criminal psychopathy: A meta-analysis. Unpublished paper. Ottawa: Department of Psychology, Carleton University.

Simourd, L. & Andrews, D. A. (1994). Correlates of delinquency: A look at gender differences. *Forum on Corrections Research*, **6**(1), 26–31.

Sutherland, E. H. & Cressey, D. R. (1970). *Principles of Criminology* (3rd edn). New York: Lippincott.

Taylor, I., Walton, P. & Young, J. (1973). *The New Criminology: For a Social Theory of Deviance.* London: Routledge and Kegan Brown.

Tennenbaum, D. J. (1977). Personality and criminality: A summary and implications of the literature. *Journal of Criminal Justice*, **5**, 225–35.

Tittle, C. R., Villimez, W. J. & Smith, D. A. (1978). The myth of social class and criminality: An empirical assessment of the empirical evidence. *American Sociological Review*, **43**, 643–56.

Vold, G. B. & Bernard, T. J. (1986). *Theoretical Criminology.* (3rd edn.) New York: Oxford University Press.

Whitehead, J. T. & Lab, S. P. (1989). A meta-analysis of juvenile correctional treatment. *Journal of Research on Crime and Delinquency*, **26**, 276–95.

Wright, R. A. (1993). The two criminologies: The divergent worldviews of textbooks and journals. *The Criminologist*, **18**(3), 1, 10.

2

Individual, Family and Peer Factors in the Development of Delinquency

DAVID P. FARRINGTON
Institute of Criminology, Cambridge University, UK

INTRODUCTION

The main aim of this chapter is to review knowledge about individual, family and peer factors in the development of delinquency. Other factors, such as biological, school or community influences, are also important, but there is not space to include them here. A second aim is to outline implications for prevention and treatment programmes, but these will not be reviewed in detail here because they are covered elsewhere in this book. This chapter is based on research carried out in the United States and England and similar Western democracies. It concentrates on offending by males, since this is generally more frequent and serious than offending by females (Farrington, 1987a), and since most of the relevant research has been conducted on males.

Within a single chapter, it is obviously impossible to review everything that is known about individual, family and peer factors. Rutter and Giller (1983), Wilson and Herrnstein (1985), Hollin (1992) and Blackburn (1993) have provided more detailed reviews of risk factors. I will be very selective in focusing on some of the more important and replicable findings obtained in some of the more methodologically adequate studies, especially longitudinal studies of large community samples. In studying the development and predictors of offending, it is essential to carry out prospective longitudinal surveys.

I will refer especially to knowledge gained in the Cambridge Study in Delinquent Development, which is a prospective longitudinal survey of over 400 London males from age 8 to age 32 (Farrington, 1995b; Farrington & West, 1990). However, similar results have been obtained in similar projects elsewhere

Clinical Approaches to Working with Young Offenders. Edited by C. R. Hollin and K. Howells.
© 1996 John Wiley & Sons Ltd.

in England (Kolvin et al., 1988b, 1990), in the United States (McCord, 1979; Robins, 1979), in the Scandinavian countries (Pulkkinen, 1988; Wikstrom, 1987), and in New Zealand (Moffitt & Silva, 1988a).

THE EPIDEMIOLOGY OF DELINQUENCY

Measurement of Offending

Offending is commonly measured using either official records of arrests or convictions or self-reports of offending. The advantages and disadvantages of official records and self-reports are to some extent complementary. In general, official records include the worst offenders and the worst offences, while self-reports include more of the normal range of delinquent activity. Self-reports have the advantage of including undetected offences, but the disadvantages of concealment and forgetting. The key issue is whether the same results are obtained with both methods. For example, if official records and self-reports both show a link between parental supervision and delinquency, it is likely that supervision is related to delinquent behaviour (rather than to any biases in measurement). This chapter focuses on such replicable results.

The prevalence of offenders varies according to the definition of offending and the method of measurement (official records or self-reports, usually). For example, in the Cambridge Study, 96% of a sample of inner-city London males admitted committing at least one of 10 common offences (including theft, burglary, violence, vandalism and drug abuse) at some time between ages 10 and 32, whereas only 33% of them had been convicted of at least one of these offences during this age range (Farrington, 1989c). In order to compare offenders and non-offenders, it is important to set a sufficiently high criterion for 'offending' (e.g. in terms of frequency, seriousness or duration, or in terms of arrests or convictions) so that the vast majority of the male population are not classified as offenders.

Officially recorded offenders and non-offenders (or, in self-report studies, more and less serious offenders) are significantly different—before, during and after their offending careers. This is basically because of consistent individual differences in underlying criminal potential or antisocial tendency. Generally, the worst offenders according to self-reports (taking account of frequency and seriousness) tend also to be the worst offenders according to official records (Farrington, 1973; Huizinga & Elliott, 1986). For example, in the Cambridge Study, between ages 15 and 18, 11% of the males admitted burglary, 62% of whom were convicted of burglary (West & Farrington, 1977). The correlates of official and self-reported offending are very similar (Farrington, 1992c). Hence, conclusions about individual characteristics of offenders can be drawn validly from both convictions and self-reports. In this chapter, 'offenders' will generally refer to officially recorded offenders, unless otherwise stated.

Natural History of Offending

The prevalence of offending increases to a peak in the teenage years and then decreases in the twenties. This pattern is seen both cross-sectionally and longitudinally (Farrington, 1986a). The peak age of official offending for English males was 15 until 1987, but it suddenly increased to 18 in 1988. The peak age for females was 14 until 1985 but then increased to 15. In the Cambridge Study, the rate of convictions increased to a peak at age 17 and then declined (Farrington, 1992a). The median age of conviction for most types of offences (burglary, robbery, theft of and from vehicles, shoplifting) was 17, while it was 20 for violence and 21 for fraud. Similarly, in the Philadelphia cohort study of Wolfgang, Thornberry & Figlio (1987), the arrest rate increased to a peak at age 16 and then declined.

The increase in the peak age of offending for English males from 15 to 18 in 1988 was the result of a number of procedural changes that caused a dramatic (but illusory) decrease in the number of recorded juvenile offenders (Farrington, 1992d). From 1985 onwards, English police forces increasingly began to use informal (unrecorded) warnings and to take no further action with apprehended juveniles whom they believed to be guilty (Barclay, 1990), thereby eliminating them from the official records. The introduction in 1986 of the Police and Criminal Evidence Act 1984, which provided increased safeguards for accused persons, caused a marked decrease in the number of detected offenders (Irving & MacKenzie, 1989). The introduction in 1986 of the Crown Prosecution Service, which transferred responsibility for the prosecution of offenders from the police to lawyers, caused a decrease in the number of persons prosecuted, and their new prosecution guidelines especially caused a decrease in the number of recorded juvenile shoplifters (Farrington & Burrows, 1993). Also, the Criminal Justice Act 1988 downgraded the offence of unauthorized taking of a motor vehicle from the indictable to the summary category, thereby eliminating about 25 000 (mostly young) offenders from the official crime statistics.

Self-report studies also show that the most common types of offending decline from the teens to the twenties. In the Cambridge Study, the prevalence of burglary, shoplifting, theft of and from vehicles, theft from slot machines and vandalism all decreased from the teens to the twenties, but the same decreases were not seen for theft from work, assault, drug abuse and fraud (Farrington, 1989c). For example, burglary (since the last interview) was admitted by 13% at age 14, 11% at age 18, 5% at age 21, and 2% at both ages 25 and 32. In their American National Youth Survey, Elliott, Huizinga and Menard (1989) found that self-reports of the prevalence of offending increased from 11–13 to a peak at 15–17 and then decreased by 19–21 years of age.

Many theories have been proposed to explain why offending peaks in the teenage years (Farrington, 1986a). For example, offending has been linked to testosterone levels in males, which increase during adolescence and early adulthood and decrease thereafter, and to changes in physical abilities or opportunities for crime. The most popular explanation focuses on social influence. From birth, children are under the influence of their parents, who generally discourage offending. However, during their teenage years, juveniles gradually break away from the control of their parents and become influenced by their peers, who may encourage offending in many cases. After age 20, offending declines again as peer influence gives way to a new set of family influences hostile to offending, originating in spouses and cohabitees.

In the Cambridge Study, the average age of the first conviction was 17.5, and the average age of the last conviction (up to age 32) was 23.3, giving an average criminal career length of 5.8 years (Farrington, 1992a). The average number of offences leading to convictions was 4.5. The males first convicted at the earliest ages (10–13) tended to become the most persistent offenders, committing an average of 8.1 offences leading to convictions in an average criminal career lasting 9.9 years. Over a quarter of all the convicted males had criminal careers lasting longer than 10 years. It is generally true that an early onset of antisocial behaviour predicts a long and serious antisocial career (Loeber & LeBlanc, 1990).

It is important to investigate developmental sequences in antisocial and criminal careers. In a study of Montreal delinquents, LeBlanc and Frechette (1989) discovered that shoplifting and vandalism tended to occur before adolescence (average age of onset 11), burglary and motor vehicle theft in adolescence (average onset 14–15), and sex offences and drug trafficking in the later teenage years (average onset 17–19). Loeber (1988) proposed that there were three different developmental pathways for antisocial behaviour, which he labelled aggressive versatile, non-aggressive and exclusive substance use. The aggressive versatile pathway included delinquent acts and had the earliest age of onset. The frequency of occurrence of any particular behaviour predicted the likelihood of transition to the next most serious behaviour.

Versatility of Offending

Juvenile delinquents are predominantly versatile rather than specialized in their offending (Klein, 1984; Farrington, Snyder & Finnegan, 1988). In other words, people who commit one type of offence have a significant tendency also to commit other types. For example, in the Cambridge Study, 86% of convicted violent offenders also had convictions for non-violent offences (Farrington, 1991b).

Just as offenders tend to be versatile in their types of offending, they also tend to be versatile in their antisocial behaviour generally. In the Cambridge Study, convicted delinquents tended to be troublesome and dishonest in their primary schools, tended to be frequent liars and aggressive at age 12–14, and tended to be bullies at age 14. By age 18, delinquents tended to be antisocial in a wide variety of respects, including heavy drinking, heavy smoking, using prohibited drugs and heavy gambling. In addition, they tended to be sexually promiscuous, often beginning sexual intercourse at under the age of 15, having several sexual partners by age 18, and usually having unprotected intercourse (West & Farrington, 1977). Because of this versatility, any prevention method that succeeds in reducing delinquency is likely also to reduce these associated social problems.

West and Farrington (1977) argued that delinquency (which is dominated by crimes of dishonesty) is only one element of a larger syndrome of antisocial behaviour which arises in childhood and usually persists into adulthood. They developed a scale of 'antisocial tendency' at age 18, based on factors such as an unstable job record, heavy gambling, heavy smoking, drug use, drunk driving, sexual promiscuity, spending time hanging about on the street, antisocial group activity, violence, and anti-establishment attitudes. Their aim was to devise a scale that was not based on the types of acts (thefts and burglaries) that usually led to convictions, and they showed that the convicted males were usually antisocial in several other respects. For example, two-thirds (67%) of the males convicted up to age 18 had four or more of these antisocial features, compared with only 15% of the unconvicted males.

These results are consistent with findings obtained in numerous other studies. For example, in a St Louis survey, Robins and Ratcliff (1980) reported that juvenile delinquency tended to be associated with truancy, precocious sex, drinking and drug use. In two American studies separated by 13 years, Donovan, Jessor and Costa (1988) concluded that a single common factor accounted for the positive correlations among a number of adolescent antisocial behaviours, including problem drinking, marijuana use, precocious sexual intercourse and delinquent behaviour. Hence, as Jessor and Jessor (1977) argued, there is a syndrome of problem behaviour in adolescence. In the literature on childhood psychopathology, it is also customary to find a single 'broad-band' syndrome of externalizing problems, including stealing, lying, cheating, vandalism, substance use, running away from home and truancy (Achenbach et al., 1987).

Offending tends to be concentrated in certain people and certain families. In the Cambridge Study, while about one-third of the males were convicted of criminal offences, it was nevertheless true that only 6% of the sample—the chronic offenders—accounted for about half of all the convictions (Farrington & West, 1993). Similarly, chronic offenders were disproportionately likely to engage in other types of antisocial behaviour. In numerous other projects such as the Philadelphia cohort study of Wolfgang, Thornberry and Figlio (1987) and the Finnish research of Pulkkinen (1988), there was a similar concentration of offending in a small proportion of the sample.

Continuity in Offending

Generally, there is significant continuity between offending in one age range and offending in another. In the Cambridge Study, nearly three-quarters (73%) of those convicted as juveniles at age 10–16 were reconvicted at age 17–24, in comparison with only 16% of those not convicted as juveniles (Farrington, 1992a). Nearly half (45%) of those convicted as juveniles were reconvicted at age 25–32, in comparison with only 8% of those not convicted as juveniles. Furthermore, this continuity over time did not merely reflect continuity in police reaction to crime. Farrington (1989c) showed that, for 10 specified offences, the significant continuity between offending in one age range and offending in a later age range held for self-reports as well as official convictions.

Other studies (e.g. McCord, 1991) show similar continuity. For example, in Sweden, Stattin and Magnusson (1991) reported that nearly 70% of males registered for crime before age 15 were registered again between ages 15 and 20, and nearly 60% were registered between ages 21 and 29. Also, the number of juvenile offences is an effective predictor of the number of adult offences (Wolfgang, Thornberry & Figlio, 1987). Farrington and Wikstrom (1994) showed that there was considerable continuity in offending between ages 10 and 25 in both London and Stockholm. A key theoretical issue is how far it is necessary to distinguish different types of delinquents. For example, Moffitt (1993) argued that offenders fell into two broad categories: 'life-course-persistent', who start offending in childhood and continue into adulthood, and 'adolescent-limited', who start and end during the teenage years.

It is not always realized that relative continuity is quite compatible with absolute change. In other words, the relative ordering of people on some underlying construct such as antisocial tendency can remain significantly stable over time, even though the absolute level of antisocial tendency declines on average for everyone. For example, Farrington (1990a) in the Cambridge Study showed that the prevalence of self-reported offending declined significantly between ages 18 and 32, but that there was a significant tendency for the worst offenders at 18 also to be the worst offenders at 32.

There is also continuity in antisocial behaviour over time. Numerous studies show that childhood conduct problems predict later offending and antisocial behaviour (Loeber & LeBlanc, 1990). For example, Spivack, Marcus and Swift (1986) in Philadelphia discovered that troublesome behaviour in kindergarten (age 3–4) predicted later police contacts; and Ensminger, Kellan and Rubin (1983) in Chicago and Tremblay, LeBlanc and Schwartzman (1988) in Montreal showed that ratings of aggressiveness by teachers and peers in the first grade (age 6–7) predicted self-reported offending at age 14–15.

Similarly, in the Cambridge Study there was evidence of continuity in antisocial behaviour from childhood to the teenage years. Farrington (1991a) developed scales of 'antisocial personality' at ages 10, 14, 18 and 32, based on offending and on other types of antisocial behaviour. The antisocial personality scale at age 10 correlated 0.50 with the corresponding scale at age 14 and 0.38 with the scale at age 18 (Farrington, 1991a). Troublesome behaviour at age 8–10 (rated by peers and teachers) was the best predictor of conviction up to age 32; 62% of troublesome boys were convicted. In regard to specific types of antisocial behaviour, troublesomeness at age 8–10 significantly predicted bullying at both ages 14 and 18 (Farrington, 1993c). Again, troublesomeness at age 8–10 was the best predictor of both truancy and aggression at age 12–14 in the secondary schools (Farrington, 1980, 1989a).

There is also continuity in antisocial behaviour from the teenage to the adult years. In the Cambridge Study, a measure of adult social dysfunction was developed at age 32, based on (in the previous five years) convictions, self-reported offending, poor home conditions, poor cohabitation history, child problems, poor employment history, substance abuse, violence and poor mental health (a high score on the General Health Questionnaire; see Farrington et al., 1988a, 1988b, and Farrington, 1989b). This measure of adult social dysfunction at age 32 was significantly predicted by the antisocial tendency measure at age 18 (Farrington, 1993a). Similarly, a measure of antisocial personality was developed at age 32 which was comparable with the earlier antisocial personality measures. Antisocial personality at age 18 had a high correlation (0.55) with antisocial personality at age 32 (Farrington, 1991a).

Expressing this another way, 60% of the most antisocial quarter of males at age 18 were still in the most antisocial quarter 14 years later at age 32. Bearing in mind the very great environmental changes between 18 and 32, as the males left their parental homes, went through a period of unstable living arrangements, and eventually settled down in marital homes, this consistency over time seems likely to reflect consistency in the individual's personality rather than consistency in the environment. It is often found that about half of any sample of antisocial children persist to become antisocial teenagers, and that about half of any sample of antisocial teenagers persist to become antisocial adults. Comparing the 0.55 correlation between ages 18 and 32 with the 0.38 correlation between ages 10 and 18, it is interesting that there was increasing stabilization of antisocial personality with age.

Zoccolillo and colleagues (1992), in a follow-up of children who had been in care, also demonstrated the continuity between childhood conduct disorder (at age 9–12) and adult social dysfunction (at age 26) in areas of work and social and sexual relationships. For example, 81% of those with three or more symptoms of conduct disorder showed adult dysfunction in two or more areas, compared with only 21% of those with less than three symptoms of conduct disorder. Approaching half (40%) of the males with three or more symptoms of conduct disorder showed persistent antisocial behaviour after age 18 and fulfilled the psychiatric criteria for adult antisocial personality disorder.

RISK FACTORS FOR OFFENDING

This chapter reviews risk factors that influence the development of offending. Fortunately or unfortunately, there is no shortage of factors that are significantly correlated with offending and antisocial behaviour; indeed, literally thousands of variables differentiate significantly between official offenders and non-offenders and correlate significantly with self-reports of offending. Loeber and Dishion (1983) and Loeber and Stouthamer-Loeber (1987) extensively reviewed the predictors of male offending. The most important predictors were poor parental child management techniques, childhood antisocial behaviour, offending by parents and siblings, low intelligence and educational attainment, and separation from parents. All of these influences are reviewed in this chapter. In contrast, low socio-economic status was a rather weak predictor, in agreement with other research casting doubt on its importance (e.g. Hindelang, Hirschi & Weis, 1981). Individual, family and peer factors may have additive, interactive or sequential effects, and they are usually intercorrelated, but I will consider them one by one.

Risk factors are prior factors that increase the risk of occurrence of events such as the onset, frequency, persistence or duration of offending. Longitudinal data are required to establish the ordering of risk factors and offending, and to avoid retrospective bias in measurement. The focus in this chapter is on risk factors for the onset or prevalence of offending. Few studies have examined risk factors for persistence or duration. However, in the Cambridge Study, Farrington and Hawkins (1991) investigated factors that predicted whether offenders convicted before age 21 persisted or desisted between ages 21 and 32. The best independent predictors of persistence included the boy rarely spending leisure time with his father at age 11–12, low intelligence at age 8–10, employment instability at age 16 and heavy drinking at age 18. Indeed, nearly 90% of the convicted males who were frequently unemployed and heavy drinkers as teenagers went on to be reconvicted after age 21.

It is often difficult to decide if any given risk factor is an indicator (symptom) or a possible cause of antisocial tendency. For example, do heavy drinking, truancy, unemployment, and divorce measure antisocial tendency, or do they cause (an increase in) it? It is important not to include a measure of the dependent variable as an independent variable in causal analyses, because this will lead to false (tautological) conclusions and an overestimation of explanatory or predictive power (Amdur, 1989).

It is not unreasonable to argue that some factors may be both indicative and causal. For example, long-term variations *between* individuals in antisocial tendency may be reflected in variations in alcohol consumption, just as short-term variations *within* individuals in alcohol consumption may cause more antisocial behaviour during the heavier drinking periods. The interpretation of other factors may be more clear-cut. For example, being exposed as a child to poor parental child-rearing techniques might cause antisocial tendency but would not be an indicator of it; and burgling a house might be an indicator of antisocial tendency but would be unlikely to cause it (although it might be argued that, when an antisocial act is successful in leading to positive reinforcement, this reinforcement causes an increase in the underlying antisocial tendency).

Cross-sectional studies make it impossible to distinguish between indicators and causes, since they can merely demonstrate correlations between high levels of one factor (e.g. unemployment) and high levels of another (e.g. offending). However, longitudinal studies can show that offending is greater (within individuals) during some periods (e.g. of unemployment) than during other periods (e.g. of employment). Because within-individual studies have greater control over extraneous influences than between-individual studies, longitudinal studies can demonstrate that changes in unemployment within individuals cause offending with high internal validity in quasi-experimental analyses (Farrington, 1988; Farrington et al., 1986). Longitudinal studies can also establish whether factors such as unemployment have the same or different effects on offending when they vary within or between individuals. Implications for prevention and treatment, which require changes within individuals, cannot necessarily be drawn from effects demonstrated only in between-individual (cross-sectional) research.

Because of the difficulty of establishing causal effects of factors that vary only between individuals (e.g. gender and ethnicity), and because such factors have no practical implications for prevention (e.g. it is not practicable to change males into females), unchanging variables will not be reviewed in this chapter. In any case, their effects on offending are usually explained by reference to other, changeable, factors (Farrington, 1987a). For example, gender differences in offending have been explained on the basis of different socialization methods used by parents with boys and girls, or different opportunities of males and females for offending.

It is important to establish which factors predict delinquency independently of other factors. In the Cambridge Study, it was generally true that each of six categories of variables (impulsivity, intelligence, parenting, criminal family, socio-economic deprivation, child antisocial behaviour) predicted offending independently of each other category (Farrington, 1990b). A theory was proposed to explain the development of male property offending in general and the major results of the Cambridge Study in particular (Farrington, 1986b, 1992b, 1993b).

INDIVIDUAL RISK FACTORS

Hyperactivity and Impulsivity

Hyperactivity and impulsivity are among the most important personality or individual difference factors that predict later delinquency. Hyperactivity usually begins before age 5 and often before age 2, and it tends to persist into adolescence (Taylor, 1986). It is associated with restlessness, impulsivity and a short attention span, and for that reason has been termed the 'hyperactivity–impulsivity–attention deficit' or HIA syndrome (Loeber, 1987). Related concepts include a poor ability to defer gratification (Mischel, Shoda & Rodriguez, 1989) and a short future time perspective (Stein, Sarbin & Kulik, 1968). Pulkkinen (1986) has usefully reviewed the various concepts and measures of hyperactivity and impulsivity.

Many investigators have reported a link between HIA and offending. For example, in a Swedish longitudinal survey, Klinteberg and colleagues (1993) found that hyperactivity at 13 (rated by teachers) predicted violent offending up to age 26. Satterfield (1987) tracked HIA and matched control boys in Los Angeles between ages 9 and 17, and showed that six times as many of the HIA boys were arrested for serious offences. Similar results were reported by Gittelman and co-workers (1985) in New York. Other studies have shown that childhood hyperactivity predicts adolescent and adult antisocial behaviour and substance use (Barkley et al., 1990; Mannuzza et al., 1991).

The major problem of interpretation in these projects centres on the marked overlap between hyperactivity and conduct disorder (Taylor, 1986). Many of the boys in these and other longitudinal studies of hyperactivity (Huessy & Howell, 1985; Nylander, 1979) probably displayed not only HIA but also conduct disorder as well, making it difficult to know how far the results might have reflected the continuity between childhood antisocial behaviour and adult antisocial behaviour.

Farrington, Loeber and van Kannen (1990) developed a combined measure of hyperactivity–impulsivity–attention deficit at age 8–10 and showed that it significantly predicted juvenile convictions independently of conduct problems at age 8–10. Hence, it might be concluded that HIA is not merely another measure of antisocial personality, but is a possible cause, or an earlier stage in a developmental sequence. For example, Richman, Stevenson and Graham (1985) found that restlessness at age 3 predicted conduct disorder at age 8. Other studies have also concluded that hyperactivity and conduct disorder are different constructs (Blouin et al., 1989; McGee, Williams & Silva, 1985). Similar constructs to HIA, such as sensation seeking, are also related to delinquency (Farley & Sewell, 1976; White, Labouvie & Bates, 1985). In the Cambridge Study, the rating of daring or risk-taking at age 8–10 by parents and peers significantly predicted convictions up to age 32 independently of all other variables (Farrington, 1990b, 1993a); 57% of daring boys were later convicted. Also, poor concentration or restlessness was the most important predictor of convictions for violence (Farrington, 1994).

It has been suggested that HIA might be a behavioural consequence of a low level of physiological arousal (Ellis, 1987). Offenders have a low level of arousal according to their low alpha frequency (brain) waves on the EEG, or according to autonomic nervous system indicators such as heart rate, blood pressure or skin conductance, or they show low autonomic reactivity (Venables & Raine, 1987). For example, violent offenders in the Cambridge Study had significantly low heart rates (Farrington, 1987b). The causal links between low autonomic arousal, consequent sensation seeking, and offending are brought out explicitly in Mawson's (1987) theory of transient criminality.

Intelligence and Attainment

As Hirschi and Hindelang (1977) showed in their review, intelligence is an important correlate of offending: at least as important as social class or ethnicity. Intelligence can be measured very early in life. For example, in a prospective longitudinal survey of about 120 Stockholm males, intelligence measured at age 3 significantly predicted officially recorded offending up to age 30 (Stattin & Klackenberg-Larsson, 1993). Frequent offenders (with four or more offences) had an average IQ of 88 at age 3, whereas non-offenders had an average IQ of 101. Official offending was also significantly predicted by language development at 6, 18 and 24 months. All of these results held up after controlling for social class. Also, in the Perry pre-school project in Michigan, intelligence at age 4 significantly predicted the number of arrests up to age 27 (Schweinhart, Barnes & Weikart, 1993).

In the Cambridge Study, West and Farrington (1973) found that twice as many of the boys scoring 90 or less on a non-verbal intelligence test (Raven's Progressive Matrices) at age 8–10 were convicted as juveniles than of the remainder. It was difficult to disentangle intelligence and attainment. Low non-verbal intelligence was highly correlated with low verbal intelligence (vocabulary, word comprehension, verbal reasoning) and with low school attainment, and all of these measures predicted juvenile convictions to much the same extent. In addition to their poor school performance, delinquents tended to leave school at the earliest possible age (which was then 15), to take no school examinations, and to be frequent truants (Farrington, 1995a).

Low non-verbal intelligence was especially characteristic of the juvenile recidivists and those first convicted at the earliest ages (10–13). Furthermore, low non-verbal intelligence predicted juvenile self-reported offending to almost exactly the same degree as juvenile convictions (Farrington, 1992c), suggesting that the link between low intelligence and delinquency was not caused by the less intelligent boys having a greater probability of being caught. Also, measures of intelligence and attainment predicted measures of offending independently of other variables such as family income and family size; 53% of boys with low non-verbal intelligence (90 or less) at age 8–10 were convicted up to age 32 (Farrington, 1990b). Similar results have been obtained in other projects (Lynam, Moffitt & Stouthamer-Loeber, 1993; Moffitt & Silva, 1988a; Wilson & Herrnstein, 1985). Delinquents often do better on non-verbal performance tests, such as object assembly and block design, than on verbal tests (Walsh, Petee & Beyer, 1987), suggesting that they find it easier to deal with concrete objects than with abstract concepts.

Intelligence may lead to delinquency through the intervening factor of school failure, as Hirschi and Hindelang (1977) suggested. The association between school failure and offending has been demonstrated consistently in longitudinal surveys (e.g. Polk et al., 1981; Wolfgang, Figlio & Sellin, 1972). In their longitudinal survey of over 200 African-American males, Robins and Hill (1966) reported that truancy and school failure were both related to early official delinquency (before age 15). They showed how the probability of offending increased according to the presence of truancy, school failure and low socio-economic status. Where none of these factors was present, only 3% of the boys became delinquent, compared with 36% when all three factors were present.

A more plausible explanatory factor underlying the link between intelligence and offending is the ability to manipulate abstract concepts. People who are poor at this tend to do badly in intelligence tests such as the Matrices and in school attainment, and they also tend to commit offences, mainly because of their poor ability to foresee the consequences of their offending and to appreciate the feelings of victims (i.e. their low empathy). Certain family backgrounds are less conducive than others to the development of abstract reasoning. For example, lower class, poorer parents tend to live for the present and to have little thought for the future, and tend to talk in terms of the concrete rather than the abstract, as Cohen (1955) pointed out many years ago. A lack of concern for the future is also linked to the concept of impulsivity.

Modern research is studying not just intelligence but also detailed patterns of cognitive and neuropsychological deficit. For example, in a New Zealand longitudinal study of over 1000 children from birth to age 15, Moffitt and Silva (1988b) found that self-reported offending was related to verbal, memory and visual–motor integration deficits, independently of low social class and family adversity. Neuropsychological research might lead to important advances in knowledge about the link between brain functioning and delinquency. For example, the 'executive functions' of the brain, located in the frontal lobes, include sustaining attention and concentration, abstract reasoning and concept formation, anticipation and planning, self-monitoring of behaviour, and inhibition of inappropriate or impulsive behaviour (Moffitt, 1990). Deficits in these executive functions are conducive to low measured intelligence and to offending. Moffitt and Henry (1989) found deficits in these executive functions especially for delinquents who were both antisocial and hyperactive.

FAMILY RISK FACTORS

Loeber and Stouthamer-Loeber (1986) completed an exhaustive review of family factors as correlates and predictors of juvenile conduct problems and delinquency. They found that poor parental supervision or monitoring, erratic or harsh parental discipline, parental disharmony, parental rejection of the child, and low parental involvement in the child's activities (as well as antisocial parents and large family size) were all important predictors of offending. Similar conclusions were drawn by Snyder and Patterson (1987) and Utting, Bright & Henricson (1993) in detailed reviews. These results are concordant with the theory (e.g. Trasler, 1962) that antisocial behaviour develops when the normal social learning process, based on rewards and punishments from parents, is disrupted by erratic discipline, poor supervision, parental disharmony or unsuitable (antisocial or criminal) parental models.

Parental Supervision, Discipline and Attitude

In the Cambridge–Somerville study in Boston, McCord (1979) reported that poor parental supervision was the best predictor of both violent and property crimes. Parental aggressiveness (which included harsh discipline, shading into child abuse at the extreme) and parental conflict were significant precursors of violent but not property crimes, while the mother's attitude (passive or rejecting) was a significant precursor of property but not violent crimes. Robins (1979), in her long-term follow-up studies in St Louis, also found that poor supervision and discipline were consistently related to later offending.

Other studies also show the link between supervision and discipline and delinquency. In a Birmingham survey, Wilson (1980) followed up nearly 400 boys in 120 large intact families, and concluded that the most important correlate of convictions, cautions and self-reported delinquency was lax parental supervision at age 10. In their English national survey of juveniles aged 14–15 and their mothers, Riley and Shaw (1985) found that poor parental supervision was the most important correlate of self-reported delinquency for girls, and that it was the second most important for boys (after delinquent friends). Also, in their follow-up of nearly 700 Nottingham children in intact families, the Newsons reported that physical punishment by parents at ages 7 and 11 predicted later convictions (Newson & Newson, 1989).

In the Cambridge Study, West and Farrington (1973) found that harsh or erratic parental discipline, cruel, passive or neglecting parental attitude, poor supervision, and parental conflict, all measured at age 8, all predicted later juvenile convictions. Generally, the presence of any of these adverse family background features doubled the risk of a later juvenile conviction. Furthermore, poor parental child-rearing behaviour (a combination of discipline, attitude and conflict) and poor parental supervision both predicted juvenile self-reported as well as official offending (Farrington, 1979). Poor parental child-rearing behaviour was related to early rather than later offending, and it predicted early convictions between ages 10 and 13 independently of all other factors (Farrington, 1984, 1986b). However, it was not characteristic of those first convicted as adults (West & Farrington, 1977). In contrast, poor parental supervision predicted both juvenile and adult convictions (Farrington, 1992b); 55% of boys who were poorly supervised at age 8 were convicted up to age 32 (Farrington, 1990b).

There seems to be significant intergenerational transmission of aggressive and violent behaviour from parents to children, as McCord's (1979) research suggested. This is also demonstrated in Widom's (1989) retrospective study of over 900 abused children in Indianapolis. Children who were physically abused up to age 11 were significantly likely to become violent offenders in the next 15 years. Similarly, harsh discipline and attitude of parents when the boys were aged 8 significantly predicted later violent as opposed to non-violent offenders up to age 21 in the Cambridge Study (Farrington, 1978). More recent research (Farrington, 1991b) showed that harsh discipline and attitude predicted both violent and persistent offending up to age 32. The extensive review by Malinosky-Rummell and Hansen (1993) confirms that being physically abused as a child predicts later violent and non-violent offending. Of course, the mechanisms underlying the intergenerational transmission of violence could be genetic as well as environmental (DiLalla & Gottesman, 1991).

Broken Homes and Separations

Most studies of broken homes have focused on the loss of the father rather than the mother, simply because the loss of a father is much more common. McCord (1982) in Boston carried out an interesting study of the relationship between homes broken by loss of the natural father and later serious offending. She found that the prevalence of offending was high for boys reared in broken homes without affectionate mothers (62%) and for those reared in united homes characterized by parental conflict (52%), irrespective of whether they had affectionate mothers. The prevalence of offending was low for those reared in united homes without conflict (26%) and—importantly—equally low for boys from broken homes with affectionate mothers (22%). These results suggest that it is not so much the broken home which is criminogenic as the parental conflict which often causes it, and that a loving mother might in some sense be able to compensate for the loss of a father.

In the Newcastle Thousand Family Study, Kolvin et al. (1988b) reported that marital disruption (divorce or separation) in a boy's first five years predicted his later convictions up to age 32. Similarly, in the Dunedin study in New Zealand, Henry and colleagues (1993) found that children who were exposed to parental discord and many changes of the primary caretaker tended to become antisocial and delinquent, and Bergman and Wangby (1993) in Sweden reported that the number of separations experienced by a child predicted later offending.

The cause of the broken home is emphasized in the English national longitudinal survey of over 5000 children born in one week of 1946 (Wadsworth, 1979). Illegitimate children were excluded from this survey, so all the children began life with two married parents. Boys from homes broken by divorce or separation had an increased likelihood of being convicted or officially cautioned up to age 21, in comparison with those from homes broken by death or from unbroken homes. Homes broken while the boy was between birth and age 4 especially predicted delinquency, while homes broken while the boy was between age 11 and age 15 were not particularly criminogenic. Remarriage (which happened more often after divorce or separation than after death) was also associated with an increased risk of delinquency, suggesting a possibly negative effect of step-parents. The meta-analysis by Wells and Rankin (1991) also shows that broken homes are more strongly related to delinquency when they are caused by parental separation or divorce rather than by death.

In the Cambridge Study, both permanent and temporary (more than one month) separations before age 10 (usually from the father) predicted convictions and self-reported delinquency, providing that they were not caused by death or hospitalization (Farrington, 1992c). However, homes broken at an early age (under age 5) were not unusually criminogenic (West & Farrington, 1973). Separation before age 10 predicted both juvenile and adult convictions (Farrington, 1992b) and predicted convictions up to age 32 independently of all other factors such as low family income or poor school attainment (Farrington, 1990b, 1993a); 56% of separated boys were convicted.

In a survey of over 1000 adults carried out for the *Sunday Times* (14 November 1993), the majority (63%) thought that it was vital for a child to grow up with both a mother and a father. Indeed, growing up in a single-parent, female-headed household is an important predictor of offending in American research (e.g. Ensminger, Kellam & Rubin, 1983). In Canada, the large-scale Ontario Child Health Study of 3300 children aged 4–16 reported that single-parent families tended to have conduct-disordered and substance-abusing children (Blum, Boyle & Offord, 1988; Boyle & Offord, 1986). However, the researchers found it difficult to disentangle the effects of single-parent families from the effects of low-income families, because most single-parent families were living in poverty. The analyses of Morash and Rucker (1989) suggest that women who have children as teenagers and then become lone mothers are particularly likely to have delinquent children.

Parental Criminality

Criminal, antisocial and alcoholic parents also tend to have delinquent sons, as Robins (1979) found. Robins, West and Herjanic (1975) followed up over 200 African-American males in St Louis and found that arrested parents tended to have arrested children, and that the juvenile records of the parents and children showed similar rates and types of offences. Similarly, McCord (1977), in her 30-year follow-up of about 250 treated boys in the Cambridge–Somerville study, reported that convicted fathers tended to have convicted sons. Whether there is a specific relationship in her study between types of convictions of parents and children is not clear. McCord found that 29% of fathers convicted for violence had sons convicted for violence, in comparison with 12% of other fathers, but this may reflect the general tendency for convicted fathers to have convicted sons rather than any specific tendency for violent fathers to have violent sons. Wilson (1987) in Birmingham also showed that convictions of parents predicted convictions and cautions of sons; more than twice as many sons with a convicted parent were convicted themselves, compared with sons with unconvicted parents.

In the Cambridge Study, the concentration of offending in a small number of families was remarkable. West and Farrington (1977) discovered that less than 5% of the families were responsible for about half of the criminal convictions of all members (fathers, mothers, sons and daughters) of all 400 families. West and Farrington (1973) showed that having convicted mothers, fathers and brothers by a boy's tenth birthday significantly predicted his own later convictions. Furthermore, convicted parents and delinquent siblings predicted self-reported as well as official offending (Farrington, 1979).

Unlike most early precursors, a convicted parent was related less to offending of early onset (age 10–13) than to later offending (Farrington, 1986b). Also, a convicted parent predicted which juvenile offenders went on to become adult criminals and which recidivists at age 19 continued offending rather than desisted (West & Farrington, 1977), and predicted convictions up to age 32 independently of all other factors (Farrington, 1990b, 1993a). As many as 59% of boys with a convicted parent were themselves convicted up to age 32 (Farrington, 1990b).

It is not entirely clear why criminal parents tend to have delinquent children. In the Cambridge Study, there was no evidence that criminal parents directly encouraged their children to commit crimes or taught them criminal techniques. On the contrary, criminal parents were highly critical of their children's offending; for example, 89% of convicted men at age 32 disagreed with the statement that 'I would not mind if my son/daughter committed a criminal offence'. Also, it was extremely rare for a parent and a child to be convicted for an offence committed together (Reiss & Farrington, 1991).

There was some evidence that having a convicted parent increased a boy's likelihood of being convicted, over and above his actual level of misbehaviour (West & Farrington, 1977). However, the fact that a convicted parent predicted self-reported offending as well as convictions shows that the labelling of children from known criminal families was not the only reason for the intergenerational transmission of criminality. It is possible that there is some genetic factor in this transmission (Mednick, Gabrielli & Hutchings, 1983). However, the main link in the chain between criminal parents and delinquent children that we could discover in the Cambridge Study was the markedly poor supervision by criminal parents.

Large Family Size

Many studies show that large families are conducive to delinquency (Fischer, 1984). For example, in the National Survey of Health and Development,

Wadsworth (1979) found that the percentage of boys who were officially delinquent increased from 9% for families containing one child to 24% for families containing four or more children. The Newsons in their Nottingham study also concluded that large family size was one of the most important predictors of offending (Newson, Newson & Adams, 1993), and similar results were reported by Kolvin and colleagues (1988b) in Newcastle upon Tyne and Ouston (1984) in Inner London.

In the Cambridge Study, if a boy had four or more siblings by his tenth birthday, this doubled his risk of being convicted as a juvenile (West & Farrington, 1973). Large family size predicted self-reported delinquency as well as convictions (Farrington, 1979), and adult as well as juvenile convictions (Farrington, 1992b). Large family size was the most important independent predictor of convictions up to age 32 in a logistic regression analysis (Farrington, 1993a); 58% of boys from large families were convicted up to this age.

There are many possible reasons why a large number of siblings might increase the risk of delinquency. Generally, as the number of children in a family increases, the amount of parental attention that can be given to each child decreases. Also, as the number of children increases, the household will tend to become more overcrowded, possibly leading to increases in frustration, irritation and conflict. In the Cambridge Study, large family size did not predict delinquency for boys living in the least crowded conditions, with two or more rooms than there were children (West & Farrington, 1973). More than 20 years earlier, Ferguson (1952) drew a similar conclusion in his study of over 1300 Glasgow boys, suggesting that an overcrowded household might be an important intervening factor between large family size and delinquency.

PEER RISK FACTORS

The reviews by Zimring (1981) and Reiss (1988) show that delinquent acts tend to be committed in small groups (of two or three people, usually) rather than alone. Large gangs are comparatively unusual; Esbensen and Huizinga (1993) in the Denver Youth Survey reported the prevalence of gang members (5%), the demographic composition of gangs and the link between gang membership and delinquency. In the Cambridge Study most officially recorded juvenile offences were committed with one or two others, but the incidence of co-offending declined steadily with age from age 10 onwards. Burglary, robbery and theft from vehicles were particularly likely to involve co-offenders, who tended to be similar in age and sex to the Study males and lived close to the boys' homes and to the locations of the offences.

The Study males were most likely to offend with brothers when they had brothers who were similar in age to them (Reiss & Farrington, 1991). In a study of delinquent boys and girls in Ottawa, Jones, Offord and Abrams (1980) proposed that there was male potentiation and female suppression of delinquency by boys. This theory was intended to explain why they found that male delinquents had relatively more brothers than sisters. However, this result was not obtained in the Cambridge Study, where the number of sisters was just as closely related to a boy's delinquency as the number of brothers (West & Farrington, 1973).

The major problem of interpretation is whether young people are more likely to commit offences while they are in groups than while they are alone, or whether the high prevalence of co-offending merely reflects the fact that, whenever young people go out, they tend to go out in groups. Do peers tend to encourage and facilitate offending, or is it just that most kinds of activities out of the home (both delinquent and non-delinquent) tend to be committed in groups? Another possibility is that the commission of offences encourages association with other delinquents, perhaps because 'birds of a feather flock together' or because of the stigmatizing and isolating effects of court appearances and institutionalization. It is surprisingly difficult to decide among these various possibilities, although most researchers argue that peer influence is an important factor. In the Rochester Youth Development Study, Thornberry and colleagues (1994) concluded that associating with delinquent peers led to an increase in delinquency and also that engaging in delinquency led to an increased association with delinquent peers. Peer (and family) influences are emphasized in Sutherland and Cressey's (1974) theory, which suggests that a child's delinquency depends on the number of persons in the immediate social environment with norms and attitudes favouring delinquency.

There is clearly a close relationship between the delinquent activities of a young male and those of his friends. Both in the United States (Hirschi, 1969) and in the United Kingdom (West & Farrington, 1973), it has been found that a boy's reports of his own offending are significantly correlated with his reports of his friends' delinquency. In the American National Youth Survey of Elliott, Huizinga and Ageton (1985), having delinquent peers was the best independent predictor of self-reported offending in a multivariate analysis. However, it is unclear how far this association reflects co-offending. In the same survey, Warr (1993) found that the importance of delinquent friends was lessened or eliminated by spending time with family members.

In the Cambridge Study, association with delinquent friends at age 14 was a significant independent predictor of convictions at the young adult ages (Farrington, 1986b). Also, the recidivists at age 19 who ceased offending differed from those who persisted, in that the desisters were more likely to have stopped going round in a group of male friends. Furthermore, spontaneous comments by the youths indicated that withdrawal from the delinquent peer group was seen as an important influence on ceasing to offend (West & Farrington, 1977). Therefore, continuing to associate with delinquent friends may be a key factor in determining whether juvenile delinquents persist in offending as young adults or desist.

Delinquent peers are likely to be most influential where they have high status within the peer group and are popular. However, studies both in the United States (Roff & Wirt, 1984) and in England (West & Farrington, 1973) show that delinquents are usually unpopular with their peers. It seems paradoxical for offending to be a group phenomenon facilitated by peer influence, and yet for offenders to be largely rejected by other adolescents (Parker & Asher, 1987). However, it may be that offenders are popular in antisocial groups and unpopular in prosocial groups, or that rejected children band together to form adolescent delinquent groups (Hartup, 1983).

PROTECTIVE FACTORS

There are several different definitions of protective factors. One is that protective factors are merely the opposite end of the scale from risk factors. For example, just as low intelligence is a risk factor, high intelligence may be a protective factor. Rae-Grant and colleagues (1989) used this definition in the Ontario Child Health Study and reported that the major protective factors for conduct disorder were getting along well with others, good academic performance and participation in organized activities.

Another possible definition of a protective factor is a variable that interacts with a risk factor to minimize the risk factor's effects (Rutter, 1985). If low intelligence was related to offending only for males from low-income families, and not for males from higher-income families, then higher income might be regarded as a protective factor against the effects of the risk factor of low intelligence. Different types of people may vary considerably in their resilience in the face of stressors. It is usual to investigate protective factors by identifying a subsample at risk (with some combination of risk factors) and then searching for factors that predict successful members of this subsample (those who do not have the antisocial outcome).

In Hawaii, Werner and Smith (1982) studied 72 children who possessed four or more risk factors for delinquency before age 2 but who nevertheless did not develop behavioural difficulties during childhood or adolescence. They found that the major protective factors included being first-born, active and affectionate infants, small family size and receiving a large amount of attention from caretakers. Kandel and colleagues (1988) studied the sons of imprisoned fathers in a Danish birth cohort of nearly 2000 males born in Copenhagen, and found that those sons who avoided imprisonment had significantly higher intelligence than those sons who were imprisoned. Hence, they considered that high intelligence was a protective factor. In the Newcastle Thousand Family Study, Kolvin et al. (1988a) studied high-risk boys (from deprived backgrounds) who nevertheless did not become offenders. The major protective factors under age 5 seemed to be good mothering, good maternal health, an employed head of household, and being an oldest child. At ages 11 and 15, the most important protective factors were high intelligence, high school attainment, good concentration, good parental supervision and membership of youth clubs.

In the Cambridge Study, Farrington et al. (1988a, 1988b) investigated vulnerable boys from typically criminogenic backgrounds (with three out of: low family income, large family size, convicted parents, poor parental child-rearing behaviour and low intelligence) who were not convicted up to age 32. The most characteristic feature of these boys was that they had few or no friends at age 8.

While they were genuinely well behaved at age 32, they were often leading relatively unsuccessful lives, for example living in dirty home conditions, not being home owners, living alone, having never married, having large debts, and having low-status, lowly paid jobs. Therefore, for boys from vulnerable backgrounds, social isolation may act as a protective factor against offending but not against other kinds of social dysfunctioning.

Factors that foster desistance may be in some sense protective, and the most important of these factors in the Cambridge Study were getting married, obtaining employment and moving out of London. Farrington and West (1995) found that a man's offending decreased after he got married, but then increased again if he became separated from his wife. Farrington and colleagues (1986) discovered that, after leaving school, the men committed fewer offences while employed than while unemployed, especially offences involving financial gain. Osborn (1980) showed that both self-reported and official delinquency of the men decreased after they moved out of London, possibly because of the effect of the move in breaking up delinquent groups.

PREVENTION AND TREATMENT

Risk Factors, Causes and Prevention

Methods of preventing or treating offending should be based on empirically validated theories about causes. In this section, implications about prevention and treatment are drawn from some of the risk factors reviewed above, assuming that they are likely causes. The major emphasis is on the early prevention of offending. Gordon and Arbuthnot (1987), Kazdin (1985, 1987) and McCord and Tremblay (1992) have provided more extensive reviews of this topic. I will focus on randomized experiments with reasonably large samples and with outcome measures of offending, since the effect of any intervention on offending can be demonstrated most convincingly in such experiments (Farrington, 1983; Farrington, Ohlin & Wilson, 1986). Many interesting experiments are not randomized (Jones & Offord, 1989), or do not have outcome measures of offending (Kazdin et al., 1987, 1989), or are based on very small samples (Shore & Massimo, 1979).

It is difficult to know how and when it is best to intervene, because of the lack of knowledge about developmental sequences, ages at which causal factors are most salient, and influences on onset, persistence and desistance. For example, if truancy leads to delinquency in a developmental sequence, intervening successfully to decrease truancy should lead to a decrease in delinquency. On the other hand, if truancy and delinquency are merely different behavioural manifestations of the same underlying construct, tackling one symptom would not necessarily change the underlying construct. Experiments are useful in distinguishing between developmental sequences and different manifestations, and indeed Berg, Hullin and McGuire (1979) found experimentally that decreases in truancy were followed by decreases in delinquency.

Causal factors may be more salient at some ages than others. For example, parental child-rearing factors are likely to be most influential before the teenage years, so that the same intervention technique targeted on parents may be more effective for children aged 8 than for those aged 16. Similarly, causal factors may have different effects on different stages of the criminal career. As an example, if delinquent peers affected continuation but not onset, an intervention technique targeted on peers should be applied after the criminal career has begun (as treatment) rather than before (as prevention).

It should be stated at the outset that many of the preventive effects on offending are rather small in magnitude and have been demonstrated with small samples, and there is rarely evidence that they are sustained over several years. The intervention methods reviewed here often provide glimmers of hope rather than solid evidence of substantial reductive effects. This may be because, as Kazdin (1987) argued, serious antisocial behaviour might be viewed as a chronic, long-lasting disease that requires continuous monitoring and intervention over the life course. It might be desirable to distinguish chronic and less seriously delinquent teenagers, and to apply different types of interventions to the two categories (LeBlanc & Frechette, 1989). If the chronics are the worst 5%, interventions applied to the next 10% may be more successful. However, success may depend on the extent to which risk factors specific to the next 10% can be identified.

An important consequence of the continuity in antisocial behaviour over time is that potential offenders can be identified at an early age with a reasonable degree of accuracy. In the Cambridge Study, Farrington (1985) developed a prediction scale based on early antisocial behaviour, convicted parents, socio-economic deprivation, low intelligence and poor parental child-rearing behaviour, all measured at age 8–10. This scale was constructed in a randomly chosen half of the sample and validated in the other half, with very little shrinkage in predictive efficiency. The 55 boys with the highest prediction scores included the majority of chronic offenders with six or more convictions up to age 25 (15 out of 23), 22 other convicted males (out of 109 with between one and five convictions) and only 18 unconvicted males (out of 265).

The ideas of early intervention and preventive treatment raise numerous theoretical, practical, ethical and legal issues. For example, should prevention techniques be targeted narrowly on children identified as potential delinquents or more widely on all children living in a certain high-risk area (e.g. a deprived housing estate)? It would be most efficient to target the children who are most in need of the treatment. Also, some treatments may be ineffective if they are targeted widely, if they depend on raising the level of those at the bottom of the heap relative to everyone else. It might be argued that early identification could have undesirable labelling or stigmatizing effects, although the most extreme cases are likely to be stigmatized anyway and there is no evidence that identification for preventive treatment in itself is damaging. The degree of stigmatization, if any, is likely to depend on the nature of the treatment. In order to gain political acceptance, it may be best to target areas rather than individuals.

The ethical issues raised by early intervention depend on the level of predictive accuracy and might perhaps be resolved by weighing the social costs against the social benefits. In the Cambridge Study, Farrington and co-workers (1988a, 1988b) found that three-quarters of vulnerable boys identified at age 10 were convicted. It might be argued that, if preventive treatment had been applied to these boys, the one-quarter who were 'false positives' would have been treated unnecessarily. However, if the treatment consisted of extra welfare benefits to families, and if it was effective in reducing the offending of the other three-quarters, the benefits might outweigh the costs and early identification might be justifiable. As already mentioned, the vulnerable boys who were not convicted had other types of social problems, including having few or no friends at age 8 and living alone in poor home conditions at age 32. Therefore, even the unconvicted males in the survey might have needed and benefited from some kind of preventive treatment designed to alleviate their problems. Blumstein, Farrington and Moitra (1985) developed an explicit method of taking social costs and benefits into account in prediction exercises.

Reducing Hyperactivity and Impulsivity

Hyperactivity is often treated, at least in the United States, using stimulant drugs such as Ritalin (Whalen & Henker, 1991). However, I will focus on psychological techniques designed to increase self-control. Hyperactivity and impulsivity might be altered using the set of techniques variously termed cognitive-behavioural interpersonal skills training, which have proved to be quite successful (Michelson, 1987). For example, the methods used by Ross to treat juvenile delinquents (Ross & Ross, 1988; Ross, Fabiano & Ewles, 1988) were solidly based on some of the known individual characteristics of offenders: impulsivity, concrete rather than abstract thinking, low empathy and egocentricity.

Ross believed that delinquents could be taught the cognitive skills in which they were deficient, and that this could lead to a decrease in their offending. His reviews of delinquency rehabilitation programmes (Gendreau & Ross, 1979, 1987) showed that those which were successful in reducing offending generally tried to change the offender's thinking. Ross carried out his own 'Reasoning and Rehabilitation' programme in Ottawa, Canada, and found (in a randomized experiment) that it led to a significant (74%) decrease in reoffending for a small sample in a short 9-month follow-up period. His training was carried out by probation officers, but he believed that it could be carried out by parents or teachers.

Ross' programme aimed to modify the impulsive, egocentric thinking of delinquents, to teach them to stop and think before acting, to consider the consequences of their behaviour, to conceptualize alternative ways of solving interpersonal problems, and to consider the impact of their behaviour on other people, especially their victims. It included social skills training, lateral thinking (to teach creative problem solving), critical thinking (to teach logical reasoning), value education (to teach values and concern for others), assertiveness training (to teach non-aggressive, socially appropriate ways to obtain desired outcomes), negotiation skills training, interpersonal cognitive problem-solving (to teach thinking skills for solving interpersonal problems), social perspective training (to teach how to recognize and understand other people's feelings), role-playing and modelling (demonstration and practice of effective and acceptable interpersonal behaviour).

The successful social skills training programme carried out by Sarason (1978) in Tacoma, Washington, is also worth mentioning here, although it was conducted in a juvenile institution. Nearly 200 male first offenders were randomly allocated to modelling, discussion or control groups. The modelling and discussion groups focused on prosocial ways of achieving goals, coping with frustrations, resisting temptation and delaying gratification. A five-year follow-up showed that the proportion of recidivists was halved in the modelling and discussion groups compared with the control group.

Pre-school Intellectual Enrichment Programmes

If low intelligence and school failure are causes of offending, then any programme that leads to an increase in school success should lead to a decrease in offending. One of the most successful delinquency prevention programmes has been the Perry pre-school project carried out in Ypsilanti (Michigan) by Schweinhart and Weikart (1980). This was essentially a 'Head Start' programme targeted on disadvantaged African-American children, who were allocated (approximately at random) to experimental and control groups. The experimental children attended a daily pre-school programme, backed up by weekly home visits, usually lasting two years (covering ages 3–4). The aim of the programme was to provide intellectual stimulation, to increase cognitive abilities, and to increase later school achievement.

About 120 children in the two groups were followed up to age 15, using teacher ratings, parent and youth interviews, and school records. As demonstrated in several other Head Start projects, the experimental group showed gains in intelligence that were rather short-lived. However, they were significantly better in elementary school motivation, school achievement at 14, teacher ratings of classroom behaviour at 6 to 9, self-reports of classroom behaviour at 15 and self-reports of offending at 15. Furthermore, a later follow-up of this sample by Berrueta-Clement and colleagues (1984) showed that, at age 19, the experimental group was more likely to be employed, more likely to have graduated from high school, more likely to have received college or vocational training, and less likely to have been arrested.

By age 27, the experimental group had accumulated only half as many arrests on average as the controls (Schweinhart et al., 1993). Also, they had significantly higher earnings and were more likely to be home-owners. More of the experimental women were married, and fewer of their children had been born out of wedlock. Hence, this pre-school intellectual enrichment programme led to decreases in school failure, to decreases in offending, and to decreases in other undesirable outcomes.

The Perry project is admittedly only one study based on relatively small numbers. However, its results become more compelling when viewed in the context of 10 other similar American Head Start projects followed up by the Consortium for Longitudinal Studies (1983) and other pre-school programmes such as the Carolina Abercedarian Project, which began at age 3 months (Horacek et al., 1987). With quite impressive consistency, all studies show that pre-school intellectual enrichment programmes have long-term beneficial effects on school success, especially in increasing the rate of high school graduation and decreasing the rate of special education placements. The Perry project was the only one to study offending, but the consistency of the school success results in all projects suggests that the effects on offending might be replicable.

Parent Management Training

If poor parental supervision and erratic child-rearing behaviour are causes of delinquency, it seems likely that parent training might succeed in reducing offending. Many different types of family therapy have been used (Kazdin, 1987; Tolan, Cromwell & Brasswell, 1986), but the behavioural parent management training developed by Patterson (1982) in Oregon is one of the most hopeful approaches. His careful observations of parent–child interaction showed that parents of antisocial children were deficient in their methods of child rearing. These parents failed to tell their children how they were expected to behave, failed to monitor the behaviour to ensure that it was desirable, and failed to enforce rules promptly and unambiguously with appropriate rewards and penalties. The parents of antisocial children used more punishment (such as scolding, shouting or threatening), but failed to make it contingent on the child's behaviour.

Patterson attempted to train these parents in effective child-rearing methods, namely noticing what a child is doing, monitoring behaviour over long periods, clearly stating house rules, making rewards and punishments contingent on behaviour, and negotiating disagreements so that conflicts and crises did not escalate. His treatment was shown to be effective in reducing child stealing and antisocial behaviour over short periods in small-scale studies (Dishion, Patterson & Kavanagh, 1992; Patterson, Chamberlain & Reid, 1982; Patterson, Reid & Dishion, 1992).

Another parenting intervention, termed functional family therapy, was evaluated by Alexander and his colleagues (Alexander & Parsons, 1973; Alexander et al., 1976; Klein, Alexander & Parsons, 1977). This aimed to modify patterns of family interaction by modelling, prompting and reinforcement, to encourage clear communication between family members of requests and solutions, and to minimize conflict. Essentially, all family members were trained to negotiate effectively, to set clear rules about privileges and responsibilities, and to use techniques of reciprocal reinforcement with each other. This technique halved the recidivism rate of status offenders in comparison with other approaches (client-centred or psychodynamic therapy). Its effectiveness with more serious offenders was confirmed in a replication study using matched groups (Barton et at., 1985).

Peer Influence Resistance Programmes

If having delinquent friends causes offending, then any programme which reduces their influence or increases the influence of prosocial friends could have a reductive effect on offending. Feldman, Caplinger and Wodarski (1983) carried out an experimental test of this prediction in St Louis. Over 400 boys (aged about 11) who were referred because of antisocial behaviour were randomly assigned to two types of activity groups, each comprising about 10–12 adolescents. The groups consisted either totally of referred youths or of one or two referred youths and about 10 non-referred (prosocial) peers. The focus was on group-level behaviour modification. On the basis of systematic observation, self-reports by the youths, and ratings by group leaders, it was concluded that the antisocial behaviour of the referred youths with prosocial peers decreased relative to that of the referred youths in homogeneously antisocial groups.

Several studies show that schoolchildren can be taught to resist peer influences encouraging smoking, drinking and marijuana use. (For detailed reviews of these programmes, see Botvin, 1990, and Hawkins, Catalano & Miller, 1992.) For example, Telch and co-workers (1982) in California employed older high school students to teach younger ones to develop counter-arguing skills to resist peer pressure to smoke, using modelling and guided practice. This approach was successful in decreasing smoking by the younger students, and similar results were reported by Botvin and Eng (1982) in New York City. Murray and colleagues (1984) in Minnesota used same-aged peer leaders to teach students how to resist peer pressures to begin smoking, and Evans and co-workers (1981) in Houston used films.

Using high-status peer leaders, alcohol and marijuana use can be reduced as well as smoking (Klepp, Halper & Perry, 1986; McAlister et al., 1980). Botvin and colleagues (1984) in New York compared the application of a substance use prevention programme by teachers and peer leaders. The programme aimed to foster social skills and teach students ways of resisting peer pressure to use these substances. They found that peer leaders were effective in decreasing smoking, drunkenness and marijuana use, but teachers were not. A large-scale meta-analysis of 143 substance use prevention programmes by Tobler (1986) concluded that programmes using peer leaders were the most effective in reducing smoking, drinking and drug use. These techniques, designed to counter antisocial peer pressures, could also help to decrease offending.

Combined Prevention Programmes

A combination of interventions may be more effective than a single method. For example, Kazdin, Siegel and Bass (1992) found that a combination of parent management training and problem-solving skills training was more effective in reducing self-reported delinquency than either method alone. Also, more complex individualized techniques including several different elements may be effective. Henggeler, Melton and Smith (1992) and Henggeler and colleagues (1993) showed that 'multi-systemic therapy', targeting the relationships between children and families, peers and schools, was effective in reducing rearrests in a two-year follow-up period, compared with the usual probation.

One of the most important prevention experiments was carried out in Montreal by Tremblay and colleagues (1991, 1992). They identified about 250 disruptive (aggressive/hyperactive) boys at age 6 for a prevention experiment. Between ages 7 and 9, the experimental group received training to foster social skills and self-control. Coaching peer modelling, role playing and reinforcement contingencies were used in small group sessions on such topics as 'how to help', 'what to do when you are angry' and 'how to react to teasing'. Also, their parents were trained using the parent management training techniques developed by Patterson (1982).

This prevention programme was quite successful. By age 12, the experimental boys committed less burglary and theft, were less likely to get drunk, and were less likely to be involved in fights than the controls. Also, the experimental boys were higher in school achievement. Interestingly, the differences in antisocial behaviour between experimental and control boys increased as the follow-up progressed.

An important school-based prevention experiment was carried out in Seattle by Hawkins, Von Cleve and Catalano (1991) and Hawkins and colleagues (1992). This combined parent training, teacher training and skills training. About 500 first-grade children (aged 6) in 21 classes in eight schools were randomly assigned to be in experimental or control classes. The children in the experimental classes received special treatment at home and school which was designed to increase their attachment to their parents and their bonding to the school, on the assumption that offending was inhibited by the strength of social bonds. Their parents were trained to notice and reinforce socially desirable behaviour in a programme called 'Catch them being good'. Their teachers were trained in classroom management, for example to provide clear instructions and expectations to children, to reward children for participation in desired behaviour, and to teach children prosocial methods of solving problems (Hawkins, Doueck & Lishner, 1988).

In an evaluation of this programme 18 months later, when the children were in different classes, Hawkins, Von Cleve and Catalano (1991) found that the boys who received the experimental programme were significantly less aggressive than the control boys, according to teacher ratings. This difference was particularly marked for Caucasian boys compared with African-American boys. The experimental girls were not significantly less aggressive, but they were less self-destructive, anxious and depressed. By the fifth grade, the experimental children were less likely to have initiated delinquency and alcohol use. It might be expected that a combination of interventions might in general be more effective than a single technique, although combining interventions makes it harder to identify the active ingredient.

CONCLUSIONS

A great deal has been learned in the last 20 years, particularly from longitudinal surveys, about risk factors for offending and other types of antisocial behaviour. Offenders differ significantly from non-offenders in many respects, including impulsivity, intelligence, family background and peer influence. Generally, these differences are present before, during and after criminal careers. While the precise causal chains that link these factors with offending, and the ways in which these factors have independent, interactive or sequential effects, are not known, it is clear that individuals at risk can be identified with reasonable accuracy.

Offending is one element of a larger syndrome of antisocial behaviour that arises in childhood and tends to persist into adulthood, with numerous different behavioural manifestations. However, while there is continuity over time in the relative ordering of people on antisocial behaviour, changes are also occurring. It is commonly found that about half of a sample of antisocial children go on to become antisocial teenagers, and about half of antisocial teenagers go on to become antisocial adults. More research is needed on factors that vary within individuals and that predict these changes over time. Research is especially needed on changing behavioural manifestations and developmental sequences at different ages. More efforts should especially be made to identify factors that protect vulnerable children from developing into delinquent teenagers. More longitudinal surveys are needed.

The interrelationships among social problems make it hard to know which are causes and which are indicators, what causes what, or when and how it is best to intervene. Prevention experiments are warranted that focus on one or more of cognitive-behavioural social skills training, pre-school intellectual enrichment programmes, parent management training, and peer influence resistance programmes. These experiments can be useful in establishing causal effects. Also, because of the link between offending and numerous other social problems, any measure that succeeds in reducing crime will have benefits that go far beyond this. Any measure that reduces crime will probably also reduce alcohol abuse, drunk driving, drug abuse, sexual promiscuity, family violence, truancy, school failure, unemployment, marital disharmony and divorce. It is clear that problem children tend to grow up into problem adults, and that problem adults tend to produce more problem children. Major efforts to tackle the roots of crime are urgently needed, especially those focusing on early development in the first few years of life.

REFERENCES

Achenbach, T. M., Verhulst, F. C., Baron, G. D. & Althaus, M. (1987). A comparison of syndromes derived from the child behaviour checklist for American and Dutch boys aged 6–11 and 12–16. *Journal of Child Psychology and Psychiatry*, **28**, 437–53.

Alexander, J. F., Barton, C., Schiavo, R. S. & Parsons, B. V. (1976). Systems-behavioural intervention with families of delinquents: Therapist characteristics, family behaviour and outcome. *Journal of Consulting and Clinical Psychology*, **44**, 656–64.

Alexander, J. F. & Parsons, B. V. (1973). Short-term behavioural intervention with delinquent families: Impact on family process and recidivism. *Journal of Abnormal Psychology*, **81**, 219–25.

Amdur, R. L. (1989). Testing causal models of delinquency: A methodological critique. *Criminal Justice and Behaviour*, **16**, 35–62.

Barclay, G. C. (1990). The peak age of known offending by males. *Home Office Research Bulletin*, **28**, 20–3.

Barkley, R. A., Fischer, M., Edelbrock, C. S. & Smallish, L. (1990). The adolescent outcome of hyperactive children diagnosed by research criteria. I. An 8-year prospective follow-up study. *Journal of the American Academy of Child and Adolescent Psychiatry*, **29**, 546–57.

Barton, C., Alexander, J. F., Waldron, H., Turner, C. W. & Warburton, J. (1985). Generalizing treatment effects of functional family therapy: Three replications. *American Journal of Family Therapy*, **13**, 16–26.

Berg, I., Hullin, R. & McGuire, R. (1979). A randomly controlled trial of two court procedures in truancy. In D. P. Farrington, K. Hawkins & S. Lloyd-Bostock (eds), *Psychology, Law and Legal Processes*. London: MacMillan, pp. 145–51.

Bergman, L. R. & Wangby, M. (1993). Adult adjustment problems of separated children: A longitudinal study from birth to the age of 23 years. *Scandinavian Journal of Social Welfare*, **2**, 10–16.

Berrueta-Clement, J. R., Schweinhart, L. J., Barnett, W. S., Epstein, A. S. & Weikart, D. P. (1984). *Changed Lives*. Ypsilanti, MI: High/Scope.

Blackburn, R. (1993). *The Psychology of Criminal Conduct*. Chichester: Wiley.

Blouin, A. G., Conners, C. K., Seidel, W. T. & Blouin, J. (1989). The independence of hyperactivity from conduct disorder: Methodological considerations. *Canadian Journal of Psychiatry*, **34**, 279–82.

Blum, H. M., Boyle, M. H. & Offord, D. R. (1988). Single-parent families: Child psychiatric disorder and school performance. *Journal of the American Academy of Child and Adolescent Psychiatry*, **27**, 214–19.

Blumstein, A., Farrington, D. P. & Moitra, S. (1985). Delinquency careers: Innocents, desisters and persisters. In M. Tonry & N. Morris (eds), *Crime and Justice*, Vol. 6. Chicago: University of Chicago Press, pp. 187–219.

Botvin, G. J. (1990). Substance abuse prevention: Theory, practice and effectiveness. In M. Tonry & J. Q. Wilson (eds). *Drugs and Crime*. Chicago: University of Chicago Press, pp. 461–519.

Botvin, G. J., Baker, E., Renick, N. L., Filazzola, A. D. & Botvin, E. M. (1984). A cognitive-behavioural approach to substance abuse prevention. *Addictive Behaviours*, **9**, 137–47.

Botvin, G. J & Eng. A. (1982). The efficacy of a multicomponent approach to the prevention of cigarette smoking. *Preventive Medicine*, **11**, 199–211.

Boyle, M. H. & Offord, D. R. (1986). Smoking, drinking and use of illicit drugs among adolescents in Ontario: Prevalence, patterns of use and sociodemographic correlates. *Canadian Medical Association Journal*, **135**, 1113–21.

Cohen, A. K. (1955). *Delinquent Boys*. Glencoe, IL: Free Press.

Consortium for Longitudinal Studies (1983). *As the Twig is Bent ... Lasting Effects of Pre-school Programmes*. Hillside, NJ: Erlbaum.

DiLalla, L. F. & Gottesman, I. I. (1991). Biological and genetic contributions to violence—Widom's untold tale. *Psychological Bulletin*, **109**, 125–9.

Dishion, T. J., Patterson, G. R. & Kavanagh, R. A. (1992). An experimental test of the coercion model: Linking theory, measurement and intervention. In J. McCord & R. Tremblay (eds), *Preventing Antisocial Behaviour*. New York: Guilford, pp. 253–82.

Donovan, J. E., Jessor, R. & Costa, F. M. (1988). Syndrome of problem behaviour in adolescence: A replication. *Journal of Consulting and Clinical Psychology*, **56**, 762–65.

Elliott, D. S., Huizinga, D. & Ageton, S. S. (1985). *Explaining Delinquency and Drug Use*. Beverly Hills, CA: Sage.

Elliott, D. S., Huizinga, D. & Menard, S. (1989). *Multiple Problem Youth*. New York: Springer-Verlag.

Ellis, L. (1987). Relationships of criminality and psychopathy with eight other apparent behavioural manifestations of sub-optimal arousal. *Personality and Individual Differences*, **8**, 905–25.

Ensminger, M. E., Kellam, S. G. & Rubin, B. R. (1983). School and family origins of delinquency. In K. T. Van Dusen & S. A. Mednick (eds), *Prospective Studies of Crime and Delinquency*. Boston: Kluwer-Nijhoff, pp. 73–97.

Esbensen, F. A. & Huizinga, D. (1993). Gangs, drugs and delinquency in a survey of urban youth. *Criminology*, **31**, 565–89.

Evans, R. I., Rozelle, R. M., Maxwell, S. E., Raines, B. E., Dill, C. A., Guthrie, T. J., Henderson, A. H. & Hill, P. C. (1981). Social modelling films to deter smoking in adolescents: Results of a three-year field investigation. *Journal of Applied Psychology*, **66**, 399–414.

Farley, F. H. & Sewell, T. (1976). Test of an arousal theory of delinquency: Stimulation-seeking in delinquent and non-delinquent black adolescents. *Criminal Justice and Behaviour*, **3**, 315–20.

Farrington, D. P. (1973). Self-reports of deviant behaviour: Predictive and stable? *Journal of Criminal Law and Criminology*, **64**, 99–110.

Farrington, D. P. (1978). The family backgrounds of aggressive youths. In L. Hersov, M. Berger & D. Shaffer (eds), *Aggression and Antisocial Behaviour in Childhood and Adolescence*. Oxford: Pergamon, pp. 73–93.

Farrington, D. P. (1979). Environmental stress, delinquent behaviour, and convictions. In I. G. Sarason & C. D. Spielberger (eds), *Stress and Anxiety*, Vol. 6. Washington, DC: Hemisphere, pp. 93–107.

Farrington, D. P. (1980). Truancy, delinquency, the home and the school. In L. Hersov and I. Berg (eds), *Out of School: Modern Perspectives in Truancy and School Refusal*. Chichester: Wiley, pp. 49–63.

Farrington, D. P. (1983). Randomized experiments on crime and justice. In M. Tonry & N. Morris (eds), *Crime and Justice*, Vol. 4. Chicago, IL: University of Chicago Press, pp. 257–308.

Farrington, D. P. (1984). Measuring the natural history of delinquency and crime. In R. A. Glow (ed.), *Advances in the Behavioural Measurement of Children*, Vol. 1. Greenwich, CT: JAI Press, pp. 217–63.

Farrington, D. P. (1985). Predicting self-reported and official delinquency. In D. P. Farrington & R. Tarling (eds), *Prediction in Criminology*. Albany, NY: State University of New York Press, pp. 150–73.

Farrington, D. P. (1986a). Age and crime. In M. Tonry & N. Morris (eds), *Crime and Justice*, Vol. 7. Chicago, IL: University of Chicago Press, pp. 189–250.

Farrington, D. P. (1986b). Stepping stones to adult criminal careers. In D. Olweus, J. Block & M. R. Yarrow (eds), *Development of Antisocial and Prosocial Behaviour*. New York: Academic Press, pp. 359–84.

Farrington, D. P. (1987a). Epidemiology. In H. C. Quay (ed.), *Handbook of Juvenile Delinquency*. New York: Wiley, pp. 33–61.

Farrington, D. P. (1987b). Implications of biological findings for criminological research. In S. A. Mednick, T. E. Moffitt & S. A. Stack (eds), *The Causes of Crime: New Biological Approaches*. Cambridge: Cambridge University Press, pp. 42–64.

Farrington, D. P. (1988). Studying changes within individuals: The causes of offending. In M. Rutter (ed.), *Studies of Psychosocial Risk*. Cambridge: Cambridge University Press, pp. 158–83.

Farrington, D. P. (1989a). Early predictors of adolescent aggression and adult violence. *Violence and Victims*, **4**, 79–100.

Farrington, D. P. (1989b). Later adult life outcomes of offenders and non-offenders. In M. Brambring, F. Losel & H. Skowronek (eds), *Children at Risk: Assessment, Longitudinal Research, and Intervention*. Berlin: De Gruyter, pp. 220–44.

Farrington, D. P. (1989c). Self-reported and official offending from adolescence to adulthood. In M. W. Klein (ed.), *Cross-national Research in Self-reported Crime and Delinquency*. Dordrecht, Netherlands: Kluwer, pp. 399–423.

Farrington, D. P. (1990a). Age, period, cohort, and offending. In D. M. Gottfredson & R. V. Clarke (eds), *Policy and Theory in Criminal Justice: Contributions in Honour of Leslie T. Wilkins*. Aldershot: Avebury, pp. 51–75.

Farrington, D. P. (1990b). Implications of criminal career research for the prevention of offending. *Journal of Adolescence*, **13**, 93–113.

Farrington, D. P. (1991a). Antisocial personality from childhood to adulthood. *The Psychologist*, **4**, 389–94.

Farrington, D. P. (1991b). Childhood aggression and adult violence: Early precursors and later life outcomes. In D. J. Pepler & K. H. Rubin (eds), *The Development and Treatment of Childhood Aggression*. Hillsdale, NJ: Erlbaum, pp. 5–29.

Farrington, D. P. (1992a). Criminal career research in the United Kingdom. *British Journal of Criminology*, **32**, 521–36.

Farrington, D. P. (1992b). Explaining the beginning, progress and ending of antisocial behaviour from birth to adulthood. In J. McCord (ed.), *Facts, Frameworks and Forecasts: Advances in Criminological Theory*, Vol. 3. New Brunswick, NJ: Transaction, pp. 253–86.

Farrington, D. P. (1992c). Juvenile delinquency. In J. C. Coleman (ed.), *The School Years* (2nd edn.). London: Routledge, pp. 123–63.

Farrington, D. P. (1992d). Trends in English juvenile delinquency and their interpretation. *International Journal of Comparative and Applied Criminal Justice*, **16**, 151–63.

Farrington, D. P. (1993a). Childhood origins of teenage antisocial behaviour and adult social dysfunction. *Journal of the Royal Society of Medicine*, **86**, 13–7.

Farrington, D. P. (1993b). Motivations for conduct disorder and delinquency. *Development and Psychopathology*, **5**, 225–41.

Farrington, D. P. (1993c). Understanding and preventing bullying. In M. Tonry & N. Morris (eds), *Crime and Justice*, Vol. 17. Chicago, IL: University of Chicago Press, pp. 381–458.

Farrington, D. P. (1994). Childhood, adolescent and adult features of violent males. In L. R. Huesmann (ed.), *Aggressive Behaviour: Current Perspectives*. New York: Plenum, pp. 215–40.

Farrington, D. P. (1995a). Later life outcomes of truants in the Cambridge Study. In I. Berg & J. Nursten (eds), *Unwillingly to School* (4th edn.). London: Gaskell, in press.

Farrington, D. P. (1995b). The development of offending and antisocial behaviour from childhood: Key findings from the Cambridge Study in Delinquent Development. *Journal of Child Psychology and Psychiatry*, **36**, 929–964.

Farrington, D. P. & Burrows, J. N. (1993). Did shoplifting really decrease? *British Journal of Criminology*, **33**, 57–69.

Farrington, D. P. & Hawkins, J. D. (1991). Predicting participation, early onset, and later persistence in officially recorded offending. *Criminal Behaviour and Mental Health*, **1**, 1–33.

Farrington, D. P. & West, D. J. (1990). The Cambridge study in delinquent development: A long-term follow-up of 411 London males. In H. J. Kerner & G. Kaiser (eds), *Criminality: Personality, Behaviour and Life History*. Berlin: Springer-Verlag, pp. 115–38.

Farrington, D. P. & West, D. J. (1993). Criminal, penal and life histories of chronic offenders: Risk and protective factors and early identification. *Criminal Behaviour and Mental Health*, **3**, 492–523.

Farrington, D. P. & West, D. J. (1995). Effects of marriage, separation and children on offending by adult males. In Z. S. Blau & J. Hagan (eds), *Current Perspectives on Aging and the Life Cycle: Delinquency and Disrepute in the Life Course*. Greenwich, CT: JAI Press, pp. 249–81.

Farrington, D. P. & Wikstrom, P.-O.H. (1994). Criminal careers in London and Stockholm: A cross-national comparative study. In E. G. M. Weitekamp & H. J. Kerner (eds), *Cross-national Longitudinal Research on Human Development and Criminal Behaviour*. Dordrecht, Netherlands: Kluwer, pp. 65–89.

Farrington, D. P., Loeber, R. & Van Kammen, W. B. (1990). Long-term criminal outcomes of hyperactivity–impulsivity–attention deficit and conduct problems in childhood. In L. N. Robins & M. Rutter (eds), *Straight and Devious Pathways from Childhood to Adulthood*. Cambridge: Cambridge University Press, pp. 62–81.

Farrington, D. P., Ohlin, L. E. & Wilson, J. Q. (1986). *Understanding and Controlling Crime*. New York: Springer-Verlag.

Farrington, D. P., Snyder, H. N. & Finnegan, T. A. (1988). Specialization in juvenile court careers. *Criminology*, **26**, 461–87.

Farrington, D. P., Gallagher, B., Morley, L., St Ledger, R. J. & West, D. J. (1986). Unemployment, school leaving, and crime. *British Journal of Criminology*, **26**, 335–56.

Farrington, D. P., Gallagher, B., Morley, L., St Ledger, R. J. & West, D. J. (1988a). A 24-year follow-up of men from vulnerable backgrounds. In R. L. Jenkins & W. R. Brown (eds), *The Abandonment of Delinquent Behaviour*. New York: Praeger, pp. 155–73.

Farrington, D. P., Gallagher, B., Morley, L., St Ledger, R. J. & West, D. J. (1988b). Are there any successful men from criminogenic backgrounds? *Psychiatry*, **51**, 116–30.

Feldman, R. A., Caplinger, T. E. & Wodarski, J. S. (1983). *The St Louis Conundrum*. Englewood Cliffs, NJ: Prentice-Hall.

Ferguson, T. (1952). *The Young Delinquent in his Social Setting*. London: Oxford University Press.

Fischer, D. G. (1984). Family size and delinquency. *Perceptual and Motor Skills*, **58**, 527–34.

Gendreau, P. & Ross, R. R. (1979). Effective correctional treatment: Bibliotherapy for cynics. *Crime and Delinquency*, **25**, 463–89.

Gendreau, P. & Ross, R. R. (1987). Revivification of rehabilitation: Evidence from the 1980s. *Justice Quarterly*, **4**, 349–407.

Gittelman, R., Mannuzza, S., Shenker, R. & Bonagura, N. (1985). Hyperactive boys almost grown up. *Archives of General Psychiatry*, **42**, 937–47.

Gordon, D. A. & Arbuthnot, J. (1987). Individual, group and family interventions. In H. C. Quay (ed.), *Handbook of Juvenile Delinquency*. New York: Wiley, pp. 290–324.

Hartup, W. W. (1983). Peer relations. In P. H. Mussen (ed.), *Handbook of Child Psychology*, Vol. 4. Toronto: Wiley, pp. 103–96.

Hawkins, J. D., Catalano, R. F. & Miller, J. Y. (1992). Risk and protective factors for alcohol and other drug problems in adolescence and early adulthood: Implications for substance use prevention. *Psychological Bulletin*, **112**, 64–105.

Hawkins, J. D., Catalano, R. F., Morrison, D. M., O'Donnell, J., Abbott, R. D. & Day, L. E. (1992). The Seattle social development project: Effects of the first four years on protective factors and problem behaviours. In J. McCord & R. Tremblay (eds), *Preventing Antisocial Behaviour*. New York: Guilford, pp. 139–61.

Hawkins, J. D., Doueck, H. J. & Lishner, D. M. (1988). Changing teaching practices in mainstream classrooms to improve bonding and behaviour of low achievers. *American Educational Research Journal*, **25**, 31–50.

Hawkins, J. D., Von Cleve, E. & Catalano, R. F. (1991). Reducing early childhood aggression: Results of a primary prevention programme. *Journal of the American Academy of Child and Adolescent Psychiatry*, **30**, 208–17.

Henggeler, S. W., Melton, G. B. & Smith, L. A. (1992). Family preservation using multi-systemic therapy: An effective alternative to incarcerating serious juvenile offenders. *Journal of Consulting and Clinical Psychology*, **60**, 953–61.

Henggeler, S. W., Melton, G. B., Smith, L. A., Schoenwald, S. K. & Hanley, J. H. (1993). Family preservation using multi-systemic treatment: Long-term follow-up to a clinical trial with serious juvenile offenders. *Journal of Child and Family Studies*, **2**, 283–93.

Henry, B., Moffitt, T., Robins, L., Earls, F. & Silva, P. (1993). Early family predictors of child and adolescent antisocial behaviour: Who are the mothers of delinquents? *Criminal Behaviour and Mental Health*, **3**, 97–118.

Hindelang, M. J., Hirschi, T. & Weis, J. G. (1981). *Measuring Delinquency*. Beverly Hills, CA: Sage.

Hirschi, T. (1969). *Causes of Delinquency*. Berkeley, CA: University of California Press.

Hirschi, T. & Hindelang, M. J. (1977). Intelligence and delinquency: A revisionist review. *American Sociological Review*, **42**, 571–87.

Hollin, C. R. (1992). *Criminal Behaviour*. London: Falmer Press.

Horacek, H. J., Ramey, C. T., Campbell, F. A., Hoffmann, K. P. & Fletcher, R. H. (1987). Predicting school failure and assessing early intervention with high-risk children. *Journal of the American Academy of Child and Adolescent Psychiatry*, **26**, 758–63.

Huessy, H. R. & Howell, D. C. (1985). Relationships between adult and childhood behaviour disorders. *Psychiatric Journal of the University of Ottawa*, **10**, 114–19.

Huizinga, D. & Elliott, D. S. (1986). Reassessing the reliability and validity of self-report measures. *Journal of Quantitative Criminology*, **2**, 293–327.

Irving, B. & MacKenzie, I. (1989). *Police Interrogation*. London: Police Foundation.

Jessor, R. & Jessor, S. L. (1977). *Problem Behaviour and Psychosocial Development*. New York: Academic Press.

Jones, M. B. & Offord, D. R. (1989). Reduction of antisocial behaviour in poor children by non-school skill-development. *Journal of Child Psychology and Psychiatry*, **30**, 737–50.

Jones, M. B., Offord, D. R. & Abrams, N. (1980). Brothers, sisters and antisocial behaviour. *British Journal of Psychiatry*, **136**, 139–45.

Kandel, E., Mednick, S. A., Kirkegaard-Sorenson, L., Hutchings, B., Knop, J., Rosenberg, R. & Schulsinger, F. (1988). IQ as a protective factor for subjects at high risk for antisocial behaviour. *Journal of Consulting and Clinical Psychology*, **56**, 224–6.

Kazdin, A. E. (1985). *Treatment of Antisocial Behaviour in Children and Adolescents*. Homewood, IL: Dorsey Press.

Kazdin, A. E. (1987). Treatment of antisocial behaviour in children: Current status and future directions. *Psychological Bulletin*, **102**, 187–203.

Kazdin, A. E., Siegel, T. C. & Bass, D. (1992). Cognitive problem-solving skills training and parent management training in the treatment of antisocial behaviour in children. *Journal of Consulting and Clinical Psychology*, **60**, 733–47.

Kazdin, A. E., Esveldt-Dawson, R., French, N. H. & Unis, A. S. (1987). Effects of parent management training and problem-solving skills training combined in the treatment of antisocial child behaviour. *Journal of the American Academy of Child and Adolescent Psychiatry*, **26**, 416–24.

Kazdin, A. E., Bass, D., Siegel, T. & Thomas, C. (1989). Cognitive-behavioural therapy and relationship therapy in the treatment of children referred for antisocial behaviour. *Journal of Consulting and Clinical Psychology*, **57**, 522–35.

Klein, M. W. (1984). Offence specialization and versatility among juveniles. *British Journal of Criminology*, **24**, 185–94.

Klein, N. C., Alexander, J. F. & Parsons, B. V. (1977). Impact of family systems intervention on recidivism and sibling delinquency: A model of primary prevention and programme evaluation. *Journal of Consulting and Clinical Psychology*, **45**, 469–74.

Klepp, K.-I., Halper, A. & Perry, C. L. (1986). The efficacy of peer leaders in drug abuse prevention. *Journal of School Health*, **56**, 407–11.

Klinteberg, B. A., Andersson, T., Magnusson, D. & Stattin, H. (1993). Hyperactive behaviour in childhood as related to subsequent alcohol problems and violent offending: A longitudinal study of male subjects. *Personality and Individual Differences*, **15**, 381–8.

Kolvin, I., Miller, F. J. W., Fleeting, M. & Kolvin, P. A. (1988a). Risk/protective factors for offending with particular reference to deprivation. In M. Rutter (ed.), *Studies of Psychosocial Risk*. Cambridge: Cambridge University Press, pp. 77–95.

Kolvin, I., Miller, F. J. W., Fleeting, M. & Kolvin, P. A. (1988b). Social and parenting factors affecting criminal-offence rates: Findings from the Newcastle Thousand Family Study (1947–1980). *British Journal of Psychiatry*, **152**, 80–90.

Kolvin, I., Miller, F. J. W., Scott, D. M., Gatzanis, S. R. M. & Fleeting, M. (1990). *Continuities of Deprivation?* Aldershot: Avebury.

LeBlanc, M. & Frechette, M. (1989). *Male Criminal Activity from Childhood Through Youth*. New York: Springer-Verlag.

Loeber, R. (1987). Behavioural precursors and accelerators of delinquency. In W. Buikhuisen & S. A. Mednick (eds), *Explaining Criminal Behaviour*. Leiden: Brill, pp. 51–67.

Loeber, R. (1988). Natural histories of conduct problems, delinquency and associated substance use: Evidence for developmental progressions. In B. B. Lahey & A. E. Kazdin (eds), *Advances in Clinical Child Psychology*, Vol. 11. New York: Plenum, pp. 73–124.

Loeber, R. & Dishion, T. (1983). Early predictors of male delinquency: A review. *Psychological Bulletin*, **94**, 68–99.

Loeber, R. & LeBlanc, M. (1990). Toward a developmental criminology. In M. Tonry & N. Morris (eds), *Crime and Justice*, Vol. 12. Chicago, IL: University of Chicago Press, pp. 375–473.

Loeber, R. & Stouthamer-Loeber, M. (1986). Family factors as correlates and predictors of juvenile conduct problems and delinquency. In M. Tonry & N. Morris (eds), *Crime and Justice*, Vol. 7. Chicago, IL: University of Chicago Press, pp. 29–149.

Loeber, R. & Stouthamer-Loeber, M. (1987). Prediction. In H. C. Quay (ed.), *Handbook of Juvenile Delinquency*. New York: Wiley, pp. 325–82.

Lynam, D., Moffitt, T. & Stouthamer-Loeber, M. (1993). Explaining the relation between IQ and delinquency: Class, race, test motivation, school failure or self-control? *Journal of Abnormal Psychology*, **102**, 187–96.

Malinosky-Rummell, R. & Hansen, D. J. (1993). Long-term consequences of childhood physical abuse. *Psychological Bulletin*, **114**, 68–79.

Mannuzza, S., Klein, R. G., Bonagura, N., Malloy, P., Giampino, T. L. & Addalli, K. A. (1991). Hyperactive boys almost grown up. V. Replication of psychiatric status. *Archives of General Psychiatry*, **48**, 77–83.

Mawson, A. R. (1987). *Transient Criminality*. New York: Praeger.

McAlister, A., Perry, C., Killen, J., Slinkard, L. A. & Maccoby, N. (1980). Pilot study of smoking, alcohol and drug abuse prevention. *American Journal of Public Health*, **70**, 719–21.

McCord, J. (1977). A comparative study of two generations of native Americans. In R. F. Meier (ed.), *Theory in Criminology*. Beverly Hills, CA: Sage, pp. 83–92.

McCord, J. (1979). Some child-rearing antecedents of criminal behaviour in adult men. *Journal of Personality and Social Psychology*, **37**, 1477–86.

McCord, J. (1982). A longitudinal view of the relationship between paternal absence and crime. In J. Gunn & D. P. Farrington (eds), *Abnormal Offenders, Delinquency, and the Criminal Justice System*. Chichester: Wiley, pp. 113–28.

McCord, J. (1991). Family relationships, juvenile delinquency, and adult criminality. *Criminology*, **29**, 397–417.

McCord, J. & Tremblay, R. (eds) (1992). *Preventing Antisocial Behaviour*. New York: Guilford.

McGee, R., Williams, S. & Silva, P. A. (1985). Factor structure and correlates of ratings of inattention, hyperactivity and antisocial behaviour in a large sample of 9-year-old children from the general population. *Journal of Consulting and Clinical Psychology*, **53**, 480–90.

Mednick, S. A., Gabrielli, W. F. & Hutchings, B. (1983). Genetic influences on criminal behaviour: Evidence from an adoption cohort. In K. T. Van Dusen & S. A. Mednick (eds), *Prospective Studies of Crime and Delinquency*. Boston, MA: Kluwer-Nijhoff, pp. 39–56.

Michelson, L. (1987). Cognitive-behavioural strategies in the prevention and treatment of antisocial disorders in children and adolescents. In J. D. Burchard & S. N. Burchard (eds), *Prevention of Delinquent Behaviour*. Beverly Hills, CA: Sage, pp. 275–310.

Mischel, W., Shoda, Y. & Rodriguez, M. L. (1989). Delay of gratification in children. *Science*, **244**, 933–8.

Moffitt, T. E. (1990). The neuropsychology of juvenile delinquency: A critical review. In M. Tonry & N. Morris (eds), *Crime and Justice*, Vol. 12. Chicago, IL: University of Chicago Press, pp. 99–169.

Moffitt, T. E. (1993). Adolescence-limited and life-course-persistent antisocial behaviour: A developmental taxonomy. *Psychological Review*, **100**, 674–701.

Moffitt, T. E. & Henry, B. (1989). Neuropsychological assessment of executive functions in self-reported delinquents. *Development and Psychopathology*, **1**, 105–18.

Moffitt, T. E. & Silva, P. A. (1988a). IQ and delinquency: A direct test of the differential detection hypothesis. *Journal of Abnormal Psychology*, **97**, 330–3.

Moffitt, T. E. & Silva, P. A. (1988b). Neuropsychological deficit and self-reported delinquency in an unselected birth cohort. *Journal of the American Academy of Child and Adolescent Psychiatry*, **27**, 233–40.

Morash, M. & Rucker, L. (1989). An exploratory study of the connection of mother's age at childbearing to her children's delinquency in four data sets. *Crime and Delinquency*, **35**, 45–93.

Murray, D. M., Luepker, R. V., Johnson, C. A. & Mittelmark, M. B. (1984). The prevention of cigarette smoking in children: A comparison of four strategies. *Journal of Applied Social Psychology*, **14**, 274–88.

Newson, J. & Newson, E. (1989). *The Extent of Parental Physical Punishment in the UK*. London: Approach.

Newson, J., Newson, E. & Adams, M. (1993). The social origins of delinquency. *Criminal Behaviour And Mental Health*, **3**, 19–29.

Nylander, I. (1979). A 20-year prospective follow-up study of 2164 cases at the child guidance clinics in Stockholm. *Acta Paediatrica Scandinavica*, supplement 276.

Osborn, S. G. (1980). Moving home, leaving London, and delinquent trends. *British Journal of Criminology*, **20**, 54–61.

Ouston, J. (1984). Delinquency, family background, and educational attainment. *British Journal of Criminology*, **24**, 2–26.

Parker, J. G. & Asher, S. R. (1987). Peer relations and later personal adjustment: Are low accepted children at risk? *Psychological Bulletin*, **102**, 357–89.

Patterson, G. R. (1982). *Coercive Family Process*. Eugene, OR: Castalia.

Patterson, G. R., Chamberlain, P. & Reid, J. B. (1982). A comparative evaluation of a parent training programme. *Behaviour Therapy*, **13**, 638–50.

Patterson, G. R., Reid, J. B. & Dishion, T. J. (1992). *Antisocial Boys*. Eugene, OR: Castalia.

Polk, K., Alder, C., Bazemore, G., Blake, G., Cordray, S., Coventry, G., Galvin, J. & Temple, M. (1981). *Becoming Adult*. Washington, DC: National Institute of Mental Health (Final Report).

Pulkkinen, L. (1986). The role of impulse control in the development of antisocial and prosocial behaviour. In D. Olweus, J. Block & M. R. Yarrow (eds), *Development of Antisocial and Prosocial Behaviour*. New York: Academic Press, pp. 149–75.

Pulkkinen, L. (1988). Delinquent development: Theoretical and empirical considerations. In M. Rutter (ed.), *Studies of Psychosocial Risk*. Cambridge: Cambridge University Press, pp. 184–99.

Rae-Grant, N., Thomas, B. H., Offord, D. R. & Boyle, M. H. (1989). Risk, protective factors, and the prevalence of behavioural and emotional disorders in children and adolescents. *Journal of the American Academy of Child and Adolescent Psychiatry*, **28**, 262–68.

Reiss, A. J. (1988). Co-offending and criminal careers. In M. Tonry & N. Morris (eds), *Crime and Justice*, Vol. 10. Chicago, IL: University of Chicago Press, pp. 117–70.

Reiss, A. J. & Farrington, D. P. (1991). Advancing knowledge about co-offending: Results from a prospective longitudinal survey of London males. *Journal of Criminal Law and Criminology*, **82**, 360–95.

Richman, N., Stevenson, J. & Graham, P. (1985). Sex differences in the outcome of pre-school behaviour problems. In A. R. Nicol (ed.), *Longitudinal Studies in Child Psychology and Psychiatry*. Chichester: Wiley, pp. 75–89.

Riley, D. & Shaw, M. (1985). *Parental Supervision and Juvenile Delinquency*. London: Her Majesty's Stationery Office.

Robins, L. N. (1979). Sturdy childhood predictors of adult outcomes: Replications from longitudinal studies. In J. E. Barrett, R. M. Rose & G. L. Klerman (eds), *Stress and Mental Disorder*. New York: Raven Press, pp. 219–35.

Robins, L. N. & Hill, S. Y. (1966). Assessing the contributions of family structure, class, and peer groups to juvenile delinquency. *Journal of Criminal Law, Criminology and Police Science*, **57**, 325–34.

Robins, L. N. & Ratcliff, K. S. (1980). Childhood conduct disorders and later arrest. In L. N. Robins, P. J. Clayton & J. K. Wing (eds), *The Social Consequences of Psychiatric Illness*. New York: Brunner/Mazel, pp. 248–63.

Robins, L. N., West, P. J. & Herjanic B. L. (1975). Arrests and delinquency in two generations: A study of black urban families and their children. *Journal of Child Psychology and Psychiatry*, **16**, 125–40.

Roff, J. D. & Wirt, R. D. (1984). Childhood aggression and social adjustment as antecedents of delinquency. *Journal of Abnormal Child Psychology*, **12**, 111–26.

Ross, R. R., Fabiano, E. A. & Ewles, C. D. (1988). Reasoning and rehabilitation. *International Journal of Offender Therapy and Comparative Criminology*, **32**, 29–35.

Ross, R. R. & Ross, B. D. (1988). Delinquency prevention through cognitive training. *New Education*, **10**, 70–5.

Rutter, M. (1985). Resilience in the face of adversity: Protective factors and resistance to psychiatric disorder. *British Journal of Psychiatry*, **147**, 598–611.

Rutter, M. & Giller, H. (1983). *Juvenile Delinquency*. Harmondsworth: Penguin.

Sarason, I. G. (1978). A cognitive social learning approach to juvenile delinquency. In R. D. Hare & D. Schalling (eds), *Psychopathic Behaviour*. Chichester: Wiley, pp. 299–317.

Satterfield, J. H. (1987). Childhood diagnostic and neurophysiological prodictors of teenage arrest rates: An 8-year prospective study. In S. A. Mednick, T. E. Moffitt & S. A. Stack (eds), *The Causes of Crime: New Biological Approaches*. Cambridge: Cambridge University Press, pp. 146–67.

Schweinhart, L. J. & Weikart, D. P. (1980). *Young Children Grow Up*. Ypsilanti, MI: High/Scope.

Schweinhart, L. J., Barnes, H. V. & Weikart, D. P. (1993). *Significant Benefits*. Ypsilanti, MI: High/Scope.

Shore, M. F. & Massimo, J. L. (1979). Fifteen years after treatment: A follow-up study of comprehensive vocationally-oriented psychotherapy. *American Journal of Orthopsychiatry*, **49**, 240–5.

Snyder, J. & Patterson, G. R. (1987). Family interaction and delinquent behaviour. In H. C. Quay (ed.), *Handbook of Juvenile Delinquency*. New York: Wiley, pp. 216–43.

Spivack, G., Marcus, J. & Swift, M. (1986). Early classroom behaviours and later misconduct. *Developmental Psychology*, **22**, 124–31.

Stattin, H. & Klackenberg-Larsson, I. (1993). Early language and intelligence development and their relationship to future criminal behaviour. *Journal of Abnormal Psychology*, **102**, 369–78.

Stattin, H. & Magnusson, D. (1991). Stability and change in criminal behaviour up to age 30. *British Journal of Criminology*, **31**, 327–46.

Stein, K. B., Sarbin, T. R. & Kulik, J. A. (1968). Future time perspective: Its relation to the socialization process and the delinquent role. *Journal of Consulting and Clinical Psychology*, **32**, 257–64.

Sutherland, E. H. & Cressey D. R. (1974). *Criminology* (9th edn.). Philadelphia, PA: Lippincott.

Taylor, E. A. (1986). Childhood hyperactivity. *British Journal of Psychiatry*, **149**, 562–73.

Telch, M. J., Killen, J. D., McAlister, A. L., Perry, C. L. & Maccoby, N. (1982). Long-term follow-up of a pilot project on smoking prevention with adolescents. *Journal of Behavioural Medicine*, **5**, 1–8.

Thornberry, T. P., Lizotte, A. J., Krohn, M. D., Farnworth, M. & Jang, S. J. (1994). Delinquent peers, beliefs and delinquent behaviour: A longitudinal test of interactional theory. *Criminology*, **32**, 47–83.

Tobler, N. S. (1986). Meta-analysis of 143 drug treatment programmes: Quantitative outcome results of programme participants compared to a control or comparison group. *Journal of Drug Issues*, **16**, 537–67.

Tolan, P. H., Cromwell, R. E. & Brasswell, M. (1986). Family therapy with delinquents: A review of the literature. *Family Process*, **25**, 619–49.

Trasler, G. B. (1962). *The Explanation of Criminality*. London: Routledge and Regan Paul.

Tremblay, R. E., LeBlanc, M. & Schwartzman, A. E. (1988). The predictive power of first-grade peer and teacher ratings of behaviour: Sex differences in antisocial behaviour and personality at adolescence. *Journal of Abnormal Child Psychology*, **16**, 571–83.

Tremblay, R. E., McCord, J., Boileau, H., Charlebois, P., Gagnon, C., LeBlanc, M. & Larivee, S. (1991). Can disruptive boys be helped to become competent? *Psychiatry*, **54**, 148–61.

Tremblay, R. E., Vitaro, F., Bertrand, L., LeBlanc, M., Beauchesne, H., Boileau, H. & David, L. (1992). Parent and child training to prevent early onset of delinquency: The Montreal longitudinal-experimental study. In J. McCord & R. Tremblay (eds), *Preventing Antisocial Behaviour*. New York: Guilford, pp. 117–38.

Utting, D., Bright, J. & Henricson, C. (1993). *Crime and the Family*. London: Family Policy Studies Centre.

Venables, P. H. & Raine, A. (1987). Biological theory. In B. J. McGurk, D. M. Thornton & M. Williams (eds), *Applying Psychology to Imprisonment*. London: Her Majesty's Stationery Office, pp. 3–27.

Wadsworth, M. (1979). *Roots of Delinquency*. London: Martin Robertson.

Walsh, A., Petee, T. A. & Beyer, J. A. (1987). Intellectual imbalance and delinquency: Comparing high verbal and high performance IQ delinquents. *Criminal Justice and Behaviour*, **14**, 370–79.

Warr, M. (1993). Parents, peers and delinquency. *Social Forces*, **72**, 247–64.

Weiss, G. & Hechtman, L. T. (1986). *Hyperactive Children Grown Up*. New York: Guilford Press.

Wells, L. E. & Rankin, J. H. (1991). Families and delinquency: A meta-analysis of the impact of broken homes. *Social Problems*, **38**, 71–93.

Werner, E. E. & Smith, R. S. (1982). *Vulnerable but Invincible*. New York: McGraw-Hill.

West, D. J. & Farrington, D. P. (1973). *Who Becomes Delinquent?* London: Heinemann.

West, D. J. & Farrington, D. P. (1977). *The Delinquent Way of Life*. London: Heinemann.

Whalen, C. K. & Henker, B. (1991). Therapies of hyperactive children: Comparisons, combinations and compromises. *Journal of Consulting and Clinical Psychology*, **59**, 126–37.

White, H. R., Labouvie, E. W. & Bates, M. E. (1985). The relationship between sensation seeking and delinquency: A longitudinal analysis. *Journal of Research in Crime and Delinquency*, **22**, 197–211.

Widom, C. S. (1989). The cycle of violence. *Science*, **244**, 160–6.

Wikstrom, P. O. (1987). *Patterns of Crime in a Birth Cohort*. Stockholm: University of Stockholm Department of Sociology.

Wilson, H. (1980). Parental supervision: A neglected aspect of delinquency. *British Journal of Criminology*, **20**, 203–35.

Wilson, H. (1987). Parental supervision re-examined. *British Journal of Criminology*, **27**, 275–301.

Wilson, J. Q. & Herrnstein, R. J. (1985). *Crime and Human Nature*. New York: Simon and Schuster.

Wolfgang, M. E., Figlio, R. M. & Sellin, T. (1972). *Delinquency in a Birth Cohort*. Chicago, IL: University of Chicago Press.

Wolfgang, M. E., Thornberry, T. P. & Figlio, R. M. (1987). *From Boy to Man, from Delinquency to Crime*. Chicago, IL: University of Chicago Press.

Zimring, F. E. (1981). Kids, groups and crime: Some implications of a well-known secret. *Journal of Criminal Law and Criminology*, **72**, 867–85.

Zoccolillo, M., Pickles, A., Quinton, D. & Rutter, M. (1992). The outcome of childhood conduct disorder: Implications for defining adult personality disorder and conduct disorder. *Psychological Medicine*, **22**, 971–86.

3

Working with Young Offenders: The Impact of Meta-Analyses

FRIEDRICH LÖSEL
University of Erlangen-Nürnberg, Germany

INTRODUCTION

Crime and delinquency are two of the most frequent behavioural problems among young people. Crime statistics reveal a clear over-representation of young men (e.g. Blumstein, Cohen & Farrington, 1988). A small population of approximately 5–8% of young males is particularly problematic. They are responsible for 50–60% of all known offences in their age cohort (e.g. Tracy, Wolfgang & Figlio 1990). Juvenile offending is frequently accompanied by other forms of problem behaviour, such as alcohol and drug abuse, traffic accidents and dangerous health behaviour (e.g. Jessor, Donovon & Costa, 1992). In high-risk groups such as young urban Afro-Americans, reciprocal violence is one of the most important causes of injuries and death (e.g. Richters, 1993).

These and other facts suggest that psychosocial treatment of young offenders—as *one* of various possible strategies for intervention and prevention—should play an important role in crime policy. However, after sometimes overoptimistic expectations of success up to the 1970s, there was a decline in treatment and rehabilitation concepts. Important reasons for this development can be found in normative arguments and changes in the political context towards retribution, deterrence and incapacitation (Allen, 1981; Cullen & Gendreau, 1989; Lösel, 1995a). However, empirical evaluation also played a role. The 'nothing works' doctrine became a widespread summary of the outcome evaluations. This stance was associated particularly with the paper by Martinson (1974) and the book from Lipton, Martinson and Wilks (1975). Other research syntheses were sceptical too, not least regarding the methodological quality and

Clinical Approaches to Working with Young Offenders. Edited by C. R. Hollin and K. Howells.
© 1996 John Wiley & Sons Ltd.

generalizability of the available studies (e.g. Bailey, 1966; Greenberg, 1977; Logan, 1972; Martin, Sechrest & Redner, 1981; Sechrest, White & Brown, 1979; Wright & Dixon, 1977). Although there were also early reviews with more positive conclusions (e.g. Blackburn, 1980; Gendreau & Ross, 1979; Hood, 1967; Palmer, 1975; Quay, 1977; Romig, 1978; and even Martinson, 1979), the discussions on treatment in crime politics remained rather undifferentiated. They mostly concerned sweeping statements for or against the 'nothing works' position.

It is remarkable how this discussion on offender treatment deviates from the development in general psychotherapy research. Here also the initial question was whether psychotherapy had any effect at all. The answer from outcome evaluation was clearly positive (e.g. Smith, Glass & Miller, 1980). A more differentiated question was how far various forms of treatment differed in their efficacy. Answers varied here: some research syntheses maintained that the differences were slight (e.g. Smith & Glass, 1977); others concluded that only the behavioural and cognitive approaches and—based on fewer controlled studies—short-term psychoanalytic or client-centred therapy could claim sufficient empirical support (e.g. Grawe, Donati & Bernauer, 1994). In this discussion, rivalries between the different therapeutic 'schools' play an important role. However, the actual scientific and practical concern is the differential indication: which disorder in which clients is best treated using which method by which therapists in which contexts? These questions have simultaneously led to increased process research. This involves a close examination of which general or specific characteristics of the therapeutic contract, bond and operations, the client's self-relatedness, the in-session impact or sequential flow lead to intended changes and which do not (Orlinsky, Grawe & Parks, 1994). 'Process' and 'outcome' became highly differentiated research topics. Overall, results suggest that the concept of an empirically founded, eclectic, and integrated professional therapy may overcome the problems arising from the hundreds of different variants of psychotherapy (Garfield & Bergin, 1994).

In the development sketched here, research integrations using meta-analysis have played an important role. The goal of meta-analysis is to perform a systematic, representative, objective and statistically founded synthesis of research findings within a specific domain. A broad variety of methods have been developed (e.g. Cooper & Hedges, 1994; Glass, McGraw & Smith, 1981; Hunter & Schmidt, 1990; Rosenthal, 1991). Naturally, meta-analyses also raise various methodological problems (e.g. Bullock & Svyantek, 1985; Lösel, 1991; Matt & Cook, 1994), but there are hardly any basic doubts regarding their adequacy. For research syntheses on psychosocial interventions, they have the following particular advantages: (1) Treatment evaluations are often based on small and non-representative samples. Meta-analytic methods make it possible to estimate sampling error and to provide a more reliable effect estimation. (2) Owing to small sample sizes in primary studies, even consistent effects may not reach an arbitrary level of significance. Therefore, computing effect sizes and confidence intervals instead of counting significances is a more sensible and adequate technique for evaluating the relevance of outcomes (see also Cohen, 1994). (3) In complex field settings, it is often not possible to avoid specific design problems.

Meta-analyses not only assess methodological shortcomings, but also test their influence on results. (4) Studies on psychosocial interventions vary greatly in treatment modes, sample characteristics, outcome measures, therapist variables, settings and so forth. The meta-analytic study of moderators uses this variety to provide information for differential indication.

Since the mid-1980s, a number of meta-analyses have also been published on the topic of offender treatment and particularly on work with young offenders (for brief overviews see Gendreau & Andrews, 1990; Hollin, 1993; Lipsey, 1988; Lösel, 1993). Not only have they contributed to revitalizing the discussion on the treatment approach (e.g. Gendreau & Ross, 1987; Lösel, 1992; McGuire & Priestley, 1992; Palmer, 1992; Thornton, 1987), but they have also delivered differentiated data that may shift the focus from 'nothing works' to 'what works' (McGuire, 1995). It is important to note that the recent meta-analyses do not differ basically from earlier research syntheses. There is a more or less continuous development from qualitative literature reviews over vote-counting of significant results to the quantitative estimation of effect sizes and analysis of its variation (Cook & Leviton, 1980). Thus, some results of quantitative meta-analyses (e.g. Lipsey, 1992a) are similar to the conclusions of qualitative reviews (e.g. Basta & Davidson, 1988). On the other hand, the messages of recent meta-analyses are in no way unequivocal. This is not surprising, because different study samples have been integrated and different meta-analytic methods used. In their conclusions regarding the treatment approach, some authors are still very sceptical (e.g. Whitehead & Lab, 1989), whereas others are fairly optimistic (e.g. Andrews et al., 1990). Critics have pointed out the need for meta-analyses to be evaluated carefully by independent experts (see Logan et al., 1991). The present chapter takes a step in this direction. The first part provides a descriptive overview of various meta-analyses on offender treatment. The second part presents an integrative evaluation of their findings. This also points out deficits in research and future perspectives. The chapter ends with a summary of findings and some conclusions.

A BRIEF OVERVIEW OF VARIOUS META-ANALYSES

In the past 30 years, about 50 reviews of research on offender treatment have been published (for references, see Antonowicz & Ross, 1994; Lösel, 1995b). It is not possible to give a comprehensive overview of this literature here. I can only analyse examples that are more or less representative. The analysis is restricted to the more recent research syntheses using at least partially quantitative methods of meta-analysis. These publications also integrate the majority of primary studies that have been reviewed earlier. A second selection is made with respect to the scope of meta-analyses. Only studies that deal specifically with the treatment of delinquency and criminality, particularly with young offenders, are reviewed. More general research syntheses on psychosocial treatment will not be discussed, although some of them also include information on delinquency, aggression, externalizing behaviour problems and so forth (e.g. Beelmann, Pfingsten &

Lösel, 1994; Corrigan, 1991; Smith, Glass & Miller, 1980; Weisz et al., 1987). According to a third principle, I review analyses from researchers that vary not only in location but also—as far as this is noticeable—in attitudes to offender treatment. Thus, subjective biases, which can even influence meta-analytic procedures, should be balanced.

To compare the results of different meta-analyses I use correlation coefficients (r, ϕ) as indicators of effect size (ES). In the range of small to medium effects, these are approximately half of the d coefficient, which is frequently used in treatment research with quantitative outcome measures (Cohen, 1988). A correlation of, for example 0.20 is equivalent to a difference of 20 percentage points between treatment and control group (Rosenthal & Rubin, 1982). If, for example, recidivism in the control group is 60%, then it is 40% in the treated group. Various coefficients reported in this chapter are only approximations, because details of computation are not fully comparable or known. In meta-analyses that have computed different coefficients, those with weighting for sample sizes are used (a more conservative estimate).

The first relevant research synthesis using quantitative meta-analysis was published by Garrett (1985). This integrated 111 studies (121 comparisons) on the treatment of adjudicated juvenile delinquents in residential settings. The primary studies had been published between 1960 and 1983. They contained randomized, quasi-experimental control-group designs as well as pre–post-test designs. The mean ES was 0.18. Behavioural and skill-oriented programmes did somewhat better than psychodynamic and other programmes, but these differences were not independent of the methodological design. In more rigorously controlled studies, there were no consistent differences between the various programmes. In these designs, the overall effect was also smaller at 0.12. Higher ES was found, particularly in pre–post comparisons with no control group. The effects of cognitive-behavioural approaches proved to be promising, but only few studies were available. Garrett (1985) also observed lower effects in outcome measures of recidivism compared with various adjustment measures.

Gottschalk and colleagues (1987a) analysed 90 evaluation studies on community based interventions with juvenile offenders. These studies had been published between 1967 and 1983 and contained 101 comparisons. In several more specific evaluations of this study sample, the research team addressed 44 studies on diversion programmes (Gensheimer et al., 1986), 25 studies on behavioural programmes (Gottschalk et al., 1987b), and 34 studies on social learning programmes within the juvenile justice system (Mayer et al., 1986). Alongside randomized and quasi-experimental control-group studies, pre–post comparisons were also analysed. The mean ES was 0.12. In the special evaluations, there were larger effects in behavioural programmes (0.20) and treatments based on a social learning approach (0.36). The evaluation of diversion programmes, in contrast, resulted in a smaller mean ES (0.09). Design quality did not have a very clear and consistent effect. The pre–post designs produced effects that tended to be smaller or larger. There were also no unified relationships between randomization and ES. In all four analyses, it became more or less clear that effects were lower on recidivism outcome measures than on various other measures of social attitudes or behaviour. Aspects of treatment integrity and intensity had a weak moderating effect, too. In programmes of longer duration or with a higher contact frequency, but also in those with a greater influence of the investigator, there were somewhat better effects.

Lösel, Köferl and Weber (1987), Lösel and Köferl (1989) and Lösel (1995a) have analysed studies on the treatment of offenders in German social-therapeutic prisons. Eight studies with 18 comparisons were published between 1978 and 1993. Because this mode of rehabilitation addresses (mostly younger) adults, results will not be presented in detail. At 0.11, the mean ES was similar to that found in the above-mentioned analyses of juvenile offender treatment. Effects were lower when construct validity was high.

The meta-analysis presented by Whitehead and Lab (1989) integrated 50 control-group evaluations on the treatment of juvenile offenders (published between 1975 and 1984). These were all studies with a recidivism outcome measure. The authors considered that an ES is only indicative for success if ϕ exceeds 0.20. By counting the number of high, modest and negative coefficients in various programme categories they concluded that the 'nothing works' hypothesis was supported. However, 40% of the effects were significantly positive and a mean ES of 0.13 can be computed from their data. System diversion appeared to be the most promising type of treatment (7 of 15 effects were above 0.20 and positive). Non-system diversion programmes, community corrections (including probation and parole) and residential corrections failed to lower recidivism. Using a more content-related grouping, the authors found no strong support for behavioural over non-behavioural programmes. In institutional settings, various effects were negative. As a trend, randomized designs showed smaller effects than quasi-experimental designs.

Andrews and colleagues (1990b) re-analysed the 50 studies in Whitehead and Lab (1989) and added 30 further evaluations that met their methodological criteria (control-group design, recidivism outcome measure). The 80 studies were published between 1950 and 1989 and contained 154 comparisons. They evaluated correctional treatment programmes within the juvenile and adult justice system, although most studies addressed juveniles. Andrews and colleagues did not code the various programmes according to formal aspects, but according to clinical–psychological and empirical–criminological ones. 'Appropriate' programmes accorded with three principles (Andrews, Bonta & Hoge, 1990). First, the *risk principle*: higher levels of service are reserved for higher risk cases, whereas lower risk cases do as well with less intensive services. Second, the *need principle*: the targets of services are matched to the specific criminogenic needs of offenders. These needs include changing antisocial attitudes and feelings, reducing antisocial peer contacts, enhancing family relationships and supervision by parents, identification with prosocial models, strengthening self-control, improving social skills, reducing drug addiction, and improving cost–utility ratios for non-criminal behaviour in various settings. Third, the *responsivity principle*: styles and modes of service are matched to the learning styles and abilities of offenders. This involves measures like anticriminal modelling, role playing, teaching concrete skills, graduated practice, reinforcement, making resources available, verbal guidance, use of authority, cognitive restructuring, and so forth. Andrews and colleagues (1990b) computed a mean ES of 0.10. Broadly independent of other study characteristics, appropriate programmes had the best outcomes (0.32). Unspecified programmes showed a weaker positive effect ES (0.10), and inappropriate services and pure criminal sanctions even showed small negative effects (−0.07 and −0.08). Appropriate programmes were predominantly (but not only) those using behavioural interventions. Appropriate correctional services had the best outcomes in both the juvenile and adult justice system. Design quality had no major impact on the results. Similar effects of treatment modality were also found in the study subsample of Whitehead and Lab (1989). In community settings, appropriate programmes produced higher mean effects than in institutional settings. However, inappropriate programmes were almost equally bad in both settings. In a related analysis, Hill, Andrews and Hoge (1991) also found that under high-integrity conditions the effects of appropriate treatment became particularly positive, while the outcome of inappropriate programmes tended to be even more negative.

The meta-analysis of Izzo and Ross (1990) integrated 46 evaluation studies (with 68 comparisons) on treatment programmes for adjudicated juvenile delinquents. The studies were published between 1970 and 1985, had experimental or quasi-experimental control-group designs, and used recidivism as the outcome criterion. Studies were categorized according to whether they were based on a sound conceptualization of antisocial behaviour and according to their programme rationale (e.g. social learning, behaviour modification, modelling, systems theory, reality therapy, interpersonal maturity-level theory, sociological theory). No detailed effect measures are reported, only results of analyses of variance. Most differences between categories were not significant, although theoretically founded programmes had higher effects than others. Two treatment characteristics significantly explained 19% of the ES variance: programmes with a cognitive component showed higher effects than others. Larger effects were also obtained in community than in institutional settings.

In the most comprehensive meta-analysis on the treatment of juvenile offenders, Lipsey (1992a) integrated 443 evaluation studies from 1950 to 1987. Programmes for school children, predelinquents and at-risk groups were also included. The methodological selection criterion was a control-group design. Results showed that 285 of the studies produced positive effects, and 131, negative effects. In 27, there was no difference in outcome. This was a highly significant positive effect, although it was low. The unweighted mean ES was 0.08; the n-adjusted and inverse-variance-weighted mean ES was 0.05. Lipsey divided the study characteristics into various clusters: 27% of the ES variance was accounted for by sampling error; 15% by measurement error; 25% by methodological factors; and 22% by treatment characteristics. In the 'treatment cluster', the type of intervention was most important. Both inside and outside the juvenile justice system, behavioural, skill-oriented, and multimodal programmes had larger effects than other treatments. At 0.10 to 0.16, their mean effects were approximately twice as high as the overall mean. Unstructured case work, individual, group or family counselling programmes, and formal measures such as probation/parole had lower effects, whereas deterrence measures even had negative outcomes. For some programmes results were not fully consistent: employment/vocational programmes, for example, overall showed about zero effects. However, a few employment programmes in the juvenile justice system were relatively successful. This might also be due to the small number of relevant studies available. In custodial institutions, public facilities and the juvenile justice system, effects were smaller than in other contexts. High-risk cases made only a slight contribution to larger effects, whereas dosage had somewhat more impact. Researcher influences on the treatment also resulted in larger ES. In the 'method cluster', there was no relationship between randomization and ES. Initial non-equivalence of treatment and control group had varying effects. There were smaller effects in studies with larger sample sizes, with higher rates of attrition, and with some 'therapeutic contact' or 'treatment as usual' in the control group. Outcome measures with low reliability, low validity and longer follow-up periods also had smaller effects. The mean ES in outcome measures of delinquency (official recidivism, self-report, other ratings) was similar to those in measures of interpersonal adjustment, school participation and vocational accomplishment. However, they were clearly lower than those for psychological measures like self-esteem and attitudes towards authority. While school participation and vocational accomplishment correlated significantly with the delinquency outcome, the psychological variables did not (Lipsey, 1992b).

Antonowicz and Ross (1994) restricted their meta-analysis to 44 rigorously controlled studies published between 1970 and 1991. Studies were included only when they dealt with officially processed juvenile or adult offenders, had experimental or quasi-experimental control-group designs, reported on community-based follow-up outcome measures such as rearrest, reconviction and reincarceration, and could be statistically analysed. There must have been some form of individual or group intervention designed to modify offenders' behaviour, attitudes, and so forth. Mere systems interventions such as restitution, intensive probation supervision, shock incarceration, or work release programmes were excluded. The same applied to studies that only compared different institutions without controlling for treatment content and the like. The authors split the studies into 20 successful versus 24 unsuccessful programmes. Effective programmes must have shown a significant difference in recidivism in favour of the treatment group. According to previous suggestions on 'what works', 40 study characteristics were compared. Unfortunately, the authors do not report separate data for juveniles and adults, but both groups seem to be similarly represented in the two study subsamples. Successful programmes more often included a sound conceptual model, the need principle, the responsivity principle, multifaceted treatment, role playing or modelling and social–cognitive skills training. The risk principle, the setting (community versus institution), offender involvement in planning and staff training or supervision showed no significant relationship to treatment success. Many other theoretically relevant variables were assessed so rarely in the primary studies that no statements could be made on their moderating effects (e.g. social perspective-taking, self-control, interpersonal problem-solving, victim awareness, client motivation, relapse prevention, supportive environment, integrity, staff motivation).

Redondo (1994) performed a meta-analysis of 57 studies on the treatment of juvenile and adult offenders in Europe (Great Britain, Spain, the Netherlands, Sweden, Germany, Israel). This was a selection of 250 European studies published between 1983 and 1993 that contained randomized and non-equivalent control-group designs as well as pre–post comparisons. The mean ES was 0.15. There were larger effects for behavioural and particularly for cognitive-behavioural interventions (about 0.25). Other therapeutic approaches, educational programmes, therapeutic communities, pure punishment and diversion showed lower and less consistent effects. For the latter categories, however, the number of studies was also smaller. Over 60% of the programmes took place in prisons, about half of them for juveniles There was no significant outcome difference as compared with community settings. Programmes in juvenile prisons and reformatories even had a slightly better effect (0.20) than community approaches (0.17). Studies with lower methodological quality showed smaller effects, particularly pre–post designs versus control-group designs. Smaller effects were also obtained when recidivism was used as an outcome criterion rather than psychological, institutional, academic or work adjustment and social skills.

WHAT THE RESEARCH SYNTHESES DO AND DO NOT TELL US

The majority of studies address young offenders, and have summarized about 500 relevant treatment evaluations. At first glance, this suggests a reliable data base. However, it is a very heterogeneous pool of primary studies. The breadth of 'treatments' ranges from interventions for predelinquent conduct problems across diversion with no further interventions in young first offenders to intensive therapies for severe and persistent offenders in custodial settings. In fact, on some specific types of programmes there still are only very few methodologically controlled studies. Because the study samples overlap in several research syntheses, results are not completely independent. Therefore, agreements between the meta-analyses should not be overinterpreted. The study samples do not just differ in size, but also on numerous other characteristics. For example, type and age of integrated offender groups vary widely. The selection criteria for design differ. For example, pre–post designs without control groups are sometimes included and sometimes not. There are great variations in the coding of the studies, for example, with respect to programme characteristics or methodological quality. Some studies focus more on formal or systems interventions; others, more on treatment content. The details in meta-analytical method differ substantially, for example, regarding whether and how ES was computed. Some studies control for sampling and measurement error, others do not. In addition, different procedures are used in the analysis of moderator effects.

Therefore, it is no surprise that the results of meta-analyses on the treatment of young offenders are not as consistent as one would expect from an objective and unbiased research integration. Because of the methodological problems in meta-analyses, we should apply the same basic empirical principle as in primary studies: evidence comes through replication. If the various meta-analyses are interpreted in this sense, they none the less reveal some fairly stable patterns. Conversely, they show that information is still inconsistent or insufficient on various important points. In the following, I shall apply both perspectives with respect to the general effect, study design, mode of treatment, outcome measure, setting type, treatment integrity and client characteristics.

Overall Effect

In all meta-analyses in which ES coefficients were computed, these were positive. However, when various types of treatment were included (and not just, for example, social learning programmes), mean ES was small. They vary only between the most conservative estimate of $r = 0.05$ or 0.08 in Lipsey (1992a) and the mean of 0.18 in Garrett (1985), which was increased by methodologically weak studies. The fact that the smallest ES is found in Lipsey (1992a) cannot be due only to his methodologically strict correction for sample size or the fact that he also included unpublished studies, that is, reduced the 'file drawer problem' (Rosenthal, 1991). The inclusion of studies with low-risk or predelinquent youngsters could also have played a role. The majority of overall effects are about 0.10. This means that, given dichotomous outcome measures such as rearrest, reconviction or reincarceration, the treated group performed on average 10 percentage points better than the control group. On quantitative criteria such as behaviour ratings, delinquency self-reports and personality measures, an ES of 0.10 means that the average treated client is better off than 58% of the control group.

For some researchers, practicians and policymakers, this small overall effect may seem disappointing. However, it does not confirm the 'nothing works' doctrine. The great number of about 500 studies with more than 80 000 subjects makes it highly significant. Even the lower confidence limit is slightly greater than zero (e.g. Lipsey, 1992a). As several meta-analyses have integrated unpublished evaluation reports, a positive effect is probably not explained sufficiently by the above-mentioned publication bias. Even a small overall effect may be relevant for practice. This is particularly the case when more successful alternatives are not available (Prentice & Miller, 1992). Cost-utility analyses have also shown that a small effect of about 0.15 can save money (e.g. Prentky & Burgess, 1992). Not infrequently, even 'unsuccessful' treatment outcomes show a delay in relapse time. According to the age curve of crime, this may help young offenders to reduce the frequency of reoffending during the period of highest risk. Not least, a small overall effect can form a basis for further developments in the contents or the cost-relatedness of treatment concepts. This makes it necessary to evaluate the effect in a broader framework.

Without doubt, the mean ES in the treatment of young offenders is lower than that found in meta-analyses of general psychotherapy, behaviour modification or social competence training (e.g. Beelmann, Pfingsten & Lösel, 1994; Shapiro &

Shapiro, 1983; Smith, Glass & Miller, 1980; Weisz et al., 1987; see also Lipsey & Wilson, 1993). In addition to inadequate programmes there can be various reasons for this small effect. Partially, it may be due to the nature of juvenile crime. As Moffitt (1993) and others suggest, one should differentiate between subgroups with 'adolescence-limited' and 'life-course-persistent antisocial behaviour'. In the first group of age-typical juvenile delinquency, problem remission can be anticipated over time due to learning processes in the normal developmental context. This may reduce treatment effects as compared with control groups (see also the risk principle mentioned above). In more persistent antisociality, severe problems are already visible in childhood. Reviews show that these are difficult to treat (Kazdin, 1987). In the subgroup of offenders in whom antisocial behaviour has commenced early in childhood, it proves to be fairly persistent (Farrington, 1987; Loeber & Dishion, 1983; Tremblay et al., 1994). Negative family and milieu conditions often contribute to a vicious circle of problem enhancement (Farrington, Ohlin & Wilson, 1986; Patterson, Reid & Dishion, 1992). Frequently, offending is immediately reinforced by self and peers (Gottfredson & Hirschi, 1990). This also holds for a broader range of problem behaviour (alcohol drinking, illegal drug use, drunken driving, early sexual contacts, truancy, etc.) that makes up the deviant life-style of many offenders (Farrington, 1989; Jessor, Donovan & Costa 1992). In contrast to many psychiatric disorders, there often is a lack of insight into personal problems and deficits in treatment motivation (Yochelson & Samenow, 1977). External constraints and expected privileges from the justice system are important motivating factors for programme participation. Traditionally, this is not viewed as promising for behavioural change. However, experiences in the field of criminality, drug use and so forth have shown that positive effects are not impossible even when the ideal of voluntary treatment is not fully met (see Sowers & Daley, 1993; Thornton & Hogue, 1993). Negative influences of custodial settings and prisonization effects may also counteract a better outcome (e.g. Bondeson, 1989). The same can be expected from the former practice of indeterminate sentences.

Last but not least, methodological aspects could contribute to lower effects as compared with other treatment areas: in offender treatment, there are normally no analogue studies or programmes in intact middle-class milieus. The outcome criteria are frequently more or less reliable indicators for recidivism. This generally involves a longer follow-up period. These 'real world' behavioural criteria are distal to the treatment content and less distorted by positive therapist's ratings or self-reports. Often outcome—like treatment—is used as only a dichotomous variable, which decreases statistical power (Cohen, 1988). All this suggests that the small effect should not be compared unrealistically with a coefficient of 1.0, but with a theoretical maximum that is much lower (see Cohen, 1988; Rosenthal, 1991). Let us take an example of 100 youngsters in the treatment group and 100 in the control group. If the recidivism rate in the control group is 50% (a realistic estimate for reincarceration), even a success rate of 100% in the treatment group would only result in a maximum ϕ of 0.58. Taking the above-mentioned problems into account, a realistic upper threshold of treatment effectivity may be about 0.30. In our example, this would mean that the success rate in the treated group is still about 80%. Thus, Whitehead and Lab

(1989, p. 291) should not consider a criterion of 0.20 as 'very generous' and suggest 0.40 to 0.50 as a 'more rigorous selection'.

Design Characteristics

The research integrations in the 1960s and 1970s did not make the general claim that 'nothing works'. However, they ascertained numerous methodological deficits and inconsistencies that prevented a sound appraisal (e.g. Bailey, 1966; Lipton, Martinson & Wilks, 1975; Logan, 1972; Sechrest, White & Brown, 1979; Wright & Dixon, 1977). A major contribution of the more recent meta-analyses has been that they have not only diagnosed the methodological problems in the primary studies but also tested their relations to ES in detail. This procedure orients itself towards a realistic estimation of the possibilities of controlled programme evaluations in complex field settings. As even very well controlled randomized experiments exhibit deficits that permit alternative explanations (Cook & Campbell, 1979), modern evaluation research questions the hope for an *experimentum crucis* that is valid in every aspect. In a differentiated manner, one tries to use the information provided by studies that fulfil the necessary but rarely sufficient methodological criteria (Cronbach et al., 1980). The quality of design is thus understood as a gradual and multidimensional evaluation system and not as an all-or-none category (e.g. Cook & Campbell, 1979; Lösel & Köferl, 1989).

In the meta-analyses on offender treatment, the effects of methodological characteristics are heterogeneous. For example, in Redondo (1994), methodological variables explained 61% of the effect-size variance, whereas in Lipsey (1992a), they explained 25%, and in Andrews, Bonta & Hoge (1990b), only approximately 5% (non-significant). The variety of the primary studies and the differentiation of methodological categories play a role here. In all, however, the studies suggest that stronger designs produce smaller effects than weaker designs (see Lösel, 1995b). When simple pre–post designs are included, they show higher effects than control-group designs. The impact of randomization on ES is less clear. Alongside zero correlations (Lipsey, 1992a), there are both weakly positive (Gottschalk et al., 1987a) and weakly negative (Whitehead & Lab, 1989) relationships. Lipsey's (1992a) findings on other methodological variables also indicate that effects tend to be smaller in designs with higher validity. As in this study, the impact of methodological variables should be analysed and weighted in a more differentiated manner in future research (Bliesener, 1994; Lösel, Köferl & Weber, 1987). Thus, corrected estimations of ES may result (e.g. Rubin, 1992). According to the present data, however, it seems unlikely that the positive overall effect and the effect-size variance can be traced back totally to methodological characteristics.

Mode of Treatment

The majority of meta-analyses show that ES depends on the type of treatment. These moderator effects are also not completely comparable, because the various meta-analyses have applied different coding categories. For example, Lipsey (1992a) discriminated between more than 20 treatment modes according to content and formal categories; Andrews and colleagues (1990b) used only three integrative categories. None the less, there is still a relatively consistent trend: forms of treatment that are oriented towards empirically sound and clinically relevant theories of criminality, are relatively structured, cognitive-behavioural and multimodal produce the best effects. This is in line with the higher mean ES in those meta-analyses that integrated special behavioural or social learning programmes (Gottschalk et al., 1987b; Mayer et al., 1986). Although the effects of the most successful programmes differ (e.g. ES is much higher in Andrews et al., 1990, than in Lipsey, 1992a), they are in each case more than twice as high as the overall effects. That some measures are more successful than others is probably the most important contribution of meta-analyses on offender treatment. The relatively positive evaluation of cognitive-behavioural techniques is also in line with qualitative reviews (e.g. Basta & Davidson, 1988; Geismar & Wood, 1985; Hollin, 1990; Kazdin, 1994).

According to several meta-analyses, one also has to anticipate negative effects for some programmes. This can be the case particularly in theoretically ill-founded, weakly structured, unspecific counselling, purely non-directive, psychodynamic or deterrence measures. Obviously, in working with young offenders, it is necessary to pay more attention not just to doing *something* but to doing the *right thing*. These results should not be misinterpreted as a simple guide for deciding between traditional 'schools' of therapy. For example, some behavioural techniques (like token economies) may be successful for shaping more prosocial behaviour, but lead to only short-term effects in controllable contexts. On the other hand, some basic elements of psychodynamic approaches (like relationship formation) are relevant for all kinds of offender treatment. However, as Andrews and Bonta (1994) show, other psychodynamic principles seem to be less adequate for the specific needs and learning styles of many offenders. One should also bear in mind that early psychoanalysts like Alfred Adler already emphasized more structured, 'cognitive-behavioural' approaches when working with antisocial youngsters.

The meta-analyses indicate which direction the further development and evaluation of programmes for young offenders must take. None the less, it is necessary to warn against falling back into the error of having overoptimistic expectations of certain programmes. We now know characteristics of relatively successful programmes that are based mostly on social-cognitive learning theories of delinquency (e.g. Hollin, 1990; Patterson, Reid & Dishion, 1992; Ross & Fabiano, 1985). However, only some of these features have been well replicated so far (Antonowicz & Ross, 1994). It also cannot be ruled out that the coding of appropriate programmes by Andrews and colleagues (1990b) was oriented, in doubtful cases, more or less implicitly towards knowledge of effects (see Lab & Whitehead, 1990; Logan et al., 1991). The responsivity principle then becomes a circular argument. Therefore, these meta-analytic results should be used as the basis for a new generation of offender treatment evaluation. Here, it would seem particularly promising not just to assess programmes according to therapeutic schools or directions, but to orient them systematically towards empirically proven risk and protective factors for juvenile delinquency (see Hawkins,

Catalano & Miller 1992; Lösel, 1994; Stouthamer-Loeber et al., 1993). This corresponds to more integrative, eclectic approaches in general psychotherapy research (Garfield & Bergin, 1994; Grawe, Donati & Bernauer, 1994). If it is possible to replicate the outcomes of relatively successful programmes with an ES of about 0.20, this would reduce, for example, a recidivism rate from 50% to 30% (a 40% reduction that is very significant in practical terms).

Outcome Measure

Various meta-analyses have shown that ES depends on the type of outcome criteria. Official recidivism repeatedly produces lower effects than, for example, measures of institutional adjustment, psychological adjustment, attitudes, personality, or other psychological criteria. This is in line with qualitative reviews (e.g. Feldman, 1989) The fact that in Lipsey (1992b), the effects for school participation, academic performance and vocational accomplishment were similar to those for delinquency may well have been related to the fact that these are also 'harder' indicators of everyday behaviour (and not just questionnaire scales). The primary delinquency measure of Lipsey additionally was not restricted to official recidivism criteria, but also covered (rarer) self-report measures and other indicators of antisocial behaviour.

In all, the impact of outcome measures on ES is not so extreme that it invalidates other differential results. Several of the research syntheses are limited in any case to primary studies with recidivism (e.g. Andrews et al., 1990b; Antonowicz & Ross, 1994; Izzo & Ross, 1990; Whitehead & Lab, 1989). The trend towards somewhat smaller effects for recidivism could be due to deficits in reliability and validity. For example, official recidivism does not just depend on actual offending, but also on the offence situation, the cleverness of the offender, selection strategies of the police, procedural decisions in the justice system, and so forth. According to Lipsey (1992a), the methodological weakness of outcome criteria correlates once more with smaller ES. However, it is not only official recidivism that is problematic. There are also similar reliability problems in the self- and external reports that form the basis of the other outcome measures.

It is probably also relevant that official recidivism involves a follow-up period, whereas this is not always the case in other measures. The length of the follow-up, in turn, seems to correlate negatively with ES (e.g. Lipsey, 1992a). In all, the meta-analyses show that more attention needs to be paid to the selection of outcome measures. Indicators of treatment efficacy are often related insufficiently to delinquent behaviour (Blackburn, 1980). Their reliability, validity and sensitivity are frequently questionable (Lipsey, 1992a). More analyses are needed in which various outcome measures are oriented systematically towards a causal chain of delinquent behaviour.

Type of Setting

Several of the meta-analyses indicate that treatment effects are somewhat larger in community settings than in custodial or institutional ones. These findings support the idea that one should prefer ambulant or community-oriented measures when working with young offenders (as far as possible according to reasons of security). This opinion has led to an expansion of programmes of diversion, victim–offender mediation, community service and the like in many countries. Avoiding custodial settings is plausible from various perspectives, as in the following examples. (1) Processes of deprivation, prisonization or institutionalization that can have a negative impact on treatment effects are circumvented. (2) Massing antisocial youngsters in institutions increases the risk of unfavourable peer-group influences. (3) In community settings, it is easier to involve the family and other important reference persons. (4) In institutions, the cognitive and behavioural skills acquired through treatment cannot be tested directly against reality but have to be transferred to a later time.

However, the results of meta-analyses do not indicate that community programmes are generally better than those in institutions. Some research syntheses have even shown no significant differences (e.g. Antonowicz & Ross, 1994; Redondo, 1994). In other analyses, the impact of the setting independent from other factors was small (e.g. Andrews et al., 1990b; Lipsey, 1992a). Only in Izzo and Ross (1990) did 'setting' explain more than 10% of effect-size variance. With appropriate programmes, substantial effects can be attained in institutions, whereas, even in community settings, inappropriate measures have no positive effect (Andrews et al., 1990b). It also has to be taken into account that primary studies normally did not directly compare a certain programme for similar offender groups in different contexts (e.g. Petersilia & Turner, 1986). This means that confounds with clients, treatment, method and other variables can exist depending on the differentiation of the analysis. In practical work with young offenders as well, the choice of setting is related closely to these other characteristics (Quay, 1987). Institutions are normally the *ultima ratio* for the most persistent or dangerous offenders. In these cases, they fulfil not only a protective role for society but also for the young persons themselves (e.g. in the risk of very severe offences, drug use, infections, etc.). Thus, treatment should not be seen as a counterpart to incapacitation. Even prison settings do not have such generally negative effects as is often maintained (see Bonta & Gendreau, 1990). Despite eventual counteracting processes, treatments under custodial conditions remain important (Agee, 1986; Garrido & Redondo, 1993; Martinson, 1979; Porporino & Baylis, 1993; Wexler, Falkin & Lipton, 1990). In addition, their disadvantages can, in some circumstances, be reduced by combining them with community-oriented approaches (Hollin, 1994).

From a scientific and practical perspective, the issue of 'community versus institution' is more of a dimension than a dichotomy. In both settings, there are various possibilities as well as transitions between the two (e.g. community residential centres, halfway houses, intensive rehabilitation supervision). On the one hand, careful offender assessment is necessary for differentiated placement (e.g. Bonta & Motiuk, 1990; Gendreau, Cullen & Bonta, 1994). On the other hand, various organizational factors moderate the influence of a formal type of setting: for example, institutional climate, extent of control, degree of isolation, crowding, features of the subculture, staff characteristics and other factors may moderate the influence of a formal type of setting (e.g. Bonta & Gendreau, 1990; Cooke, Baldwin

& Howison, 1990; Farrington & Nuttall, 1980; Moos, 1975; Toch & Grant, 1989; Zamble & Porporino, 1990). Unfortunately, such data have too rarely been assessed in treatment studies, and are thus under-represented in the meta-analyses.

Treatment Integrity

A certain treatment label can be rather misleading regarding what actually happens in a programme (e.g. Quay, 1977; Rezmovic, 1984; Sechrest, White & Brown, 1979), Treatment integrity is often questionable. The issue of integrity is complex and not an unidimensional variable (Hollin, 1995). Partially, it is related to characteristics of the setting. Here as well, meta-analyses can provide only limited information, because integrity has frequently not been studied in detail in the primary studies (see Antonowicz & Ross, 1994). Available data indicate that high programme integrity is associated with better outcomes (e.g. Hill, Andrews & Hoge, 1991; Lipsey, 1992a). It is clear that this only holds for programmes that are successful in principle. In the case of inappropriate treatment, integrity does not improve outcome. Indirect information on the role of integrity is also provided by the moderator effects of dosage variables and of researcher influences in treatment implementation (Gensheimer et al., 1986, Lipsey, 1992a). The latter may have led to better monitoring, but also to positive biases in outcome measurement. The practical importance of treatment integrity is greater than the small proportions of explained variance in meta-analyses reveal. However, whereas process analyses have become a central topic in general psychotherapy research, many studies on offender treatment limit themselves to analysing outcome. This is regrettable, because the concrete contents of the programmes seem to be more important than their formal definition in the justice system.

Lack of integrity leads to a low reliability of treatment (see Lösel & Wittmann, 1989). Just as with the lack of reliability of outcome measures, this results in a smaller effect. Thus, high treatment integrity is important for an effective programme. Low integrity may have many causes (see Rossi & Freeman, 1985). Only some factors can be mentioned here (see, for example, Hollin, 1995; Palmer, 1992; Roberts, 1995): (a) weakly structured programmes with no detailed treatment manuals; (b) insufficient staff training in general care skills and knowledge, awareness of professional issues, and treatment skills; (c) organizational barriers and staff resistance to proper programme implementation; (d) critical incidents like prisoner escapes or violent acts that lead to a change in political climate; (e) implicit learning processes that modify programme implementation in an unsystematic way; and (f) lack of a common basic philosophy regarding criminality, rehabilitation and treatment paradigms. The last point is revealed very clearly in a study that we have carried out on subjective theories of juvenile crime (Averbeck & Lösel, 1994). Various professional groups including prison governors, judges, prison officers, psychologists, social workers and probation officers had rather different ideas on the factors that are relevant for juvenile crime and recidivism.

Naturally, in a basically individual process like treatment, it is not possible (and also, from the perspective of therapeutic bonds, not desirable) to 'standardize' working with young offenders. However, in order to ensure treatment integrity, measures are needed regarding the organizational structure, the communication and decision rules, the selection and training of staff and so forth (e.g. Dionne et al., 1994; Hollin, 1994; Lösel & Bliesener, 1989). These need to be included in treatment evaluation through systematic process analyses and monitoring.

Client Characteristics

One essential feature of differential indication is that a successful treatment is tailored to the individual characteristics of a client. Most of the meta-analyses are not very differentiated here and they also produce only weak moderator effects. For example, Gottschalk and colleagues (1987a) differentiated only between characteristics such as age, sex or legal status, and found that studies with a higher proportion of males and non-adjudicated juveniles tended to show higher effects. Client variables received a more differentiated coding in Lipsey (1992a). This included age, sex, ethnicity, level of delinquency (risk), prior offence history, predominant types of offence, sources of treatment (voluntary, mandatory, etc.) and heterogeneity of the sample. None the less, the 'subjects cluster' did not make a significant contribution to the explanation of variance. The only tendency was that risk level correlated with ES. According to Lipsey, this requires further exploration, which is in agreement with Antonowicz and Ross (1994). Although Andrews and colleagues (1990b) could confirm the importance of risk, in their meta-analysis this is not tested independently from the need and responsivity principle (Andrews et al., 1990b). Perhaps the relation between risk and treatment efficacy is not linear but follows an inverse U function: in low-risk cases, there are small differences to the control group because of spontaneous remissions; these are not seen in high-risk cases, because of stabilized deviant behaviour patterns that are hard to modify.

That relatively undifferentiated client characteristics have little impact in the meta-analyses may also be related to characteristics of juvenile delinquency. For example, the structure of offences tends to be heterogeneous (Klein, 1984) and there are hardly any specializations, as in, for example, sex offenders. However, a low differentiation according to client characteristics is unsatisfactory. Early treatment approaches already particularly emphasized this aspect (e.g. Palmer, 1984; Sparks, 1968). This is supported by the positive effects of programmes that are oriented towards the need and responsivity principle or towards a sound conceptual model (e.g. Andrews et al., 1990; Antonowicz & Ross, 1994). Such programmes are based on a matching of intervention strategy to specific clients. However, the characteristics summarized in these principles tend to be more generally relevant for the modification of delinquent behaviour and not primarily for specific types of offenders.

One aspect that should be considered more in differential indication is the *development* of antisocial behaviour. As mentioned above, Moffitt (1993) has discriminated between life-course-persistent and adolescence-limited antisocial behaviour. In the former, neuropsychological deficits are already apparent during childhood, and these are strengthened by a disadvantaged milieu and unfavourable parental behaviour. This reveals itself at an early age in conduct disorders. Serious delinquency results from a successive interaction between personality-determined antisociality and reactions in the environment. In contrast to this, Moffitt considers that the causes of adolescence-limited antisociality are mainly found in temporary status problems, the reinforcement gained from deviant behaviour, and the peer group. These can also lead to severe delinquency. However, 'normal' formal and informal reactions of the environment suffice to dissuade from antisocial behaviour in late adolescence. Although there are still problems in predicting such subgroups reliably, models of different developmental pathways to delinquency are very important for intervention strategies (see also Farrington, 1992; LeBlanc & Loeber, 1993; Loeber, 1990; Lösel 1995c), For example, life-course-persistent antisociality overlaps with antisocial personality disorder and sociopathy (Hare, Hart & Harpur, 1991). In these groups, in turn, treatment effects are rare or even negative (e.g. Hart, Kropp & Hare, 1988; Rice, Harris & Cormier 1992). In addition, cognitive deficits and biases of offenders, which are emphasized in cognitive-behavioural pro- grammes, are probably not equally relevant for all offender groups. For example, it has been shown that hostile attributional biases are particularly found in undersocialized aggressive conduct disorders but not in socialized delinquency and non-violent crimes (Dodge et al., 1990).

Evaluation studies also provide little information on the therapeutic moderator function of *protective* client factors. The risk concept is oriented primarily towards negative predictors and deficits. However, research on resilience has shown that even with a comparably high risk load, more favourable chances of development exist when certain social or personal resources are available (e.g. Lösel, 1994; Rutter, 1990; Stouthamer-Loeber et al., 1993). The former can be a positive reference person, social support from non-deviant persons or adequate education by authorities; and the latter, cognitive abilities, temperament characteristics, and experiences of self-efficacy in prosocial activities (Lösel & Bliesener, 1994; Rutter, 1990; Werner & Smith, 1992). Such 'natural' protective factors are similar to the characteristics of appropriate treatment. Like professional interventions, they can help to create turning points in a delinquent career (e.g. Sampson & Laub, 1993; Werner & Smith, 1992). Correlational- longitudinal research on protective processes and the influence on risk constellations is growing rapidly (Cichetti & Garmezy, 1993). Because the everyday social context (family, school, peer group) plays a very important role in work with young offenders, more attention should be paid to natural protective mechanisms in treatment research as well.

SUMMARY AND CONCLUSION

Meta-analyses on the treatment of young offenders have integrated an impressive number of outcome evaluations. In all, the results do not support the nothing works doctrine. However, effects are mainly small and only partially consistent. The various moderators make it very difficult to estimate valid corrected effect sizes. Thus, meta-analyses do not yet provide empirically well founded knowledge on differential indication. However, we have converging indications on how to aim towards realistic successes, and on which conditions these depend. The value of meta-analyses is not only that they summarize the available primary studies in a relatively objective and representative way. They also point to problems that have received insufficient attention and to 'blind spots' in research. From both these perspectives, the following points emerge from the present chapter.

1. The mean of all outcome evaluations is a small positive effect of treatment programmes for young offenders. This has to be judged realistically in the light of various problems of offender treatment. In this case, even a small effect may have practical relevance.
2. Various types of programme vary in their effectiveness. Programmes with a theoretically sound conceptualization, that consider specific criminogenic needs and learning styles of offenders, that have a cognitive-behavioural, multimodal and skill orientation clearly surpass the general effect. Theoretically ill-founded programmes, unspecific counselling, low-structured non-directive and psychodynamic interventions, pure formal measures, or deterrent approaches reveal lower and sometimes even negative effects.
3. There are still frequent deficits in study design. Their impact on the results is not fully consistent, particularly as far as randomization is concerned. In general, the meta-analyses suggest that effects tend to be overestimated in weaker designs with less reliable measures.
4. Somewhat lower effects have to be anticipated with outcome measures of delinquent behaviour or recidivism than with more proximal and subjective measures of psychological adaptation, attitude change and the like. There is a lack of systematically graded findings on the causal links between various effect indicators and offending.
5. Programmes in community settings tend to do somewhat better than those in institutional settings. However, the various contexts are still contrasted too sweepingly. More studies on specific institutional characteristics, moderators of custodial effects, and the interaction between positive and negative setting variables are needed.
6. Although treatment integrity is a precondition of successful interventions, insufficient attention is paid to this in evaluation. This also applies to the influence of organizational resistance, staff motivation, training or supervision. More process evaluations are needed, as well as integrations of clinical and organizational approaches in working with offenders.
7. A dynamic assessment of the individual offender's risk and needs and an appropriate matching with the level of service seem to be important. In contrast, many programmes and evaluations are not well adapted to psychologically meaningful subject characteristics. More use should be made of findings from developmental psychopathology, particularly the research on different pathways to delinquency and on the interplay between risk and protective factors in natural settings.

Despite a respectable number of evaluation studies, findings on theoretically and practically important issues in offender treatment are still insufficiently replicated.

Even for those types of programmes that have proved to be particularly successful, only a few carefully controlled and well documented studies are available. Thus, the impact of meta-analyses on actual work with young offenders consists of guiding not only answers but also questions. The promising results up to now should serve as a basis for a new generation of theoretically elaborated, methodologically controlled, process-oriented, and replicated evaluation studies (see, also, Andrews & Bonta, 1994; Palmer, 1992). There is a need for more combinations of correlational-longitudinal and experimental-intervention designs (Loeber & Farrington, 1994). An explicit developmental perspective can also help to draw attention to the characteristics that offender treatment shares with programmes of prevention or early intervention. In recent times, these measures have shown more promise (see McCord & Tremblay, 1992; Tremblay & Craig, 1995; Yoshikawa, 1994). However, programmes and research efforts in this field should not be understood as an alternative to the treatment approach. Coping with the problems of delinquency calls for improvements in both areas (and other approaches as well). It may be superfluous to emphasize this, but in criminal policy there is sometimes a similar problem to that found in many young offenders: thinking in undifferentiated categories such as black or white and good or bad.

AUTHOR NOTE

My work on the meta-evaluation of offender treatment was supported by grants from the German Federal Government and the Council of Europe. I thank Jonathan Harrow, University of Bielefeld, for his help with the translation.

REFERENCES

Agee, V. L. (1986). Institutional treatment programs for the violent juvenile. In S. J. Apter & A. P. Goldstein (eds), *Youth Violence: Programs and Prospects*. Elmsford, NY: Pergamon Press, pp. 75–88.

Allen, F. A. (1981). *The Decline of the Rehabilitative Ideal: Penal Policy and Social Purpose*. New Haven, CT: Yale University Press.

Andrews, D. A. & Bonta, J. (1994). *The Psychology of Criminal Conduct*. Cincinnati, OH: Anderson.

Andrews, D. A., Bonta, J. & Hoge, R. D. (1990a). Classification for effective rehabilitation. *Criminal Justice and Behavior*, **17**, 19–51.

Andrews, D. A., Zinger, I., Hoge, R. D., Bonta, J., Gendreau, P. & Cullen, F. T. (1990b). Does correctional treatment work? A clinically relevant and psychologically informed meta-analysis. *Criminology*, **28**, 369–404.

Antonowicz, D. & Ross, R. R. (1994). Essential components of successful rehabilitation programs for offenders. *International Journal of Offender Therapy and Comparative Criminology*, **38**, 97–104.

Averbeck, M. & Lösel, F. (1994). Subjektive Theorien über Jugendkriminalität [Subjective theories on juvenile delinquency]. In M. Steller, K.-P. Dahle & M. Basqué (eds), *Straftäterbehandlung*. Pfaffenweiler: Centaurus, pp. 213–26.

Bailey, W. C. (1966). Correctional outcome: An evaluation of 100 reports. *Journal of Criminal Law, Criminology and Police Science*, **57**, 153–60.

Basta, J. M. & Davidson II, W. S. (1988). Treatment of juvenile offenders: Study outcomes since 1980. *Behavioral Sciences and the Law*, **6**, 353–84.

Beelmann, A., Pfingsten, U. & Lösel, F. (1994). The effects of training social competence in children: A meta-analysis of recent evaluation studies. *Journal of Clinical Child Psychology*, **23**, 260–71.

Blackburn, R. (1980). *Still not working? A look at recent outcomes in offender rehabilitation*. Paper presented at the Scottish Branch of the British Psychological Society Conference on Deviance, Stirling, UK.

Bliesener, T. (1994). Der Einfluß der Forschungsqualität auf das Forschungsergebnis. [The relationship between methodological rigour and effect size.] Habilitationsschrift, Universität Erlangen-Nürnberg.

Blumstein A., Cohen, J. & Farrington, D. P. (1988). Criminal career research: Its value for criminology. *Criminology*, **26**, 1–35.

Bondeson, U. V. (1989). *Prisoners in Prison Societies*. New Brunswick, NJ: Transaction Books.

Bonta, J. & Gendreau, P. (1990). Reexamining the cruel and unusual punishment of prison life. *Law and Human Behavior*, **14**, 347–72.

Bonta, J. & Motiuk, L. L. (1990). Classification to halfway-houses: A quasi-experimental evaluation. *Criminology*, **28**, 497–506.

Bullock, J. R. & Svyantek, D. J. (1985). Analyzing meta-analysis: Potential problems, an unsuccessful replication, and evaluation criteria. *Journal of Applied Psychology*, **70**, 108–15.

Cichetti, D. & Garmezy, N. (1993). Editorial. Prospects and promises in the study of resilience. *Development and Psychopathology*, **5**, 497–502.

Cohen, J. (1988). *Statistical Power Analysis for the Behavioral Sciences*, 2nd edn. New York: Academic Press.

Cohen, J. (1994). The earth is round ($p < .05$). *American Psychologist*, **49**, 997–1003.

Cook, T. D. & Campbell, D. T. (1979). *Quasi-experimentation. Design and Analysis Issues for Field Settings*. Chicago, IL: Rand-McNally.

Cook, T. D. & Leviton, L. C. (1980). Reviewing the literature. A comparison of traditional methods with meta-analysis. *Journal of Personality*, **48**, 449–72.

Cooke, D. J., Baldwin, P. J. & Howison, J. (1990). *Psychology in Prisons*. London: Routledge.

Cooper, H. M. & Hedges, L. V. (eds) (1994). *The Handbook of Research Synthesis*. New York: Russell Sage Foundation.

Corrigan, P. W. (1991). Social skills training in adult psychiatric populations: A meta-analysis. *Journal of Behavior Therapy and Experimental Psychiatry*, **22**, 203–10.

Cronbach, L. J., Ambron, S. R., Dornbusch, S. M., Hess, R. D., Hornik, R. C., Philips, D. C., Walker, D. F. & Weiner, S. S. (1980). *Toward Reform of Program Evaluation*. San Francisco: Jossey Bass.

Cullen, F. T. & Gendreau, P. (1989). The effectiveness of correctional rehabilitation: Reconsidering the 'Nothing Works' doctrine. In L. Goodstein & D. L. Mackenzie (eds), *The American Prison: Issues in Research Policy* New York: Plenum Press, pp. 23–44.

Dionne, J., LeBlanc, M., Grégoire, J. C., Proulx, J. & Trudeau-LeBlanc, P. (1994). Staff training. The corner stone of a differential approach project with delinquent adolescents. *Research and Evaluation in Group Care*, in press.

Dodge, K. A., Price, J. M., Bachorowski, J.-A. & Newman, J. P. (1990). Hostile attributional biases in severely aggressive adolescents. *Journal of Abnormal Psychology*, **99**, 385–392.

Farrington, D. P. (1987). Early precursors of frequent offending. In J. Q. Wilson & G. C. Loury (eds), *From Children to Citizens: Families, Schools, and Delinquency Prevention*. New York: Springer, pp. 27–50.

Farrington, D. P. (1989). Later adult life courses of offenders and nonoffenders. In M. Brambring, F. Lösel & H. Skowronek (eds), *Children at Risk: Assessment, Longitudinal Research, and Intervention*. Berlin: de Gruyter.

Farrington, D. P. (1992). Psychological contributions to the explanation, prevention, and treatment of offending. In F. Lösel, D. Bender & T. Bliesener (eds), *Psychology and Law: International Perspectives*. Berlin: de Gruyter, pp. 35–51.

Farrington, D. P. & Nuttall, C. P. (1980). Prison size, overcrowding, prison violence, and recidivism. *Journal of Criminal Justice*, **8**, 221–31.

Farrington, D. P., Ohlin, L. E. & Wilson, J. Q. (1986). *Understanding and Controlling Crime*. New York: Springer.

Feldman, P. (1989). Applying psychology to the reduction of juvenile offending and offences: Methods and results. *Issues in Criminological and Legal Psychology*, **14**, 3–32.

Garfield, S. L. & Bergin, A. E. (1994). Introduction and historical overview. In A. E. Bergin & S. L. Garfield (eds), *Handbook of Psychotherapy and Behavior Change*, 4th edn. New York: Wiley, pp. 3–18.

Garrido, V. & Redondo, S. (1993). The institutionalisation of young offenders. *Criminal Behaviour and Mental Health*, **3**, 336–48.

Garrett, P. (1985). Effects of residential treatment of adjudicated delinquents: A meta-analysis. *Journal of Research in Crime and Delinquency*, **22**, 287–308.

Geismar, L. L. & Wood, K. M. (1985). *Family and Delinquency: Resocializing the Young Offender*. New York: Human Sciences Press.

Gendreau, P. & Andrews, D. A. (1990). Tertiary prevention: What the meta-analyses of the offender treatment literature tell us about 'What works'. *Canadian Journal of Criminology*, **32**, 173–84.

Gendreau, P. & Ross, R. R. (1979). Effective correctional treatment: Bibliotherapy for cynics. *Crime and Delinquency*, **25**, 463–89.

Gendreau, P. & Ross, R. R. (1987). Revivication of rehabilitation: Evidence from the 1980s. *Justice Quarterly*, **4**, 349–407.

Gendreau, P., Cullen, F. T. & Bonta, J. (1994). Intensive rehabilitation supervision: The next generation in community corrections? *Federal Probation*, **58**, 72–8.

Gensheimer, L. K., Mayer, J. P., Gottschalk, R. & Davidson II, W. S. (1986). Diverting youth from the juvenile justice system: A meta-analysis of intervention efficacy. In S. J. Apter & A. Goldstein (eds), *Youth Violence: Programs and Prospects*. Elmsford, NY: Pergamon Press, pp. 39–57.

Glass, G. V., McGaw, B. & Smith, M. L. (1981). *Meta-analysis in Social Research*. Beverly Hills, CA: Sage.

Gottfredson, M. R. & Hirschi, T. (1990). *A general Theory of Crime*. Stanford, CA: Stanford University Press.

Gottschalk, R., Davidson II, W. S., Gensheimer, L. K. & Mayer, J. P. (1987a). Community-based interventions. In H. C. Quay (ed.), *Handbook of Juvenile Delinquency*. New York: Wiley, pp. 266–89.

Gottschalk, R., Davidson II, W. S., Mayer, J. & Gensheimer, L. K. (1987b). Behavioral approaches with juvenile offenders. A meta-analysis of long-term treatment efficacy. In E. K. Morris & C. J. Braukmann (eds), *Behavioral Approaches to Crime and Delinquency*. New York: Plenum Press, pp. 399–423.

Grawe, K., Donati, R. & Bernauer, F. (1994). *Psychotherapie im Wandel: Von der Konfession zur Profession*. [Psychotherapy in change: From confession to profession]. Göttingen: Hogrefe.

Greenberg, P. F. (1977). The correctional effects of corrections: A survey of evaluations. In D. F. Greenberg (ed.), *Corrections and Punishment*. Beverly Hills, CA: Sage, pp. 111–48.

Hare, R. D., Hart, S. D. & Harpur, T. J. (1991). Psychopathy and the DSM-IV criteria for antisocial personality disorder. *Journal of Abnormal Psychology*, **100**, 391–8.

Hart, S. D., Kropp, P. R. & Hare, R. D. (1988). Performance of male psychopaths following conditional release from prison. *Journal of Consulting and Clinical Psychology*, **56**, 227–32.

Hawkins, J. D., Catalano, R. F. & Miller, J. Y. (1992). Risk and protective factors for alcohol and other drug problems in adolescence and early adulthood: Implications for substance abuse prevention. *Psychological Bulletin*, **112**, 64–105.

Hill, J. K., Andrews, D. A. & Hoge, R. D. (1991). Meta-analysis of treatment programs for young offenders: The effect of clinically relevant treatment on recidivism. *Canadian Journal of Program Evaluation*, **6**, 97–109.

Hollin, C. R. (1990). *Cognitive-behavioral Interventions with Young Offenders*. Elmsford, NY: Pergamon Press.

Hollin, C. R. (1993). Advances in the psychological treatment of delinquent behaviour. *Criminal Behaviour and Mental Health*, **3**, 142–57.

Hollin, C. R. (1994). Designing effective rehabilitation programmes for young offenders. *Psychology, Crime & Law*, **1**, 193–9.

Hollin, C. R. (1995). The meanings and implications of 'programme integrity'. In J. McGuire (ed.), *What Works: Reducing Reoffending*. Chichester: Wiley pp. 195–208.

Hood, R. (1967). Research on the effectiveness of punishments and treatments. In European Committee on Crime Problems (ed), *Collected Studies in Criminological Research*, Vol. I. Strasbourg: Council of Europe, pp. 73–113.

Hunter, J. E. & Schmidt, F. L. (1990). *Methods of Meta-analysis*. Newbury Park, CA: Sage.

Izzo, R. L. & Ross, R. R. (1990). Meta-analysis of rehabilitation programs for juvenile delinquents. A brief report. *Criminal Justice and Behavior*, **17**, 134–42.

Jessor, R., Donovan, J. E. & Costa, F. M. (1992). *Beyond Adolescence*. Cambridge: Cambridge University Press.

Kazdin, A. (1987). Treatment of antisocial behavior in children: Current status and future directions. *Psychological Bulletin*, **102**, 187–203.

Kazdin, A. E. (1994). Psychotherapy for children and adolescents. In A. E. Bergin & S. L. Garfield (eds), *Handbook of Psychotherapy and Behavior Change*, 4th edn. New York: Wiley, pp. 543–94.

Klein, M. W. (1984). Offence specialisation and versatility among juveniles. *British Journal of Criminology*, **24**, 185–94.

Lab, S. P. & Whitehead, J. T. (1990). From 'nothing works' to 'the appropriate works': The latest stop on the search for the secular grail. *Criminology*, **28**, 405–17.

LeBlanc, M. & Loeber, R. (1993). Precursors, causes and the development of criminal offending. In D.F. Hays & A. Angold (eds), *Precursors and Causes in Development and Psychopathology*. New York: Wiley.

Lipsey, M. W. (1988). Juvenile delinquency intervention. In H. S. Bloom, D. S. Cordray & R. Light (eds), *Lessons from Selected Program and Policy Areas. New Directions for Program Evaluation*, No. 37. San Francisco: Jossey Bass, pp. 63–84.

Lipsey, M. W. (1992a). Juvenile delinquency treatment: A meta-analytic inquiry into variability of effects. In T. D. Cook, H. Cooper, D. S. Cordray, H. Hartmann, L. V. Hedges, R. L. Light, T. A. Louis & F. Mosteller (eds), *Meta-analysis for Explanation*. New York: Russell Sage Foundation, pp. 83–127.

Lipsey, M. W. (1992b). The effect of treatment on juvenile delinquents: Results from meta-analysis. In F. Lösel, D. Bender & T. Bliesener (eds), *Psychology and Law. International Perspectives*. Berlin, New York: de Gruyter, pp. 131–43.

Lipsey, M. W. & Wilson, D. B. (1993). The efficacy of psychological, educational, and behavioral treatment. *American Psychologist*, **48**, 1181–1209.

Lipton, D., Martinson, R. & Wilks, J. (1975). *The Effectiveness of Correctional Treatment*. New York: Praeger.

Loeber, R. (1990). Disruptive and antisocial behavior in childhood and adolescence: Development and risk factors. In K. Hurrelmann & F. Lösel (eds), *Health Hazards in Adolescence*. Berlin, New York: de Gruyter, pp. 223–57.

Loeber, R. & Dishion, T. (1983). Early predictions of male delinquency: A review. *Psychological Bulletin*, **94**, 68–99.

Loeber, R. & Farrington, D. P. (1994). Problems and solutions in longitudinal and experimental treatment studies of child psychopathology and delinquency. *Journal of Consulting and Clinical Psychology*, **62**, 887–900.

Logan, C. (1972). Evaluation research in crime and delinquency: A reappraisal. *Journal of Criminal Law, Criminology and Police Science*, **63**, 378–87.

Logan, C. H., Gaes, G. G., Harer, M., Innes, C. A., Karacki, L. & Saylor, W. G. (1991). *Can Meta-Analysis Save Correctional Rehabilitation?* Washington, DC: Federal Bureau of Prison.

Lösel, F. (1991). Meta-analysis and social prevention: Evaluation and a study on the family-hypothesis in developmental psychopathology. In G. Albrecht & H.-U. Otto (eds), *Social Prevention and the Social Sciences*. Berlin: de Gruyter, pp. 305–32.

Lösel, F. (1992). Sprechen Evaluationsergebnisse von Meta-Analysen für einen frischen Wind in der Straftäterbehandlung? [Are meta-analyses a 'fresh breeze' in offender treatment?] In M. Killias (ed.), *Rückfall und Bewährung/Récidive et Réhabilitation*. Chur, Switzerland: Rüegger, pp. 335–53.

Lösel, F. (1993). The effectiveness of treatment in institutional and community settings. *Criminal Behaviour and Mental Health*, **3**, 416–37.

Lösel, F. (1994). Protective effects of social resources in adolescents at high risk for antisocial behavior. In E. Weitekamp & H.-J. Kerner (eds), *Cross-National Longitudinal Research on Human Development and Criminal Behavior*. Dordrecht, Netherlands: Kluwer, pp. 281–301.

Lösel, F. (1995a). Increasing consensus in the evaluation of offender rehabilitation? Lessons from research syntheses. *Psychology, Crime and Law*, **2**, 19–39.

Lösel, F. (1995b). The efficacy of correctional treatment: A review and synthesis of meta-evaluations. In J. McGuire (ed.), *What Works: Reducing Reoffending*. Chichester: Wiley, pp. 77–111.

Lösel, F. (1995c). Die Prognose antisozialen Verhaltens im Jugendalter: Eine entwicklungsbezogene Perspektive [Prediction of antisocial behavior in adolescence: A developmental perspective]. In D. Dölling (ed), *Die Täter-Individual prognose*. Heidelberg, Germany: Kriminalistik Verlag, 21–61.

Lösel, F. & Bliesener, T. (1989). Psychology in prison: Role assessment and testing of an organizational model. In H. Wegener, F. Lösel & J. Haisch (eds), *Criminal Behavior and the Justice System: Psychological Perspectives*. New York: Springer, pp. 419–39.

Lösel, F. & Bliesener T. (1994). Some high-risk adolescents do not develop conduct problems: A study on protective factors. *International Journal of Behavioral Development*, **17**, 753–77.

Lösel, F. & Köferl, P. (1989). Evaluation research on correctional treatment in West Germany: A meta-analysis. In H. Wegener, F. Lösel & J. Haisch (eds), *Criminal Behavior and the Justice System: Psychological Perspectives*. New York: Springer, pp. 334–55.

Lösel, F. & Wittmann, W. W. (1989) The relationship of treatment integrity and intensity to outcome criteria. In R. F. Conner & M. Hendricks (eds), *International Innovations in Evaluation Methodology. New Directions for Program Evaluation*, No. 42. San Francisco: Jossey-Bass, pp. 97–108.

Lösel, F., Köferl, P. & Weber, F. (1987). *Meta-Evaluation der Sozialtherapie. [Meta-evaluation of Social Therapy]*. Stuttgart, Germany: Enke.

Martin, S. E., Sechrest, L. B. & Redner, R. (1981). *New Directions in the Rehabilitation of Criminal Offenders*. Washington, DC: National Academy Press.

Martinson, R. (1974). What works? Questions and answers about prison reform. *The Public Interest*, **10**, 22–54.

Martinson, R. (1979). New findings, new views: A note of caution regarding sentencing reform. *Hofstra Law Review*, **7**, 242–58.

Matt, G. E. & Cook, T. (1994). Threats to the validity of research syntheses. In H. Cooper & L. V. Hedges (eds), *The Handbook of Research Synthesis*. New York: Russell Sage Foundation, pp. 503–20.

Mayer, J. P., Gensheimer L. K., Davidson II, W. S. & Gottschalk, R. (1986). Social learning treatment within juvenile justice: A meta-analysis of impact in the natural environment. In S. J. Apter & A. Goldstein (eds), *Youth Violence: Programs and Prospects*. Elmsford, NY: Pergamon Press, pp. 24–38.

McCord, J. & Tremblay, R. (eds) (1992). *Preventing Antisocial Behavior: Interventions from Birth through Adolescence*. New York: Guilford Press.

McGuire, J. (ed.) (1995). *What Works: Reducing Reoffending*. Chichester: Wiley.

McGuire, J. & Priestley, P. (1992). Some things do work: Psychological interventions with offenders and the effectiveness debate. In F. Lösel, D. Bender & T. Bliesener (eds), *Psychology and Law: International Perspectives*. Berlin: de Gruyter, pp. 163–174.

Moffitt, T. E. (1993). Adolescence-limited and life-course-persistent antisocial behavior: A developmental taxonomy. *Psychological Review*, **100**, 674–701.

Moos, R. (1975). *Evaluating Correctional and Community Settings*. New York: Wiley.

Orlinsky, D. E., Grawe, K. & Parks, B. K. (1994). Process and outcome in psychotherapy—noch einmal. In A. E. Bergin & S. L. Garfield (eds), *Handbook of Psychotherapy and Behavior Change*, 4th edn. New York: Wiley, pp. 270–376.

Palmer, T. (1975). Martinson revisited. *Journal of Research in Crime and Delinquency*, **12**, 133–52.

Palmer, T. (1984). Treatment and the role of classification: A review of basics. *Crime and Delinquency*, **30**, 245–67.

Palmer, T. (1992). *The Re-emergence of Correctional Intervention*. Newbury Park, CA: Sage.

Patterson, G. R., Reid, J. B. & Dishion, T. J. (1992). *Antisocial Boys*. Eugene, OR: Castalia Publishing.

Petersilia, J. & Turner, S. with J. Peterson (1986). *Prison versus Probation in California*. Santa Monica, CA: Rand Corporation.

Porporino, F. J. & Baylis, E. (1993). Designing a progressive penology: the evolution of Canadian federal corrections. *Criminal Behaviour and Mental Health*, **3**, 268–89.

Prentice, D. A. & Miller, D. T. (1992). When small effects are impressive. *Psychological Bulletin*, **112**, 160–4.

Prentky, R. & Burgess, A. W. (1992). Rehabilitation of child molesters: A cost–benefit analysis. In A. W. Burgess (ed), *Child trauma I: Issues and Research*. New York: Garland, pp. 417–42.

Quay, H. C. (1977). The three faces of evaluation: What can be expected to work? *Criminal Justice and Behavior*, **4**, 341—54.

Quay, H. C. (1987). Institutional treatment. In H. C. Quay (ed.), *Handbook of Juvenile Delinquency*. New York: Wiley.

Redondo, S. (1994). *El tratamiento de la delinquencia en Europa: Un estudio meta-analitico*. Tesis Doctoral. Barcelona, Spain: Universidad de Barcelona.

Rezmovic, E. L. (1984). Assessing treatment implementation amid the slings and arrows of reality. *Evaluation Review*, **2**, 187–204.

Rice, M. E., Harris, G. T. & Cormier, C. A. (1992). An evaluation of a maximum security therapeutic community for psychopaths and other mentally disordered offenders. *Law and Human Behavior*, **16**, 399–412.

Richters, J. E. (1993). Community violence and children's development: Toward a research agenda for the 1990s. *Psychiatry*, **56**, 3–6.

Roberts, C. (1995). Effective practice and service delivery. In J. McGuire (ed.), *What Works: Reducing Reoffending*. Chichester: Wiley, pp. 221–36.

Romig, A. D. (1978). *Justice for our Children. An Examination of Juvenile Delinquent Rehabilitation Programs*. Lexington, MA: Lexington Books.

Rosenthal, R. (1991). *Meta-analytic Procedures for Social Research*, 2nd edn. Newbury Park, CA: Sage.

Rosenthal, R. & Rubin, D. B. (1982). A simple general purpose display of magnitude of experimental effect. *Journal of Educational Psychology*, **74**, 166–9.

Ross, R. R. & Fabiano, E. A. (1985). *Time to Think: A Cognitive Model of Delinquency Prevention and Offender Rehabilitation*. Johnson City, TN: Institute of Social Sciences and Arts.

Rossi, P. H. & Freeman, H. E. (1985). *Evaluation. A Systematic Approach*, 3rd edn. Beverly Hills, CA: Sage.

Rubin, D. B. (1992). Meta-analysis: Literature-synthesis or effect-size surface estimation. *Journal of Educational Statistics*, **17**, 363–74.

Rutter, M. (1990). Psychosocial resilience and protective mechanisms. In J. Rolf, A. Masten, D. Cicchetti, K. Nuechterlein & S. Weintraub (eds), *Risk and Protective Factors in the Development of Psychopathology*. New York: Cambridge University Press, pp. 181–214.

Sampson, R. J. & Laub, H. H. (1993). *Crime in the Making: Pathways and Turning Points Through Life*. Cambridge, MA: Harvard University Press.

Sechrest, L. B., White, S. O. & Brown, E. D. (1979). *The Rehabilitation of Criminal Offenders: Problems and Prospects*. Washington, DC: National Academy of Sciences.

Shapiro, D. A. & Shapiro, D. (1983). Meta-analysis of comparative therapy outcome studies: A replication and refinement. *Psychological Bulletin*, **92**, 581–604.

Smith, M. L. & Glass, G. V. (1977). Meta-analysis of psychotherapy outcome studies. *American Psychologist*, **32**, 752–760.

Smith, M. L., Glass, G. V. & Miller, T. I. (1980). *The Benefits of Psychotherapy*. Baltimore, MD: Johns Hopkins University Press.

Sowers, W. E. & Daley, D. C. (1993). Compulsory treatment of substance use disorders. *Criminal Behaviour and Mental Health*, **3**, 403–15.

Sparks, R. F. (1968). Types of treatment for types of offenders. In European Committee on Crime Problems (ed.), *Collected Studies in Criminological Research*, Vol. 3. Strasbourg: Council of Europe, pp. 129–69.

Stouthamer-Loeber, M., Loeber, R., Farrington, D. P., Zhang, Q., van Kammen, W. & Maguin, E. (1993). The double edge of protective and risk factors for delinquency: Interrelations and developmental patterns. *Development and Psychopathology*, **5**, 683–701.

Thornton, D. M. (1987). Treatment effects on recidivism: A reappraisal of the 'nothing works' doctrine. In B. J. McGurk, D. M. Thornton & M. Williams (eds), *Applying Psychology to Imprisonment*. London: HMSO, pp. 181–9.

Thornton, D. & Hogue, T. (1993). The large-scale provision of programmes for imprisoned sex offenders. Issues, dilemmas and progress. *Criminal Behaviour and Mental Health*, **3**, 371–80.

Toch, H. & Grant, D. (1989). Noncoping and maladaptation in confinement. In L. Goodstein & D. L. MacKenzie (eds), *The American Prison: Issues in Research and Policy*. New York: Plenum Press.

Tracy, P. E., Wolfgang, M. E. & Figlio, R. M. (1990). *Delinquency Careers in Two Birth Cohorts*. New York: Plenum Press.

Tremblay, R. E. & Craig, W. (1995). Developmental prevention of crime. From pre-birth to adolescence. In N. Morris & M. Tonry (eds), *Crime Prevention. Crime and Justice: An Annual Review of Research*. Chicago, IL: The University of Chicago Press, pp. 151–236.

Tremblay, R. E., Pihl, R. O., Vitaro, F. & Dobkin, P. L. (1994). Predicting early onset of male antisocial behavior from preschool behavior. *Archives of General Psychiatry*, **51**, 732–9.

Weisz, J. R., Weiss, B., Alicke, M. D. & Klotz, M. L. (1987). Effectiveness of psychotherapy with children and adolescents: A meta-analysis for clinicians. *Journal of Consulting and Clinical Psychology*, **55**, 542–9.

Werner, E. E. & Smith, R. S. (1992). *Overcoming the Odds*. Ithaca, NY: Cornell University Press.

Wexler, H. K., Falkin, G. P. & Lipton, D. S. (1990). Outcome evaluation of a prison therapeutic community for substance abuse treatment. *Criminal Justice and Behavior*, **17**, 71–92.

Whitehead, J. T. & Lab, S. P. (1989). A meta-analysis of juvenile correctional treatment. *Journal of Research in Crime and Delinquency*, **26**, 276–95.

Wright, E. W. & Dixon, M. C. (1977). Community prevention and treatment of juvenile delinquency. A review of evaluations. *Journal of Research in Crime and Delinquency*, **14**, 35–67.

Yochelson, S. & Samenow, S. (1977). *The Criminal Personality*, Vol 2. *The Change Process*. New York: Jason Aronson.

Yoshikawa, H. (1994). Prevention as cumulative protection: Effects of early family support and education on chronic delinquency and its risks. *Psychological Bulletin*, **115**, 28–54.

Zamble, E. & Porporino, F. J. (1990). Coping, imprisonment, and rehabilitation: Some data and their implications. *Criminal Justice and Behavior*, **17**, 53–70.

Part 2

Settings for Working with Young Offenders

4

Working in Institutions

MICHAEL A. MILAN
Georgia State University, USA

INTRODUCTION

Training schools are typically portrayed as the facilities that exist for the incarceration of adjudicated youths who have committed the most serious of criminal offenses for which, if adults, they would be sentenced to periods of imprisonment. As anyone familiar with the juvenile justice system knows, however, many training schools also incarcerate large numbers of youths who have committed lesser crimes for which judges and the juvenile justice system will not or cannot utilize alternative, less restrictive placements. Such inappropriate placements invariably stretch the already limited resources of the training schools. In addition, training school resources are being further stretched by a continuing increase in the commission of the types of serious offenses that all but mandate the long-term incarceration of youthful offenders in training schools under existing and proposed 'get tough' laws in the United States.

The bulk of the serious offenses that typically mandate training school placement consist of the violent 'index' crimes of murder and non-negligent manslaughter, forcible rape, robbery and aggravated assault that are tracked by the US Department of Justice. Offense data for 1992 (Snyder, 1994), the most recent data for crimes committed by juveniles available at the time of writing, indicate that there were approximately 200 violent crime arrests for every 100 000 persons under the age of 18 in the US population. These data represent a 38% increase during the five-year period ending with 1992. However, the inclusion of children younger than 10 years of age in the 1992

Clinical Approaches to Working with Young Offenders. Edited by C. R. Hollin and K. Howells.
© 1996 John Wiley & Sons Ltd.

population base presents a somewhat misleading picture of the incidence of juvenile crime.

Violent crime data for 1991 (Allen-Hagen & Sickmund, 1993) focused on youths between 10 and 17 years of age, rather than considering all youths below 18 years of age, and provide a more accurate depiction of juvenile crime per se than do the 1992 data. The 1991 data indicate that there were approximately 450 violent crime arrests per 100 000 juveniles between 10 and 17 years of age. Violent crime arrests for these youthful offenders were relatively stable during the 1970s and most of the 1980s. However, their arrest rates for violent index crimes increased dramatically during the late 1980s and into the early 1990s, and in 1991 had reached the highest rates in the past 20 years.

Juveniles accounted for 17% of all violent crime arrests in the United States in 1991. During the five-year period ending in 1991, juveniles' violent crimes increased by 50% overall, twice the increase for persons 18 years of age and older. During the same five-year period, juveniles' arrests for murder and non-negligent manslaughter increased by 85%, four times the increase for persons 18 years of age and older. The violent crime arrest rate for black youths was five times greater than that for white youths.

Turning briefly to juveniles as victims rather than as perpetrators of crimes, approximately 6700 of every 100 000 teenagers were victims of violent crime each year during the five-year period ending in 1991, a victimization rate that is 2.5 times greater than that of persons 20 years of age or older. The homicide victimization rate for teenagers more than doubled in the five years ending in 1991, with the homicide victimization rate for black teenagers more than six times higher than that for white teenagers. If they signify anything, the perpetrator and victimization rates are a sad commentary on the disadvantaged conditions under which so many minority group members must live in this country. Not surprisingly, therefore, prevalence rates of mental disorders among youths in the juvenile justice system have been found to be considerably higher than in the general population (Otto et al., 1992).

THE CASE AGAINST TRAINING SCHOOLS

A national survey (Camp & Camp, 1993) of 48 states plus the District of Columbia (Alaska and Arkansas apparently did not respond) indicated that there were approximately 122 000 youthful offenders in their juvenile correctional programs on 1 January, 1993. Of these, approximately half (48%) were in residential programs. Although training schools consisted of only 23% of the residential facilities housing juvenile offenders (including detention centers), the training schools incarcerated 66% of all juveniles in residential placements. The ethnic composition of the residential programs consisted of approximately 46% black, 32% white, and 18% hispanic juveniles, with orientals, native Americans, and others comprising the remainder. The heavy reliance upon training schools evidenced by these data may well be uncalled for. There is good reason to believe that more effective and less costly services for most, if not all but the rarest of exceptions, may be provided in less restrictive, community-based non-residential and short-term residential programs.

The Massachusetts Experiment

The 'Massachusetts Experiment' (Miller, 1991) is often taken as a prime example of why training schools should be closed and how doing so may affect rehabilitation efforts and public safety. In the early 1970s, Massachusetts responded to the abusive and ineffective programs of its state training schools by closing the schools and providing community-based treatment for its youthful offenders. The community-based alternatives to training school placement included outreach programs, day treatment programs, wilderness programs, foster care, group homes, and a small number of beds in secure residential programs. A summary of several reports assessing the impact of the Massachusetts training school closings (Krisberg & Austin, 1923) indicates that the closings were not followed by a juvenile crime wave but instead by a decrease in the juvenile crime rate, which may or may not have been a result of the closings.

Similarly, recidivism rates did not increase following the Massachusetts training school closures but instead may have decreased. In addition, the volume and severity of the crimes committed by the recidivists did not increase following the closing of the training schools but instead decreased which, again, may or may not have been a result of the closure. Cause-and-effect relationships are notoriously difficult to discern in the naturalistic, quasi-experimental evaluations of the Massachusetts experiment. None-the-less, Massachusetts has one of the lowest juvenile arrest rates (ranking 46th out of the 50 states) in a juvenile justice system with a cost per committed youth that is considerably lower than many states with significantly higher arrest rates. It certainly appears that community treatment of most youthful offenders is a viable and most probably preferred alternative to placement in training schools.

Placement of Training Schools

Despite findings such as those generated by the Massachusetts experiment, training schools continue to be a significant placement option in most state juvenile justice systems. The physical structure of the typical training school emphasizes security and control. Training schools are typically placed in remote locations that are thought to discourage escape attempts geographically and psychologically, and to facilitate the speedy apprehension of those who do escape. The design and placement of the typical training school provide a concerned and increasingly safety-minded public with a sense of protection from the youthful offenders who have been removed from the community and placed in a distant and secure training school. As a consequence, the country's heavy reliance on training schools in its programs for youthful offenders is likely to continue for the foreseeable future. Although a number of euphemisms (e.g. client, resident, student) have been used to refer to youths incarcerated in training school, the youths are typically thought of and treated like inmates, and will be referred to as such herein.

Unfortunately, rural placement of the typical training school is also far removed from the urban homes and communities from which most inmates have come. The remoteness of the training schools makes it difficult, if not impossible, for families to maintain their relationship with inmates, for the school to involve families in rehabilitation and treatment programs, for volunteers and service organizations to contribute to school programs, for schools to take advantage of community recreational events and cultural activities, and for inmates to arrange and participate in school, job and community program interviews and activities as they prepare to return to their homes. The design, placement and pay scale of the typical training school also impede the ability of its mental health, psychosocial rehabilitation, academic, special education and vocational training programs to attract and retain the most qualified professionals and paraprofessionals. The average turnover rate for training school counselors, for example, was 15% in 1992, with a range from 2.2% to 46% (Camp & Camp, 1993). The turnover rate for professionals and paraprofessionals may well be higher.

It should be noted that juvenile justice professionals are not unaware of the many problems occasioned by the placement of training schools in remote rural areas where inmates are far from their families and the urban communities to which they will return, and where the schools themselves are cut off from the rich urban pool of professionals and paraprofessionals who can provide needed services on full- and part-time bases. However, attempts by juvenile justice planners and administrators to locate training schools in or near urban centers are often thwarted by large and vocal groups of urban citizens, often despairingly labeled 'NIMBYs' (for Not-In-My-Back-Yard). Paradoxically, the efforts of the urban resisters are often supported by other large and vocal groups of rural citizens and politicians who see a training school as a financial boon, and campaign equally vigorously for its placement in their economically depressed and unemployment-ravaged communities. Under such circumstances, it is not surprising that even now, new training schools tend to be built in remote rural areas.

Effectiveness of Rehabilitation and Management

It is now *de rigueur* to begin a discussion of the effectiveness of offender rehabilitation programs by citing the well known bromide that 'nothing works' or, more accurately, 'the rehabilitation efforts that have been reported so far have had no appreciable effect on recidivism' (Martinson, 1974, p. 25). Unfortunately, that early conclusion, as inaccurate as it may be, is considerably better known and more frequently reported than either its subsequent rebuttals (e.g. Palmer, 1975; Ross & Gendreau, 1980) or more recent meta-analyses (e.g. Garrett, 1984; Gendreau & Andrews, 1990) documenting the effects of at least some treatment modalities with some offenders.

The results of meta-analytic 'research' are reported in terms of average effect size. The effect size in a sample of studies subjected to meta-analysis is the average difference between comparison conditions, reported in standard deviation units. For example, if the effect size of a particular treatment condition is 1.00 relative to a no-treatment condition, the average of the means for the treatment condition falls 1.00 standard deviations above the average of the means for the no-treatment condition. Perusal of the standard normal distribution that may be found in the appendix of most introductory statistics texts reveals that the 'average' individual in the treatment condition would score better than 84% of the individuals in the no-treatment condition (or 50% of the treatment individuals would score better than 84% of the no-treatment individuals). Similarly, if the effect size of one treatment condition is 0.50 relative to a second treatment condition, the average of the means of the first treatment condition falls 0.50 standard deviations above the average of the means of the second treatment condition. The standard normal distribution indicates that the 'average' individual in the first treatment condition would score better than 69% of the individuals in the second treatment condition (or 50% of the individuals receiving the first treatment would score better than 69% of the individuals receiving the second treatment).

A recent review of institutional treatment (Quay, 1987) summarized the results of a large meta-analysis (Garrett, 1984) of the effects of rehabilitation programs for youthful offenders across a number of treatment outcome variables, such as recidivism, academic performance and psychological adjustment. The analysis involved a total of 225 treatment versus control comparisons and 433 effect sizes. An analysis of broad categories of treatment modalities yielded effect sizes of 0.63 for the behavioral orientation, 0.31 for general interventions focusing on life skills, and 0.17 for psychodynamic approaches.

An analysis of more specific intervention procedures within the broad categories of treatment yielded effect sizes of 0.86 for contingency management programs, 0.56 for cognitive-behavioral approaches, 0.31 for milieu therapy, and 0.24 for guided group interaction/positive peer culture programs. Subsequent analyses considering the experimental rigor of the studies, the specific outcome measures examined, individual differences, and the like temper these findings somewhat, but the general thrust of the findings remain little changed. None-the-less, the meta-analytic literature is not without its inconsistencies, with some analyses (e.g. Davidson et al., 1990) indicating that the effectiveness of intervention with offenders has not yet been demonstrated. Critiques of meta-analyses (e.g. Gendreau & Andrews, 1990) report, however, that even when the overall effectiveness of intervention with offenders is not documented in meta-analytic studies, the analyses commonly find that particular interventions, typically those involving behavioral and cognitive-behavioral applications, are effective. Perhaps a meta-analysis of the meta-analyses is now in order.

An analysis of why this culture continues to place so heavy a reliance upon training schools in its attempts to deal with its juvenile justice problems, why it continues to ignore findings that indicate the relative superiority of certain forms of intervention within the juvenile justice system over others that are more frequently employed, and why those who have developed and can employ those interventions have turned away from the juvenile justice system to concentrate their efforts elsewhere is beyond the scope of this chapter. Those interested in considering coherent answers to such questions are referred to Ellis' (1991) insightful conceptual analysis of the array of societal, systemic and institutional metacontingencies that underlie today's sad state of affairs.

BEHAVIOURAL AND COGNITIVE-BEHAVIOURAL PROGRAMS

A sizable behavioral and, to a lesser degree, cognitive-behavioral literature further documents the potential and describes the content of those two approaches to the rehabilitation of both youthful and adult offenders. Although the behavioral and cognitive-behavioral literature in the area of crime and delinquency has focused upon community-based interventions, it also addresses programs conducted in closed institutions. Unfortunately, however, much of the literature describes research conducted more than a decade ago, indicating that with the noteworthy exceptions of substance abusers (e.g. Sobell, Wilkinson & Sobell, 1990) and sexual offenders (e.g. McConaghy, 1990), behaviorists and cognitive-behaviorists have all but abandoned the problems of crime and delinquency. This is particularly discouraging in light of both the many meta-analytic findings favoring the behavioral and cognitive-behavioral approaches, and the quality of those early programs even when considered within the context of the many advances in theory and practice that have taken place since those programs were designed and tested.

A number of excellent anthologies and texts spanning the past 25 years describe the major behavioral and cognitive-behavioral contributions to crime and delinquency. Stumphauzer collected and commented upon some of the earliest work in his two pioneering anthologies (Stumphauzer, 1973; 1979). These anthologies document the early applications of behavioral and cognitive-behavioral interventions, ranging from individual and group contingency management through assertiveness training to self-control and self-instruction training. Ayllon and colleagues (1979) presented detailed descriptions of two early rehabilitation and management programs in closed institutions of youthful and adult offenders, and Nietzel (1979) provided a behavioral (social learning) perspective on crime, delinquency, and the criminal and juvenile justice systems.

A subsequent anthology by Ross and Gendreau (1980) updated the earlier works and described the continuing development of behavioral and cognitive-behavioral approaches to the prevention of crime and delinquency and to the rehabilitation of criminals and delinquents. In two more recent texts, Goldstein and Glick (1987) described what may best be categorized as a cognitive-behavioral approach to anger control training for delinquent youths, and Hollin (1990) provided a more encompassing formulation of cognitive-behavioral approaches to intervention with young offenders. Finally, Morris and Braukman's (1987) comprehensive text presents original contributions describing the full range of behavioral approaches to crime and delinquency. The Morris and Braukman work includes chapters describing the use of basic behavioral procedures (Milan, 1987a) and more comprehensive token economy programs

(Milan, 1987b) in closed institutions for delinquent youths and adult offenders. For that reason, a review of such procedures and programs in closed institutions will not be repeated here.

Much of the early behavioral work in closed institutions was designed with two purposes in mind. These were first to create a positive psychological environment within which institutional rehabilitation programs could be conducted, and to then develop and encourage participation in those programs. The need to transform the psychological environment of institutions has been commented upon over the years. For example, Moos (1975) found that the psychological climate within correctional institutions can contribute to or detract from prosocial and antisocial behavior in important ways, and Miller (1991) pointed to the failure to change the regressive psychological environment within training schools as a major factor underlying his advocacy of the closing of the Massachusetts schools. Similarly, the Johnson and Toch (1982) anthology presents a vivid picture of the many factors that contribute to the pains of imprisonment. However, a recent review of the imprisonment literature (Bonta & Gendreau, 1990) indicates that the effects of incarceration may not be as universally destructive as these authors claim, and that it may now be appropriate to turn our attention to the particular ways in which particular individuals are impacted by particular conditions.

One set of factors that contributes in several significant ways to the regressive psychological effects of incarceration when they do occur may well be a training school's heavy reliance upon punishment practices to suppress prohibited behavior and to ensure the performance of required behaviors (with the latter technically termed escape and avoidance procedures). Although the contemporary use of punishment focuses upon the loss of privileges, placement in solitary confinement (also known as administrative segregation), and extensions of the period of confinement, it should not be concluded that the use of physical punishment is a discredited practice that was long ago abandoned or prohibited by the juvenile justice system. At the time of writing, for example, the National Center for Youth Law (Lambert, 1995) is joined in litigation with the State of Washington seeking to ban the use of peppergas spray (Mace) in a training school for what is alleged to be the suppression of undesirable behavior and the motivation of desirable behavior.

The use of punishment to stop and/or deter prohibited behavior and to coerce required behavior has long been recognized as both inappropriate and undesirable. The American Correctional Association's (ACA) behavior management in juvenile correctional facilities correspondence course (ACA, 1993), for example, discusses the use of punishment with offenders and concludes that punishment has little value in deterring rule violations and inappropriate behavior in institutions for youthful offenders. The use of the threat of punishment to force individuals to comply with orders and requirements is also discussed by Sidman (1989) who concludes that when all of its effects are taken into account, punishment's success in eliminating undesirable behavior is inconsequential. Moreover, he notes that a consideration of other effects of punishments on the person who is being punished, as well as its effects on the person who is administering the punishment, leads to the inescapable conclusion that punishment is a most unwise, undesirable, and fundamentally destructive method of controlling conduct.

REHABILITATION AND TREATMENT REQUIREMENTS

The relatively long-term and self-contained nature of training schools, in conjunction with the characteristics of the youths placed within them, requires that the schools provide a range of academic, vocational and treatment services. Those working in institutions must have a model to guide them in the creation of an institutional environment that fosters the rehabilitation of youthful offenders and in the development and staffing of treatment and education programs. Moreover, the specification of minimally adequate conditions of confinement provides a basis for the procurement of resources necessary to establish a safe institutional environment for youthful offenders and to develop a range of services and programs necessary to meet mental health and rehabilitative needs. The sources for these minimally adequate conditions consist of several 'landmark' class action legal cases, professional organizations, and commissions that have prescribed conditions of confinement, treatment services and educational programs necessary for the minimally adequate care and rehabilitation of youthful offenders incarcerated in training schools. The requirements established in legal cases, such as *Morales v. Turman*, 383 F. Supp. 53 (E. D. Tex. 1974) are often referenced and provide the basis of standards prescribed by professional organizations and commissions which, in turn, provide justification for requirements prescribed in subsequent class action legal cases.

Perhaps the three most influential sets of standards bearing upon the care and rehabilitation of training school inmates are the Standards for the Administration of Juvenile Justice promulgated by the National Advisory Committee for Juvenile Justice and Delinquency Prevention (1980), the Standards for Training Schools prescribed by the American Correctional Association (1991), and the Standards for Health Services in Correctional Institutions established by the American Public Health Association (1986). The most comprehensive of the standards that focus more directly upon mental health treatment within institutions are those promulgated by the American Association for Correctional Psychology (1980). However, the requirements of these four sets of standards frequently overlap or complement each other. The following material will therefore abstract and present in a unified manner the requirements specified in these four sets of standards that are most relevant to psychologists and other mental health professionals who are or will become involved in the design and operation of institutional rehabilitation programs for youthful offenders. However, special requirements, such as those to be applied to high security units within training schools, will not be addressed in this general overview.

The Institution

To start with, training schools should be co-educational to the greatest degree possible. The National Advisory Committee for Juvenile Justice and Delinquency

Prevention bases this seemingly radical requirement on the assumption that co-educational experiences are necessary for the normal development of youths whether they are in the community or confined in a secure facility. The benefits of co-educational programs, including creating a more normal and normalizing environment, providing more meaningful counseling and rehabilitation programs, and reducing situational homosexuality, far outweigh the problems they might involve, such as increased conflict, pregnancies and venereal disease among inmates. Moreover, these problems may be minimized through adequate education, counseling and supervision.

For reasons discussed previously, training schools should be located in or near the communities from which they draw their populations. The training schools themselves should house no more than a total of 100 inmates in living units of no more than 20 inmates each. These units should include private and semi-private rooms, as well as study areas, staff offices, group rooms, and indoor and outdoor recreational areas adequate to meet program needs that go beyond the requirements of the education program. The living units should function in a semi-autonomous manner so that the inmates and living unit staff (e.g. houseparents, caseworkers, associate psychologists, and the like) cooperate in the development of their cottage program. As such, the cottages should serve as the focus of all significant rehabilitation, treatment, education, recreation and management activities.

Staffing Patterns and Qualifications

The minimum staffing ratios for training schools call for one half-time psychiatrist for every 100 inmates, one psychologist for every 100 inmates, one associate psychologist for every 50 inmates, one caseworker for every 20 inmates, one houseparent on duty for every 10 inmates during working hours, one houseparent on duty for every 20 inmates during sleeping hours, one educational diagnostician for every 100 inmates, one vocational counselor for every 100 inmates, one academic counselor for every 100 inmates, one special education teacher for every eight inmates in need of special education services, and one academic or vocational teacher for every 12 inmates. In addition, a medical doctor and a dentist should be on staff or on call at all times, and a registered nurse should be in attendance on a 24-hour, seven-day-per-week basis.

The staff should meet minimal experience, education, and certification or licensure standards. For example, the psychiatrist, psychologist, medical doctor and dentist should all be licensed as such in the jurisdiction of the training school. Similarly, the associate psychologist, vocational counselor, academic counselor and registered nurse should be licensed or certified in the jurisdiction of the training school. The caseworker should have a bachelor's degree with coursework in social work, psychology or a related field plus at least one year's full-time, paid experience working with adolescents. The houseparent should have a high school degree or its equivalent plus at least one year's full-time, paid experience working with adolescents. The educational diagnostician should have a master's degree in special education with graduate-level coursework in assessment. The special education teachers should be certified as such and have experience in diagnosing and providing remedial instruction to the educationally disadvantaged. Finally, the academic and vocational teachers should be certified to teach the subject matter for which they are responsible in the public schools of the jurisdiction of the training school.

Treatment Plans

New inmates should be screened for medical and psychological problems, including personality disturbances and suicide potential, upon their admission to the training school. Youths testing positive in these areas should then be evaluated individually and procedures implemented for the protection of the new inmate or others as appropriate. Within 15 days of admission, inmates should be assessed by a multidisciplinary team, the team should meet to discuss findings and recommendations, and the initial program plan (also known as the treatment plan or rehabilitation plan) should be developed. The 15-day assessments should include direct observations of behavior, tests of social maturity, individual tests of intelligence and psychomotor capacity, tests of vocational interest and aptitude, and tests to determine educational achievement and handicapping conditions.

Inmates' program plans should contain individualized long-term and short-term goals with specific time frames that address their problems by building upon their competencies. The individualization of goals therefore requires the identification of the unique competencies and problems of each inmate. The competencies and problems should be stated in clear and unambiguous terms requiring at most a minimum of inference or interpretation. The needs and goals within inmates' initial performance contract should be based upon the competencies and problems identified during the initial assessment. Subsequent needs and goals should be based upon the changing assessment of competencies and problems that takes place as inmates progress through the program.

Inmates' goals should specify the expected result or outcome of the services that will be provided as when, for example, an expected effect of social skills training is identified not only as the mastery of the skills taught but also as the elimination of the fights with peers that led to the prescription of social skills training in the first place. By so doing, the importance of each goal is clear to inmates and to staff, the likelihood that inmates and staff will work together to achieve each goal increases, and inmates and staff have an objective basis for determining when each goal has been achieved.

Formal progress reviews should be conducted by the multidisciplinary assessment team, typically at 30 days after admission, again at 90 days after admission, and then every 90 days thereafter. The purpose of the progress reviews is to determine an inmate's progress and to take corrective action when appropriate. The reviews should be based upon progress notes that are written on a regular basis by both those staff who supervise inmates throughout the day and by those staff who are responsible for providing the services prescribed in the inmates' program plan. The progress notes should be written on a regular basis and should address adjustment and progress towards performance contract goals in an objective manner. Most importantly, the formal progress reviews should address the problems youths are experiencing in the program, perhaps by modifying the program plan and/or making follow-up the responsibility of a designated staff member who is to ensure that corrective action is taken and then report back to the review team.

Rehabilitation Programs

A range of individual and group counseling and therapy programs should be provided to meet inmates' treatment and rehabilitation needs. The quality of the services within training schools should be no less than that of services generally available in the community. Counseling and therapy groups should be limited to no more than 10 inmates so that the group leaders may maintain leadership of the group, so that the group members have a meaningful opportunity to participate in the group process, and so that no one will be overwhelmed or intimidated by the size of the group. While the potential contribution of houseparents and other paraprofessional staff to individual and group counseling and therapy programs is recognized, these staff members must have the training, experience and professional supervision necessary to function in this role if expected to do so.

The education program should address the diverse educational needs of training school inmates, and should include academic, vocational and special education components. The program should emphasize the academic and vocational skills necessary for successful reintegration into the community. Inmates should be provided with career counseling that enables them to choose between academic and vocational areas of emphasis. Younger inmates should be allowed to participate in limited vocational training as a complement to their academic education program if they wish. Older inmates should be allowed to choose between an academic and vocational emphasis in their education program. The education curriculum should be comparable to that required in the community, and should meet all requirements necessary for the transfer of earned academic credits to the school to which the inmates will return.

Finally, the training school should have a structured program to reintegrate inmates successfully into community life. The program should include presentations and discussions concerning release and community reintegration, counseling and therapy addressing inmates' general and individual community re-entry and adjustment needs, prerelease visits by the aftercare worker who will be responsible for inmates when they return to the community, and graduated release through short pre-release furloughs. Aftercare workers should participate in the development of youths' treatment plans early in the youths' stay at the school so that the course of treatment may take into account the youths' community adjustment needs. Similarly, the aftercare workers should remain informed about their youths' progress and any changes in program plans that may impact upon community placement as they prepare for the youths' release.

Each initial treatment plan should include a tentative re-entry plan that should be modified as progress reviews dictate. In addition, prerelease efforts should intensify as the youths' release approaches. Ideally, aftercare workers should meet with training school staff and inmates concerning re-entry programming. As was indicated previously, however, the remote location of the training schools often makes adequate personal contact difficult given current aftercare staffing patterns. Telephone contacts have been used in place of personal contacts, but this is a weak substitute for face-to-face meetings. The training schools, in conjunction with aftercare workers, should therefore develop a final re-entry plan that takes into account the insights training school staff have about youths, the community needs that the staff have identified, the services that the training school will provide to meet those needs, and the services the aftercare program should provide to build upon and complete what the training school has accomplished.

ETHICS AND INSTITUTIONS

Psychologists working in the juvenile and criminal justice systems are bound by the same ethical principles and code of conduct (American Psychological Association (APA; 1992) that apply to psychologists working in other settings and with different clients. However, the unique environment, demands and expectations encountered by psychologists working with youthful and adult offenders in general, and in training schools and correctional institutions in particular, sometimes cloud professional issues and ethical decisions in ways seldom encountered elsewhere. The many issues and concerns bearing upon the ethical practice of psychology in the juvenile and criminal justice system were initially the subject matter of a number of early books (e.g. Martin, 1975; Monahan, 1980; Schwitzgebel, 1979), and are now routinely discussed in texts dealing with ethical principles in general (e.g. Carroll, Schneider & Wesley, 1985; Keith-Spiegel & Koocher, 1985). Nothing that follows should be construed as legal advice or opinion.

Psychologists and other mental health professionals working in institutions for youthful offenders must consider exactly who their clients are and how this affects their professional relationships with other groups. Although it might first appear that the inmates to whom mental health professionals provide direct services should be considered the clients, in fact at least three groups of potential clients are often identified. These three groups consist of the inmates of the institutions, the staff and administrators who work with the inmates in the institution, and members of the community to which the inmates will eventually return.

Deciding which of the three groups the mental health professional is serving at any particular time can be problematic for several reasons. First, of course, the mental health professionals providing services to inmates of institutions for youthful offenders are typically paid by the state. It is traditional to think of the person who pays for the services of a professional as the client of the professional. In addition, institutions may seek to involve their mental health professionals in a range of activities related to the management and operation of the institution. These activities may include participation in the selection, retention, and promotion of employees, staff training, consultation on matters relating to the management of difficult inmates, the development of suicide prevention policies, and the like.

Institutions for youthful offenders may also seek to involve their mental health professionals in the design and implementation of education and rehabilitation programs to prepare inmates to adjust successfully to community life after they leave the institution. Here, mental health professionals may become involved developing incentive programs to maximize performance in the classroom, conducting social skills training and anger management programs for those with a history of violent acting-out, and leading court-mandated therapy groups for sex offenders. Finally, mental health professionals may be asked to participate in the review of inmates who are being considered for release.

The ethical issues surrounding inmates' consent to psychological treatment and the confidentiality of material that inmates share with the psychologist may well be the most difficult ethical areas confronting psychologists working in institutions for youthful offenders. These two ethical issues, as well as the others confronting psychologists engaged in institutional work, should be addressed in a proactive manner. Psychologists must first decide for themselves how the ethical principles and code of conduct of their profession translate into day-to-day practices in the environment of their particular institution. They must then clarify with institutional administrators how the profession's ethical requirements will govern their activities in the institution.

If the psychologists' job description or the administration's expectations are incompatible with the psychologists' ethical stance, psychologists should consider whether they can and should work within the institution. If the administration's expectations are compatible with the ethics of the profession, the procedures the psychologists will follow should be described in writing, if only in memos summarizing the results of discussions of ethics between the psychologists and the administration. The resulting documentation may then guide both psychologists and administrators as ethical issues are encountered and questions concerning professional practices arise, as they undoubtedly will.

Confidentiality

Perhaps the most important ethical requirement, as well as the most difficult to preserve, is the confidentiality of the material the inmate shares with the therapist, the conclusions the therapist draws about the inmate on the basis of the therapeutic relationship, and the files documenting these aspects of psychological treatment. In general, the bonds of confidentiality may be broken only when therapists have reason to believe that clients present a threat to themselves or to others. Under such conditions, therapists must act to protect clients and others who are in jeopardy and, when necessary to do so, must disclose information and conclusions arising from the therapeutic relationship. While psychologists working in institutions for youthful offenders are bound by the same general rules of confidentiality as psychologists working elsewhere, psychologists in the institutions are typically confronted by more frequent and more difficult ethical questions than their colleagues in other settings.

The ethical questions concerning confidentiality that are encountered in institutional work are not easily answered. When, for example, clients share with their therapist information of a minor rule infraction involving reading other inmates' institutional files while working as a clerk in the classification officer's office, should the therapist inform the classification officer so that the confidentiality of inmate records may be preserved by transferring the client to another job and, perhaps, punishing the client by taking away accumulated good-time? When clients tell their therapist of their own or others trafficking in illegal drugs within the institution, should the therapist pass that information on to the administration so that the dealers may be arrested and brought to trial, and the supply of drugs at least temporarily interrupted? When clients inform their therapist of their own or others' escape plans, should the therapist alert the correctional staff so that it can act to thwart the escape by separating those involved, placing them in segregation, and charging them with attempted escape?

Each of these very real scenarios can be construed as a situation in which the client poses a danger to self or others. Should therapists interpret all of them as such? If not, should the therapist construe any of them as such? Although the therapist in these examples may consider the inmate to be the client, given the client's problem and the manner in which the client entered into therapy, does the therapist have any obligations to the institution as employer and to the community as possible victim?

If therapists maintain confidentiality and the administration and staff of the institution learn of the therapists' knowledge (as they most certainly will), how will the therapists' credibility and effectiveness be affected when advocating for inmates or recommending programmatic changes? Conversely, if therapists break confidentiality and inmates learn that they have done so (as they most certainly will), how will the therapists' credibility and effectiveness be affected as they attempt to provide individual and group therapy, intervene in crises, and participate in rehabilitation programs?

Psychologists should clarify their ethical responsibilities to the inmates of the institution in general and to their clients in particular. All should be informed of the circumstances under which confidentiality will not hold, both generally and because of the special conditions within an institution for youthful offenders. By explicitly enunciating and then abiding by the policies governing confidentiality, psychologists may best preserve their relationship, trust and credibility with both inmates and institutional personnel.

Psychologists should also make it clear that others are not bound by the ethical requirements of their profession. This is particularly important when mental health paraprofessionals or other therapists participate as apprentices or co-therapists in psychologists' individual and group therapy. The clients should know that while the psychologists will honor the bonds of confidentiality, the paraprofessionals and other therapists need not and very well may not, unless they are members of professions with similar ethical standards.

Cohen (1985) suggests that psychologists break confidentiality to inform administrative personnel of their findings or conclusions in seven circumstances. These circumstances are when an inmate is identified as suicidal; homicidal; presenting a reasonably clear danger of injury to self or others as a function of their conduct or their verbal statements; presenting a clear and present risk of escape or the creation of an internal disorder or a riot; receiving psychotropic medication; requiring movement to a special unit or program within the facility for observation, evaluation or treatment; and requiring transfer to another facility or a hospital for treatment.

As Cohen (1985) points out, breaking confidentiality when an inmate is suicidal, homicidal or represents a clear danger of non-lethal but serious injury to self or others is in accord with psychologists' duty to preserve life and prevent harm. Breaking confidentiality when learning of a planned escape or uprising is not only in accord with the duty to preserve life and prevent injury, but is also in accord with common laws that require the reporting of discussions of future crimes, as escape and riot typically are. The use of psychotropic medications can sometimes underlie altered states of behavior and consciousness and as a result it is in the inmate's best interests that administrators know of these possibilities. Similarly, if an inmate requires a transfer within the institution or to a different institution, it is in the inmate's best interests that administrators be informed so that they may approve and arrange the transfer. Although these exceptions to confidentiality seem reasonable and appropriate, it remains the psychologists' responsibility to determine under what conditions they will break the confidentiality of their relationship with clients.

Consent to Treatment

A competent citizen is typically empowered with a constitutional right to refuse treatment, even when that treatment is considered to be necessary for the preservation of life. However, exceptions to the right to refuse treatment do exist, and involve such diverse examples as the unconscious emergency room patient and the involuntarily committed psychiatric patient. The same holds for inmates of correctional institutions. Summarizing the judicial findings existent at the height of the controversy concerning the enforced treatment of criminal offenders, Schwitzgebel (1979) concluded that the state may impose treatment (broadly defined) without consent when it has a compelling interest to do so, and when the treatment itself does not constitute cruel and unusual punishment. The protection of the citizenry through the rehabilitation of offenders is one such compelling interest. The right of the state to impose treatment upon inmates has remained substantially the same to this date.

In the absence of inmates' constitutional right to refuse treatment in which the state has a compelling interest, the right to refuse treatment is often more of a professional issue than a legal one in most correctional institutions. It should therefore not be surprising that the ethical requirement that psychologists secure their clients' written consent for treatment is probably the second most difficult ethical issue faced by psychologists working in institutions for youthful offenders. In closed institutions, the issues surrounding consent are generally as difficult when the treatment is a generally accepted one as when it is experimental in nature. Consent must be informed, rational, and freely given.

Informed consent

For consent to be informed, therapists must provide clients with the now-routine description of the nature of any assessment or intervention that is being offered, the purpose of the assessment or intervention, and, of special importance in institutions for youthful offenders, whether and to whom information obtained from assessment or concerning treatment will be made known. Inmates should also be informed of the anticipated beneficial results of treatment, any possible short-term and long-term iatrogenic side-effects, and any reasonable alternatives to the treatment that is being offered. Therapists must also inform clients of the expected duration of treatment, any inconveniences it will entail, and whether the treatment is of documented effectiveness or is experimental in nature.

Finally, therapists must inform their clients that the clients are free to choose whether or not to participate in therapy, and that they are also free to withdraw their consent and participation in therapy at any time. All information should be conveyed in a manner that is fully comprehensible by clients. It is not uncommon to call upon the services of a translator to ensure that all information is fully comprehended when the client's native language is other than the official or native language of the jurisdiction.

Rational consent

For consent to be rational, clients must be competent to give that consent as prescribed by the jurisdiction in which the consent is given. In general, five criteria must be satisfied if a youthful offender is to be considered competent to consent to treatment (Schwitzgebel, 1979). First, of course, competent persons are able to communicate a decision about whether or to which treatment the person consents. A mute schizophrenic's refusal or inability to communicate in any way would, for example, call that person's competency to consent into question. The second criterion specifies that competent persons are able to make what appear to be reasonable choices about whether to accept or refuse treatment, that is, they make the same decisions that most reasonable individuals would make when presented with the same scenarios.

Third, competent persons base their decisions on rational reasons to accept or refuse treatment. A delusional person's refusal to participate in therapy on the grounds that it is a CIA mind control plot would, for example, call that person's competency into question. Mental illness *per se*, however, does not constitute adequate grounds on which to base a decision of incompetency. Another person with delusions of CIA persecution who refuses a form of treatment that emphasizes early childhood relationships on the grounds that the person does not want to dwell upon and re-experience those painful memories but instead wants to get on with life in the here-and-now might very well be completely rational about treatment options and competent to give or withhold informed consent.

The fourth criterion specifies that competent persons are able to understand the risks, benefits and alternatives to treatment. The person must have the ability to at least generally weigh the pros and cons of treatment in a minimally adequate manner, but not necessarily in the manner one would expect of a high school graduate, much less a professionally trained individual. Finally, competent people have an understanding of the actual benefits, risks and alternatives to the treatment that is being considered. This final criterion goes beyond the general ability to weigh the pros and cons of treatment by specifying that persons actually have knowledge of and understand the pros and cons of the treatment to which they are being asked to consent.

Freely given consent

Ensuring that consent is freely given in institutions for youthful offenders is more problematic than ensuring that it is informed and competent. However, the problems involved in ensuring voluntary participation in treatment may not be unique to institutions for youthful offenders but may simply be more obvious than in other settings. It is not uncommon for judges to order treatment for specific problems, such as sexual assaults, exhibited by youthful offenders who are placed in institutions and community programs. Should psychologists working in these settings provide the court-mandated treatment to all for whom it is ordered? Should psychologists provide therapy only to those who admit their problems and agree to treatment? When these offenders do agree to treatment, should psychologists consider to what degree the offenders' agreement is a product of their recognition that their failure to comply with the court order will block their release from the institution or program, rather than a sincere desire to overcome their problems? Similarly, when the administration refers inmates to psychologists for behavior problems they are experiencing in the institution, should the correctional psychologists provide treatment to all for whom it is ordered?

The difficulty of distinguishing between voluntary and coerced participation in treatment is addressed by Carroll and colleagues (1985). They note that merely making one form of treatment more desirable than another form of treatment or no treatment at all may be interpreted as destroying free choice. If this point of view was adopted, offering potential psychotherapy clients a small amount of money to participate in an outcome study comparing two forms of treatment, offering welfare clients small gifts for increased involvement in prenatal and well baby programs, and offering institutionalized offenders additional token economy points for achieving in a rehabilitation program would all be coercive and in violation of the requirement that participation in treatment be freely given. Carroll and colleagues point out, however, that adoption of this point of view would mean that most of what is thought of as voluntary behavior would be redefined as coerced.

Carroll and colleagues (1985) argue that in making the distinction between voluntary and coerced decisions, the profession must distinguish between what they term temptation and coercion. In the three examples provided above, the psychotherapy clients, the welfare clients, and the inmates were certainly tempted to participate in programs, but were the temptations so irresistible that their decisions to participate were coerced? A choice may be said to be freely made when it would be reasonable to expect that the typical person would be able resist the temptation in the situation and under the conditions the choice is offered. Most would agree that all three of the examples constitute a free choice where consent would be considered to be freely given.

Conversely, most would agree that offering an exorbitant amount of money to impoverished potential psychotherapy clients, threatening welfare clients with the removal of their children, and promising the immediate release of institutionalized offenders with long-term sentences would constitute an irresistible temptation for the average person. Under such circumstances, consent would be considered to be involuntarily given even if some individuals did resist the temptations.

Finally, for consent to be voluntary, the alternatives among which the client may choose must be meaningful. That is, the typical person could be reasonably expected to choose at least one of the alternatives when the choice is between that alternative and no treatment at all. For example, most would agree that offering sex offenders a choice between either 50 years to life in prison with no chance of early parole or surgical castration does not constitute a meaningful choice. Whatever the choice, it would be coerced and involuntarily given. Although these and other forms of coercion might well be found to be legal, the profession might well hold that to participate in such practices would be unethical.

APA's Ethical Guidelines for Criminal Justice Psychologists

In conclusion, APA's 12 guidelines for psychologists working in the criminal justice system will be summarized, with occasional clarifying comments included when called for. The guidelines are a product of APA's Task Force on the Role of Psychology in the Criminal Justice System (1980), and represent the profession's position at the time of APA's most recent systematic review of the issues confronting criminal justice system psychologists. The guidelines address both the ethical issues the criminal justice system creates for psychologists and the ethical issues the psychologists create for the criminal justice system.

The first three of the eight recommendations by APA pertaining to psychologists working in the criminal justice system address questions of loyalty within the context of the question 'Who is the client?'.

Recommendation 1. Psychologists in criminal justice settings, as elsewhere, should inform all parties to a given service of the level of confidentiality that applies and should specify any circumstances that would constitute an exception to confidentiality. This should be done in advance of the service, preferably in writing.

Recommendation 2. The ideal level of confidentiality of therapeutic services in criminal justice settings should be the same as the level of confidentiality that exists in voluntary non-institutional settings.

Recommendation 3. Other than for legitimate research purposes, psychological assessments of offenders should be performed only when the psychologist has a reasonable expectation that such assessments will serve a useful therapeutic or dispositions function.

The remaining five of the eight recommendations pertaining to the ethical issues the criminal justice system causes psychologists address questions of competence.

Recommendation 4. Psychologists who work in the criminal justice system, as elsewhere, have an ethical obligation to educate themselves in the concepts and operations of the system in which they work.

Recommendation 5. Since it is not within the professional competence of psychologists to offer conclusions on matters of law, psychologists should resist pressure to offer such conclusions. In competency to stand trial hearings, for example, it is well within psychologists' area of expertise to testify to what are often considered to be the three ingredients of this form of competency: detainees' comprehension of the nature and severity of the charges against them, detainees' ability to participate meaningfully in their own defense, and the likelihood that detainees will exhibit appropriate courtroom demeanor during trial. It would be inappropriate, however, for psychologists to offer a professional conclusion concerning whether detainees are or are not competent to stand trial because competency itself is a matter of law.

Recommendation 6. Psychologists should be clear about what they are trying to accomplish in the criminal justice system and the state of the empirical evidence in support of their ability to accomplish it. This recommendation does not mean that procedures and programs that have not been tested at all or have not been tested with offenders should not be deployed within the criminal justice system. To bar such procedures and programs would freeze our understanding of delinquent and criminal behavior and of 'what works with what problem experienced by what offender under what conditions' at their current primitive state. Instead, whether empirical, conceptual or theoretical support exists for the practices in which psychologists engage should be made clear to offenders, correctional administrators and the public alike, and when empirical support is lacking empirical evaluations should be fostered. Indeed, this constitutes an ethical obligation (see below).

Recommendation 7. There is an ethical obligation on psychologists who perform services in the criminal justice system, as elsewhere, to encourage and cooperate in the evaluation of those services.

Recommendation 8. Psychological research in prisons should conform to the ethical standards proposed by the National Commission for the Protection of Human Subjects. The National Commission for the Protection of Human Subjects of Biomedical and Behavioral Research (1977) identified three categories of research in correctional institutions. The first two are research that documents the effects of psychological treatments that have the goal or likelihood of improving the health or the well-being of the inmate participants, and research that does not impact directly upon the inmate participants but will increase our understanding of delinquent and criminal behavior and the effects of the justice system and incarceration upon offenders. The commission recommended that both types of research be allowed in correctional institutions, provided such research projects are first reviewed by an appropriately constituted and charged human subjects or institutional review board. Interestingly, the criteria suggested for approval of the second type of research are somewhat more stringent than for the first type in that the procedures should also involve at most a minimal risk to participants and no more than mere inconvenience while participating.

The third type of research identified by the commission is that which uses inmates only because they are readily available as subjects for studies unrelated to their status as offenders or inmates. Perhaps the most common of this type of research is psychopharmacological testing. Approval of this research requires the closest scrutiny. Not only must the research proposal be approved by a review board, but it must also satisfy three additional criteria. The research must fill an important social and scientific need, it must satisfy conditions of equity and it must involve a high degree of voluntariness for those offered the opportunity to participate. The commission goes on to describe the conditions necessary to maximize the voluntary nature of participation. These include a grievance committee, adequate food, recreation and living space, work opportunities that pay the same as participation in the research if monetary incentives are offered, adequate mental health services and the like.

A further two of APA's 12 guidelines address the ethical issues psychologists create for the criminal justice system:

Recommendation 9. Psychologists should be exceedingly cautious in offering predictions of criminal behavior for use in imprisoning or releasing individual offenders. If a psychologist decides that it is appropriate in a given case to provide a prediction of criminal behavior, he or she should clearly specify (a) the acts being predicted, (b) the estimated probability that these acts will occur during a given time period, and (c) the factors on which the predictive judgement is based. This recommendation is based in part on the conclusion that 'the validity of psychological predictions of violent behavior, at least in the sentencing and release situations we are considering, is extremely poor, so poor that one could oppose their use on the strictly empirical grounds that psychologists are not professionally competent to make such judgements' (p. 14).

Recommendation 10. Psychologists should be strongly encouraged to offer treatment services to offenders who request them.

The final two guidelines address the implementation of the task force's recommendations.

Recommendation 11. The American Psychological Association should strongly encourage graduate and continuing education in the applied ethics of psychological intervention and research.

Recommendation 12. The American Psychological Association should take steps to increase awareness among psychologists and those with whom they work of mechanisms to investigate and act upon complaints of violations of its Ethical Standards. Formal advisory opinions should continue to be offered to psychologists requesting an interpretation of the Ethical Standards in specific fact situations. In these last two recommendations, the task force is encouraging a pro-active stance in which information and consultation are made available to criminal justice psychologists as they carry out their day-to-day activities, not merely reactive enforcement of sanctions on those who have erred in their well intentioned scientist and practitioner endeavors.

CONCLUSIONS

Although often overlooked, the similarities among individuals are far more striking than are the differences. In a similar vein, it has been the author's observation that the similarities among offenders and non-offenders are far more striking than are the differences, and that many or most offenders have as much or more in common with non-offenders than they do with other offenders. Offenders commonly experience the same anxiety and depression as do non-offenders, and for much the same reasons as do non-offenders. Offenders commonly respond to the same interventions for these problems as do non-offenders, in the much same ways as do non-offenders. The mental health professional working with offenders in institutions for offenders will encounter the same psychological disturbances and adjustment problems with their clients as will their colleagues working with non-offenders in non-institutional settings.

Mental health professionals contemplating a career in correctional psychology should not be intimidated by either their prospective clients or those clients' mental health and rehabilitation needs. Correctional mental health professionals quickly learn that their professional training stands them in as good stead in the correctional setting as it does elsewhere, although additional training in the manner in which they should function and additional training in the manner in which they should deploy their therapeutic skills in that setting are certainly called for. However, additional training of this type is called for whenever mental health professionals enter a new setting, be it the psychiatric hospital, the community mental health center, or the correctional institution.

Current policies calling for the imprisonment of larger numbers of offenders for longer periods of time dictate that correctional psychology may well be one of the few 'growth industries' in the mental health field for the foreseeable future. Mental health professionals choosing to work with offenders in institutions will find themselves working in a natural laboratory that will allow them to develop their own and, through research and publication, the profession's understanding and treatment of serious forms of psychopathology and debilitating rehabilitation needs that is all but impossible elsewhere. Where else but in a correctional institution do psychologists have the opportunity to study in depth and in relatively large numbers persons with a range of personality disorders, persons exhibiting various sexual deviancies, and persons manifesting the spectrum of mental health and rehabilitation needs exhibited by offenders themselves?

Research and practice in correctional psychology have much to recommend them. Although the challenges facing the correctional psychologist are many, the potential for meaningful service, personal satisfaction, and professional contribution are proportional to those challenges. Correctional psychology in general, and in correctional institutions in particular, remain areas in which the individual scientist-practioner can still make a difference.

REFERENCES

Allen-Hagen, B. & Sickmund, M. (1993). *Juveniles and Violence: Juvenile Offending and Victimization*. Washington, DC: US Department of Justice.

American Association for Correctional Psychology (1980). Standards for psychological services in adult jails and prisons. *Criminal Justice and Behavior*, **7**, 81–127.

American Correctional Association (ACA). (1991). *Standards for Training Schools*. Laurel, MD: American Correctional Association.

American Correctional Association (ACA). (1993). *Behavior Management in Juvenile Facilities*. Laurel, MD: American Correctional Association.

American Psychological Association (APA) (1992). *Ethical Principles of Psychologists and Code of Conduct*. Washington, DC: American Psychological Association.

American Public Health Association (1986). *Standards for Health Services in Correctional Institutions*. Washington, DC: American Public Health Association.

Ayllon, T., Milan, M. A., Roberts, M. D. & McKee, J. M. (1979). *Correctional Rehabilitation and Management*. New York: Wiley.

Bonta, J. & Gendreau, P. (1990). Reexamining the cruel and unusual punishment of prison life. *Law and Human Behavior*, **14**, 347–72.

Camp, G. M & Camp, C. G. (1993). *The Corrections Yearbook*. South Salem, NY: Criminal Justice Institute.

Carroll, M. A., Schneider, H. G. & Wesley, G. R. (1985). *Ethics in the Practice of Psychology*. Englewood Cliffs, NJ: Prentice-Hall.

Cohen, F. (1985). Legal issues and the mentally disordered inmate. In National Institute of Corrections, *Sourcebook on the Mentally Disordered Offender*. Washington, DC: US Government Printing Office, pp. 32–90.

Davidson II, W. S., Redner, R., Amdur, R. L. & Mitchell, C. M. (1990). *Alternative Treatment for Troubled Youth*. New York: Plenum.

Ellis, J. (1991). Contingencies and metacontingencies in correctional settings. In P. A. Lamal (ed.), *Behavioral Analysis of Societies and Cultural Practices* New York: Hemisphere, pp. 201–17.

Garrett, C. J. (1984). *Meta-analysis of the Effects of Institutional and Community Residential Treatment on Adjudicated Delinquents*. Unpublished doctoral dissertation, University of Colorado.

Gendreau, P. & Andrews, D. A. (1990). Tertiary prevention: What the meta-analyses of the offender treatment literature tell us about 'what works', *Canadian Journal of Criminology*, **32**, 173–84.

Gendreau, P. & Ross, R. R. (1980). Effective correctional treatment: Bibliotherapy for cynics. In R. R. Ross & P. Gendreau (eds), *Effective Correctional Treatment*. Toronto, Canada: Butterworth, pp. 13–36.

Goldstein, A. P. & Glick, B. (1987). *Aggression Replacement Training*. Champaign, IL: Research Press.

Hollin, C. R. (1990). *Cognitive-behavioral Interventions with Young Offenders*. New York: Pergamon.

Johnson, R. & Toch, H. (1982). *The Pains of Imprisonment*. Beverly Hills, CA: Sage.

Keith-Spiegel, P. & Koocher, G. P. (1985). *Ethics in Psychology*. New York: Random House.

Krisberg, B. & Austin, J. F. (1993). *Reinventing Juvenile Justice*. Newbury Park, CA: Sage.

Lambert, D. (1995). Pepperspray: Coming soon to an institution near you! *Youth Law News*, **XVI**, 1–3.

Martin, R. (1975). *Legal Challenges to Behavior Modification*. Champaign, IL: Research Press.

Martinson, R. (1974). What works? Questions and answers about prison reform. *Public Interest*, **35**, 22–54.

McConaghy, N. (1990). Sexual deviation. In A. S. Bellack, M. Hersen & A. E. Kazdin (eds), *International Handbook of Behavior Modification and Therapy*. New York: Plenum, pp. 565–80.

Milan, M. A. (1987a). Basic behavioral procedures in closed institutions. In E. K. Morris & C. J. Braukman (eds), *Behavioral Approaches to Crime and Delinquency*. New York: Plenum., pp. 161–94.

Milan, M. A. (1987b). Token economy programs in closed institutions. In E. K. Morris & C. J. Braukman (eds), *Behavioral Approaches to Crime and Delinquency*. New York: Plenum, pp. 195–222.

Miller, J. S. (1991). *Last One Over the Wall*. Columbus, OH: Ohio State University Press.

Monahan, J. (ed.) (1980). *Who is the Client? The Ethics of Psychological Intervention in the Criminal Justice System*. Washington, DC: American Psychological Association.

Moos, R. (1975). *Evaluating Correctional and Community Settings*. New York: Wiley.

Morris, E. K. & Braukman, C. J. (eds). (1987). *Behavioral Approaches to Crime and Delinquency*. New York: Plenum.

National Advisory Committee for Juvenile Justice and Delinquency Prevention (1980). *Standards for the Administration of Juvenile Justice*. Washington, DC: US. Government Printing Office.

National Commission for the Protection of Human Subjects of Biomedical and Behavioral Research (1977). Research involving prisoners: Report and recommendation. *Federal Register*, **42**, 3075–91.

Nietzel, M. T. (1979). *Crime and its Modification*. New York: Pergamon.

Otto, R. K., Greenstein, J. J., Johnson, M. K. & Freidman, R. M. (1992). Prevalence of mental disorders among youth in the juvenile justice system. In J. J. Cocozza (ed.), *Responding to the Mental Health Needs of Youths in the Juvenile Justice System*. Seattle, WA: National Coalition for the Mentally Ill in the Criminal Justice System, pp. 7–48.

Palmer, T. (1975). Martinson revisited. *Journal of Research in Crime and Delinquency*, **12**, 133–52.

Quay, H. C. (1987). Institutional treatment. In H. C. Quay (ed.), *Handbook of Juvenile Delinquency* New York: Wiley, pp. 224–65.

Ross, R. R. & Gendreau, P. (eds.) (1980). *Effective Correctional Treatment*. Toronto, Canada: Butterworth.

Schwitzgebel, R. K. (1979). *Legal Aspects of the Enforced Treatment of Offenders*. Washington, DC: US Government Printing Office.

Sidman, M. (1989). *Coercion and its Fallout*. Boston, MA: Authors Cooperative.

Snyder, H. A. (1994). *Juvenile Violent Crime Arrest Rates 1972–1992*. Washington, DC: US Department of Justice.

Sobell, M. B., Wilkinson, D. A. & Sobell, L. C. (1990). Alcohol and drug problems. In A. S. Bellack, M. Hersen & A. E. Kazdin (eds), *International Handbook of Behavior Modification and Therapy* New York: Plenum, pp. 415–36.

Stumphauzer, J. S. (1973). *Behavior Therapy with Delinquents*. Springfield, IL: Charles C. Thomas.

Stumphauzer, J. S. (1979). *Progress in Behavior Therapy with Delinquents*. Springfield, IL: Charles C. Thomas.

Task Force on the Role of Psychology in the Criminal Justice System (1980). Report of the Task Force on the Role of Psychology in the Criminal Justice System. In J. Monahan (ed.), *Who is the Client? The Ethics of Psychological Intervention in the Criminal Justice System*. Washington, DC: American Psychological Association, pp. 1–17.

5

Diversion Programs

RAYMOND E. LEGLER, BARBARA A. SCHILLO, TIMOTHY W. SPETH AND WILLIAM S. DAVIDSON II
Department of Psychology, Michigan State University, USA

INTRODUCTION

Juvenile delinquency continues to present itself as a major social problem in many countries throughout the world. This is particularly true in the United States, as witnessed in recent statistics on juvenile crime. For example, youth custody rates increased 46% throughout the 1980s at a time when the youth population in the US was declining (US Department of Justice, 1992a). An estimated 2.2 million arrests of persons under the age of 18 occurred in 1990, accounting for 16% of all arrests (US Department of Justice, 1992b). Furthermore, the beginning of this decade was witness to a considerable increase in juvenile arrests for violent offenses (US Department of Justice, 1992b). While overall crime rates have seen a slight decrease recently, this increase in violent crimes attributed to juveniles has raised concern within communities and brought the issue of juvenile crime to the forefront of national attention.

Numerous strategies have been applied to the problem of juvenile crime since the inception of the juvenile court system, with little success. Dissatisfaction with traditional treatment strategies for juvenile offenders, such as institutionalization and therapy-based approaches, was particularly strong during the 1960s and 1970s. During this period, concerns arose regarding the legal system's ability to deal effectively with the problem of juvenile crime. Several early reviews of the research found that traditional strategies relied upon within the juvenile justice system have not proven effective in reducing the prevalence of juvenile delinquency (Grey & Dermody, 1972; Kahn, 1965; Levitt, 1971; Lipton,

Clinical Approaches to Working with Young Offenders. Edited by C. R. Hollin and K. Howells.
© 1996 John Wiley & Sons Ltd.

Martinson & Wilks, 1975). In 1974, Dean and Repucci reported that half of all juveniles released from institutions are subsequently reincarcerated.

More recent reviews of the literature have offered similar conclusions. A review of 829 outcome studies spanning a period of 56 years concluded that few traditional intervention strategies have provided effective solutions to the problem of juvenile delinquency (Romig, 1978). A meta-analysis of the literature on traditional treatments from 1967 to 1983 found no evidence to support the overall efficacy of treatment interventions with young offenders (Davidson et al., 1990). Similarly, a meta-analysis by Lipsey and Wilson (1993) reported that the average effect size among delinquency treatment studies represented only a 10% reduction in delinquency.

A Call for Alternative Strategies

Over 25 years ago the President's Commission on Law Enforcement and Crime (1967) called for new methods for reducing juvenile crime and addressing the needs of youthful offenders. Common criticisms included: (1) inhumane treatment of juveniles; (2) violation of their rights; (3) inflated caseloads; and (4) the inneffectiveness of large institutional programs. Each of these criticisms led to the development of several alternative approaches for addressing delinquency (Davidson & Rapp, 1976). The hope was that innovative policies and procedures that emphasized prevention and early intervention could succeed where traditional strategies had failed. These same developments drive the demand for effective alternatives today.

Diversion of young offenders from the legal system represents one of the innovations that developed out of these dissatisfactions. Diversion involved the use of policies which limited the contact young offenders had with the justice system. This policy was based on the argument that the interaction with the justice system may actually contribute to further delinquency (Bullington et al., 1990). Subsequently, the past 25 years have seen a proliferation of diversion programs designed to provide alternative services to juvenile offenders.

Current Debate

Today, however, it appears that juvenile justice policy in the US has come full circle. The focus on alternatives prevalent in the 1960s and 1970s shifted back to more punitive approaches in the 1980s. It has been suggested that this shift emanated from the conservative agenda that dominated the national discussion of crime in the US during the late 1970s and the 1980s (Krisberg & Austin, 1993). Conservatives argued that the courts had become 'soft' on juvenile offenders and attacked the use of diversion and other alternative methods. They asserted that the most effective way to reduce criminal behavior among young people was through the use of deterrence and punishment. Krisberg and Austin argued, however, that since many communities had failed to develop or adequately fund the types of alternative programs that had been called for by the President's Commission of 1967, innovative approaches involving prevention and early intervention were never given a serious chance. As it currently stands, the juvenile justice system is struggling to provide services for a large number of young offenders detained primarily for property, drug and other minor offenses (Krisberg & Austin, 1993). Increasing rates of incarceration and recidivism have accentuated the need to reconsider innovative strategies such as diversion.

This chapter presents an overview of the practice of diversion and a summary of the review literature that has examined the outcomes of diversion programs. Following this, components of the Michigan State University Adolescent Diversion Project (ADP) are discussed in detail. Next, practical guidance for the implementation of diversion programs based on the literature and the experiences of the ADP is presented. Finally, the future of diversion within the juvenile justice system is examined in the context of the current sociopolitical climate in the United States.

OVERVIEW OF DIVERSION

History of Diversion

The roots of diversion can be traced back to the conception of the juvenile justice system. The establishment of juvenile courts was itself an attempt to divert young offenders from the adult court system (Mennel, 1972). Diversion was one of the many alternative programs created to redirect young people out of the legal system in order to prevent them from experiencing the stigmatization and subsequent crime-producing effects often seen as a result of contact with that system (Whitehead & Lab, 1990). In addition, these programs provided services that would reduce the likelihood of recidivism.

Diversion has been generally defined as 'the formal channeling of youths away from further penetration into the juvenile justice system to an alternative, non-judicial means of handling the juvenile' (Gensheimer et al., 1987, p. 41). Diversion methods vary widely depending on where and when within the system the youth is diverted. The youth might be diverted by police officers before any charges are filed, after charges are filed but before any further processing by the court, after intake, or after adjudication before disposition.

Theoretical Foundations

Diversion programs also vary in regard to the theoretical basis of the particular intervention. Depending on which theory of juvenile delinquency is involved, there are many possible approaches to implementing a diversion program. Social labeling theory is the basis for many diversion programs (Davidson et al., 1990). The fundamental assumption of this perspective is that the juvenile justice system, by labeling a youth as delinquent, actually serves to increase the likelihood of recidivism. The more exposure the young person has to the legal system, the more that youth and the significant people in their life come to believe the truth of the 'deviant' label—leading to continued criminal behavior. For example, labeling can increase the youth's chances of rearrest if they begin to believe and act like criminals. In addition, people in the community such as parents, neighbors, teachers or police officers may more closely attend to the youth's behavior if they become aware that the youth has been labeled delinquent. Since most diversion programs view the labeling process as detrimental, the philosophy of these interventions usually includes a deliberate effort to limit the youth's exposure to the legal system.

Another frequent theoretical foundation of diversion programs is the environmental differences model. The environmental differences model of delinquency posits that the environment, rather than the individual, is the cause of delinquency (Davidson et al., 1990). Such a perspective leads many diversion programs to focus on a youth's environment and her or his ability to find and take advantage of opportunities within the environment. This approach would include an attempt to alter the young person's opportunity structure through the use of skills training, educational and vocational programs.

The other main theoretical bases for diversion programs are the social control and social learning models. When a youth does not feel bonded to the traditional values and goals of society, social control theory predicts that this individual will be more likely to violate the laws of the society (Davidson et al., 1990). In addition, social learning theory suggests that juvenile offenders have learned that their illegal behavior is rewarded (Davidson et al., 1990). Diversion programs based on these theories attempt to strengthen the youth's beliefs in social norms or try to change the youth's reward structure in order to reinforce prosocial behavior. This approach often involves significant individuals in the young person's life, such as family members and friends.

In summary, diversion programs vary greatly as a function of the different points at which the juvenile is diverted from the system as well as the different theories that drive these programs. Diversion may involve police officers releasing youths after arrest with no further processing. A diversion program might simply provide information regarding community resources to young offenders. It might also include a service brokerage or referral component that directs youths to community agencies for services. Finally, a diversion intervention may involve alternative, community-based programs designed to provide offenders with direct services.

LITERATURE REVIEW

A substantial body of literature has grown out of the systematic evaluation of diversion programs. This analysis of the literature is limited to major review articles that summarize the diversion literature, providing the reader with an overview of different models of diversion and evidence regarding their effectiveness.

Diversion Programs

As a result of the different points at which the juvenile is diverted from the system as well as the different theories that drive these programs, diversion encompasses a wide range of practices. A meta-analysis of diversion programs (Gensheimer et al., 1987) identified 14 different types of intervention strategies used in diversion programs (see Table 5.1). A review of the literature by Whitehead and Lab (1990) also revealed a variety of interventions referred to as diversions. One early diversion program, known as the Sacramento (California) 601 Diversion Program provided counseling to youths and their families who had been referred by police, families and schools. The Youth Services Program in Dallas, Texas included lectures about the juvenile justice system and the young offender's behavior along with intake assessment, skills training and follow-up.

Many diversion programs were established as youth service bureaus. These bureaus provided service brokerage by referring youths to outside agencies for counseling, recretion, and academic and crisis intervention. An example of this type of program was the Memphis (Tennessee) Metro Youth Diversion Program which coordinated community services, placed youths with service providers, and monitored their progress (Whitehead & Lab, 1990).

Beyond these more typical approaches, Whitehead and Lab (1990) noted a number of other widely varying approaches to the practice of diversion. So-called 'scared straight' programs attempt to deter future illegal behavior by taking young offenders to visit a penitentiary and exposing them to the realities of prison life. Wilderness experience programs take youthful offenders out to natural areas and utilize activities such as hiking, climbing, and camping to teach the youths self-esteem and teamwork. Other programs use approaches such as dispute resolution training or community service and restitution when working with diverted youths. Finally, the Michigan State University Adolescent Diversion Project uses trained undergraduate students to work one-on-one with juvenile offenders who were being considered for formal charges, and is described in detail in the second half of this chapter.

The Effectiveness of Diversion

The multitude of approaches to diversion and methodologies used in the evalution of these programs makes any attempt to reach conclusions regarding its

Table 5.1 Intervention strategies of diversion programs

Type of intervention	Number	Percentage
Service brokerage	20	45
Group therapy	18	41
Academic	16	36
Vocational	16	36
Advocacy	15	34
Intensive casework	8	18
Modeling role play	6	14
Behavioral contracting	5	11
Positive reinforcement	5	11
Token economy	3	7
Probation	3	7
Psychodynamic	2	5
Cognitive	2	5
Client centered	1	2

effectiveness extremely difficult. Several researchers, however, have undertaken reviews in an attempt to establish the effectiveness of diversion programs as an alternative strategy for dealing with youthful offenders. In an extensive meta-analysis of the literature, Gensheimer and colleagues (1987) examined outcome studies of programs that serviced officially delinquent youth diverted from the formal justice system. In considering outcomes such as recidivism, self-reported delinquency and various types of behavior, the authors rated the effectiveness of each study in addition to noting reported effect sizes. Gensheimer and colleagues reported that 41% of studies reviewed showed overall positive results, 52% had no effect and 7% produced a negative effect. They concluded that there is no substantial evidence for the efficacy of diversion programs overall, while stating that the wide range of services offered as 'diversion' along with the generally poor research methodology regarding design, control groups and random assignment make it difficult to determine the true effectiveness of this approach.

Within a comprehensive review of approaches to dealing with juvenile offenders, Basta and Davidson (1988) compared diversion to behavioral, counseling and deterrence methods. Of the diversion studies examined, only three out of seven showed positive results, leading the authors to conclude that they found no substantial evidence for the efficacy of diversion programs. Whitehead and Lab (1990) concluded that there is conflicting evidence regarding diversion's ability to reduce recidivism. They discussed the difficulty of identifying a 'typical' successful diversion program, noted mixed findings among counseling approaches, and hypothesized a maturation effect among subjects as a possible explanation of studies showing positive results.

Although the overall evidence for the effectiveness of diversion programs is mixed, research on the University of Illinois Adolescent Diversion Project (ADP) from 1973 to 1976, and subsequent assessments of the Michigan State University ADP through 1983, have demonstrated positive results (Davidson et al., 1990). The initial evaluation of this diversion project utilized an experimental design, in which juvenile offenders were randomly assigned to experimental and control groups. Undergraduate students were trained in behavioral contracting and youth advocacy techniques, and worked one-on-one with young offenders 6–8 hours per week for 18 weeks. An examination of recidivism two years after the intervention showed that those in the experimental group had a 45% recidivism rate, while the control group had a 96% recidivism rate (Davidson et al., 1977).

Further research on the ADP was designed to identify the effective components of the initial model by manipulating various aspects of intervention strategies (Davidson et al., 1990). This second phase of research replicated the first program, and also included a family-focused group, a relationship-therapy group, a group administered through the juvenile court, an attention placebo group, and a control group. A two-year follow-up of this phase showed that while the family and relationship groups showed lower recidivism than the attention placebo group, only the original model showed a reduction in recidivism that was statistically different from the attention placebo group.

The next two phases of research on the original ADP model studied the effects of manipulating the service provider and setting. Phase three compared university students, community college students, and community volunteers, and found that all three groups were equally effective in significantly reducing recidivism. Phase four implemented the ADP in a large urban setting and used paid staff as service providers, comparing this group to a group released to parents with no further intervention, and a traditional court-processed group. A follow-up one year after the program showed that the experimental group had significantly lower recidivism than the other two groups (Davidson et al., 1990).

Criticisms of Diversion

Aside from the positive findings from the Illinois and Michigan State Adolescent Diversion Programs, the overall evidence for the effectiveness of diversion appears to be inconclusive. In addition to the question of whether or not diversion works, questions remain as to whether diversion is truly an alternative and humane strategy for dealing with youthful offenders and the degree to which it is cost-effective.

It has been questioned whether diversion is an alternative or merely an extension of the legal system. For example, the voluntary nature of diversion programs has been called into question. Davidson, Snellman and Koch (1981) noted that youths who have been arrested are often given the 'choice' of entering a diversion program as an alternative to continued formal processing, but may be coerced into this choice by family members or court officials. Other issues of due process may be violated if youths are referred into diversion programs without formal determination of guilt or if it is 'suggested' that they admit their guilt so that things will go easier for them. By failing to meet the requirements for due process, diversion programs can be susceptible to the same critiques directed at the juvenile court system in terms of failing to observe the rights of young offenders or treat them in a humanitarian way.

It has also been suggested that diversion does not prevent the labeling of juvenile offenders (Whitehead & Lab, 1990) and that the labeling effects of adjudication may cancel out the positive impact of diversion (Gensheimer et al., 1987). The majority of participants in diversion programs have been referred by police or the courts and have been accused of some offense. These offenders who have had contact with the court may have already experienced a significant degree of labeling despite efforts to divert them out of the justice system.

Lastly, critics have raised concerns over the cost-effectiveness of diversion programs. Whitehead and Lab (1990) argue that diversion is not cost-effective if adolescents diverted from the legal system are replaced by other youths who would not have entered the system before the diversion program was in place. This 'net widening' would actually result in an overall increase in costs. Davidson, Snellman and Koch (1981) point out that the cost of most diversion programs in comparison to the costs of formal processing in the legal system are considerably lower—in the case of the Michigan State University program as low as one-seventh the cost. However, in agreement with Whitehead and Lab, Davidson and colleagues caution that net widening may increase the number of individuals receiving services and that careful assessment of programs is necessary in order to make accurate statements regarding cost-effectiveness.

In contrast, it can be argued that the radiating financial savings from reduced recidivism and incarceration, and subsequent reduced property, personal and social costs, is well worth the minimal investment. In addition, as youthful criminal activity becomes young adult criminal activity, the individual's employment status and tax-paying ability can be affected, as well as the individual's ability to support his or her family and prevent the need for unemployment and other public assistance benefits.

Davidson, Snellman and Koch (1981) argued that the toughest obstacles to effective diversion interventions were the issues of net widening, closeness of relationships with the legal system, and inconsistent implementation of programs. Despite these criticisms, there are several strong arguments to support the practice of diversion. Whitehead and Lab (1990) pointed out that the formal system is doing no better. They asserted that society has an obligation to attempt to aid young people in trouble, that some diversion programs actually are effective, and that net widening might simply be an indication of latent need. The reviewers went on to argue that evaluation of diversion programs might do better to focus on qualitative improvements in behavior, such as educational achievement, family adjustment, and employment, rather than focusing strictly on quantitative assessments of delinquency and recidivism.

This review of the literature on diversion programs has shown that the outcome evidence regarding the efficacy of the diversion approach is quite mixed. The next section discusses components of effective diversion programs. This section begins with a detailed description of the Michigan State University Adolescent Diversion Program as an illustration of an effective program. This is followed by a summary of effective elements of diversion programs based on the experiences of the MSU ADP and the preceding review of the literature.

THE MICHIGAN STATE UNIVERSITY ADOLESCENT DIVERSION PROJECT

Following the series of research studies discussed earlier in this chapter, the ADP was established exclusively as a service program in 1982. Since that year, the project has been supported cooperatively by county and University funding. The ADP currently receives referrals from the Intake Department of the county probate court and provides services to approximately 125 adolescents a year. In order to gauge the continued effectiveness of the project, the court records of youths who participated in the ADP have periodically been examined. These findings support earlier results and demonstrate that the ADP continues to be an effective program for youthful offenders.

Program Philosophy

There are several central tenets that guide the operations of the MSU Adolescent Diversion Project. The guiding principle of the program is that intervention activities must take place in the youth's natural environment in order to produce lasting effects. Equally important, the cooperation of non-professional college students as change agents helps to ensure the effective and cost-efficient operation of the project. In order to limit the labeling and exposure to criminal behavior that often occurs with involvement in the juvenile justice system, the ADP intervenes early in the lives of juvenile offenders. Finally, by building on the competencies and abilities of adolescents, this project attempts to avoid a victim-blaming approach that focuses on individual deficits (Davidson et al., 1977).

Participant Referral

Young people accused of a crime attend a preliminary hearing in juvenile court. If the accused individual admits to the offense, the intake referee has the option of referring the juvenile to the ADP. Since only those adolescents who have admitted guilt are referred to the ADP, their right to due process is ensured. Intake referees refer only those youths who would normally be processed through the court system and not individuals who would simply be warned and released. This helps limit net widening by only diverting juveniles who would have been in formal contact with the legal system. Most youths referred to the ADP have admitted to serious misdemeanor or non-serious felony charges. Most charges involve property offenses such as larceny or retail fraud (shoplifting); however, the ADP works with juveniles who have committed a wide variety of offenses. In 1993, property crimes accounted for 51.5% of referrals while 23.8% of referrals involved assault charges.

If the intake referee determines that a youth is an appropriate referral for the ADP, they describe the program to the youth and their parents and allow them to decide if they would like to participate. If the youth and their parent(s) or guardian decide to participate, they meet with a project staff member who reviews the program requirements and asks them to sign a participation agreement and a release of information form. After the young person has agreed to participate, the court is informed of their decision. Diversion laws passed in Michigan in 1988 state that the record of charges against those individuals participating in the ADP must be kept separate, and are open only to those individuals with a legitimate interest. The file is destroyed 28 days after the adolescent turns 17 years of age.

Training Procedures

The ADP trains undergraduate college students to work as change agents. These students enroll in a two-semester course sequence and are trained and supervised by graduate students and a faculty advisor. During the first ten weeks of the course students undertake an intensive instruction period designed to familiarize them with the juvenile justice system, relationship and assessment techniques, behavioral and advocacy methods, and methods of implementing and monitoring intervention mechanisms. An emphasis on having the change agents teach the youth and their family many of these techniques allows the adolescents to acquire skills they can continue to use once their participation in the ADP has ended.

The training period is highly structured and involves readings, homework, weekly quizzes and in-class activities. The progress of the students is carefully monitored to ensure that they have acquired the skills necessary to function effectively in the community. Near the end of the training segment, change agents are assigned to a youth, and the class is broken into groups of six to eight students which are each supervised by two graduate students. These groups continue to meet for 2–3 hours per week during which students give detailed reports of their past week's activities. Students are expected to participate actively in the small group discussion of cases, in order to share information and generate ideas for possible intervention strategies. Research has shown that this intensive, small group format is crucial to the success of the ADP (Kantrowitz, 1979).

Students spend 6–8 hours per week with their youth over an 18-week period. After an initial period that centers on the student and the youth becoming acquainted with each other, the focus turns to the identification of goal areas to be addressed during the intervention. Supervisors and students discuss the implementation of intervention strategies and carefully monitor these strategies to allow for continual reassessment and adjustment when necessary. As the end of the 18-week period approaches, youths are encouraged to become more involved in the intervention activities so that they will have the tools to continue these strategies once they leave the program.

The Intervention

The primary intervention strategies of the ADP are the behavioral contracting model and the child advocacy model. The behavioral contracting model is designed to improve the relationships in the youth's life by establishing agreements between him or her and the significant adults in their environment. The child advocacy model is designed to identify resources for the youth and implement strategies to gain access to those resources. These resources often include recreation, education and employment. The two models are used in conjunction with each other in order to tailor the intervention to the specific needs of each youth. Students constantly work at instructing and demonstrating how the youth and her or his family can employ these strategies.

There are four main intervention components that are considered critical to the success of the ADP. These include a *highly structured program for the training and supervision* of change agents and *intensive intervention* involving 6–8 hours of weekly contact with the youth. Most importantly, the ADP involves a pro-active intervention that includes multiple components and *operates in the youth's natural environment.* By conducting intervention activities in the youth's environment, change agents can meet significant individuals such as parents, teachers and friends, and determine the specific needs of their youth. This allows for an individualized plan of action—leading to substantive changes in the youth's life that will continue once the intervention is over. Finally, the ADP *emphasizes the youth's strengths and competencies.* By focusing on the youth's abilities and helping to build skills and interests, the ADP is effective in increasing prosocial behaviors among youths—and consequently decreasing undesirable behaviors.

The following case studies are provided to illustrate the principles, techniques, activities and possible outcomes of the intervention strategies utilized within the ADP. Two case studies are presented—one illustrating behavioral contracting, and the other illustrating child advocacy.

Behavioral Contracting Case Study

Rachael was a 14-year-old who was petitioned to the court's juvenile division for larceny. The female volunteer who was assigned to work with Rachael called her at home and arranged for a time to get together. During their initial meeting, the volunteer met briefly with Rachael and her parents and reviewed the terms of their participation in the project. Rachael and the volunteer then spent some time alone to begin the process of becoming acquainted. Rachael was initially quiet and appeared hesitant to share information about herself and her situation. During the next two weeks, however, Rachael began to feel more comfortable around her volunteer and began sharing some of the details of the various areas of her life. Rachael indicated that she had been placed on a half-day schedule at school because of her truancy but was still not attending classes on a regular basis. She also explained that she liked to hang out with her friends and did not spend a lot of time at home.

After establishing a positive working relationship with Rachael and her parents, the volunteer began to work on assessing Rachael's situation more specifically in order to initiate a behavioral contract. The volunteer set up separate meetings with Rachael and her parents to discuss what they would like to see from each other. The volunteer explained the idea of behavioral contracting and what was required by both parties. Both parties were initially resistant to the idea of contracting. Rachael's parents were not convinced that contracting alone would change their daughter's behaviors, while Rachael believed that the contract would be used to punish her. The volunteer worked hard to help both parties understand how they would benefit from a contract and eventually got both sides to agree to give it a try.

During the initial contracting session, Rachael's parents stated that they wanted Rachael to attend school and to come home every night at a mutually agreed upon curfew. Rachael expressed that she wanted an allowance and rides for her and friends to and from activities. At the next meeting, the volunteer prompted the parents to specify the responsibilities they wanted from Rachael. They felt that she should: (1) attend half days at school every day; (2) spend school nights at home; and (3) ask for permission when spending the weekend nights at a friend's house. Rachael stated that she wanted (1) a $10.00 weekly allowance and (2) transportation to and from activities on weekends.

On the basis of this information, the volunteer helped Rachael and her parents to negotiate the following contract:

Rachael agrees to:	Rachael's parents agree to:
• Return home by curfew (Sunday–Thursday).	• Pay her $0.50 for each night she returns home by curfew.
• Attend classes.	• Pay her $0.50 for each class she attends.
• Ask for permission to spend the weekend night at a friend's house.	• Provide rides to and from a mutually agreed upon activity the following weekend.

Bonus
If Rachael performs at 80% or better on all of the above listed agreements for a week, her parents will pay her an additional $5.00.

At this time the volunteer also set up daily checklists on each of the terms of the contract to be used jointly by Rachael and her parents to record each other's performance. For the first two weeks, the volunteer monitored the contract daily, by checking the monitoring sheet every time she was at the youth's home or when she called. The volunteer prompted the youth and parents to fulfill their responsibilities and praised their efforts in meeting the terms of the agreement. In addition, she met weekly with all parties to review their progress. The volunteer took these opportunities to model, prompt, and praise positive behaviors.

Rachael's performance on the contract was 100% with the exception of school attendance. Eventually, however, Rachael's performance in this area increased as well. Both Rachael and her parents reported that they were more satisfied with their situation. When the initial contract was up for renegotiation, both parties agreed to expand the original contract to include additional privileges and responsibilities.

During the last weeks of the intervention, the volunteer-engaged in termination activities with Rachael and her parents. They discussed the contracting approach and its use on an ongoing basis and role-played negotiations of several situations in which contracting would be useful. The volunteer coached them in specifying what each party wanted, stating requests in positive terms, negotiating reciprocal agreements, and monitoring the contract.

Child Advocacy Case Study

Michael was a 15-year-old who was referred to the ADP for assault and battery. Following intake and pre-assessment, Michael was assigned to a volunteer who spent the first few weeks of the intervention getting to know Michael, his family and his environment. This period of assessment revealed that Michael's primary unmet needs centered around the area of education. Michael, a ninth grader, had been repeatedly suspended from school and was experiencing serious academic problems as a result. In addition to the area of school, the volunteer assessed several other unmet needs in the areas of employment and recreational activities.

Following this initial assessment, the volunteer implemented advocacy strategies to address Michael's educational needs. The volunteer determined that school officials were relying heavily on suspension when disciplining Michael. Although Michael had been previously suspended for fighting, many of his subsequent suspensions were for minor infractions. The volunteer took a strong stand in making school officials aware that their current approach in disciplining Michael was excessive, ineffective and was denying the youth his right to an education. As a result of the volunteer's repeated efforts, the school officials agreed to try less punitive measures when disciplining Michael. The volunteer also assisted Michael in making up work that he had missed when suspended. As a result of these efforts, Michael's academic performance greatly improved.

In addressing other areas of unmet needs, the volunteer and the youth engaged in several activities designed to assist Michael in securing a part-time job. Michael and his volunteer practised filling out applications and role-played interviews before submitting actual applications. In addition, the volunteer showed Michael how to keep track of and follow up on applications. Although it took several weeks of intensive efforts, eventually Michael secured a part-time position in a fast-food restaurant. The volunteer and the youth also spent several hours together accessing various recreational resources and enrolled Michael in a driver's education course.

Throughout the intervention, the advocate was active in monitoring each of the chosen intervention strategies and engaging in follow-up advocacy strategies when necessary. The advocate included Michael and his parents at each stage of the intervention to assist them in developing self-advocacy skills. During the final weeks of the intervention, the volunteer reviewed the advocacy strategies they had utilized throughout the intervention and discussed possible advocacy strategies in order to prepare Michael to advocate for his own needs in the future.

ELEMENTS OF EFFECTIVE DIVERSION PROGRAMS

Strategy

Based on the literature reviewed in the first section of this chapter and the experiences of the ADP, there seem to be some essential elements necessary to a successful diversion program. On a basic level, outcome evidence shows a link between number of hours of intervention and effectiveness. Gensheimer and colleagues (1987) observed that the number of hours of intervention is positively related to positive outcome. Whether it is an advocacy, behavioral or counseling strategy, amount of direct service intervention appears to matter.

Location of Intervention

Conducting an intervention strategy in the youth's natural environment appears to be another critical characteristic of successful diversion programs. It has been argued that these types of approaches—those that mobilize resources for youths in their natural environments—are more successful than traditional treatment strategies in addressing issues of delinquency (Rappaport, Laimell & Seidman, 1980). By dealing with aspects of the youth's life such as family, friends, school, employment and recreation, diversion programs conducted in the natural environment hope to make substantial, lasting changes in the beliefs, opportunities and actions of the young offender. In addition, it appears important that diversion programs operate relatively independently from the juvenile justice system, as evidence suggests that advocates who work within the system may be compromised in their abilities to advocate effectively on behalf of their youth's needs (Blakely, 1981).

IMPLEMENTING DIVERSION PROGRAMS

The Legal System

Several critical components in the process of developing and operating an effective diversion program have been identified throughout the history of the ADP. The primary component in this process is convincing people that whoever runs this project knows and understands the problems of young offenders (Ku & Blew, 1977). Briefing judicial officials about the purpose, nature, and operations of the project along with the potential impact that this program may have on juvenile court operations or caseloads is critical in avoiding future misunderstandings. This process of establishing credibility and selling the project may need to occur at multiple levels, from law enforcement officers and court staff to prosecutors and judges.

Another critical element in this process involves working directly with those who will be responsible for diverting youths (Ku & Blew, 1977). In order to convince officials to divert offenders, it is necessary to meet with these people and assure them that the program will be able to handle both potentially delinquent juveniles, and those with records of serious illegal activity. Those responsible for diverting youths must understand how diversion operates and be aware that, in order for it to have a significant impact on the justice system, they should not divert youths who would ordinarily be informally diverted anyway (warned and released). It is also important to provide referral officials with timely feedback about the performance of the youth who have been diverted.

Communication

It has been the experience of the MSU Diversion Program that an ongoing dialogue with court referees is essential to maintaining a cooperative working relationship with the legal system. Alternative programs such as diversion can be viewed by court officials as a threat, especially if the program is effective in reducing recidivism. Perceptions by referees that the ADP is in competition with the juvenile court system for resources can undermine the referral process and subsequently threaten the operation of the project. By keeping the lines of communication open, ADP staff continually work to foster a collaborative relationship with court officials.

Organizational Setting

The other half of the process of establishing an alternative program, such as the ADP, involves identifying available resources for the operation of the project. The initial decision to be made in this process is whether to locate the program within or outside the formal justice system. While it may be logical to locate some types of diversion programs within the justice system (e.g. the diversion of juveniles by police officers), the objectives of other programs may be compromised by such actions. Research on the ADP revealed that volunteers who worked under the supervision of the formal justice system were limited in their abilities to address the needs of their youth effectively (Blakely, 1981).

Funding

Regardless of where the program is located, a source(s) of funding for the project will need to be secured. Various levels of government (city, county and state) and private sources (foundations) all represent possible sources of funding for alternative programs. In localities with access to university or college resources, there exists the potential to establish collaborative agreements with these institutions for the development and operation of an alternative program. In the case of the ADP, Michigan State University has provided the resources—office space, staff and a pool of volunteers—that allow the ADP to operate at a fraction of the cost of a court-run program. It should be noted, however, that the use of college students is not essential to the operation of a project such as the ADP, as this project has been successfully replicated with contractual staff (Davidson & Johnson, 1987).

THE FUTURE OF DIVERSION

The history of diversion within the juvenile justice system provides an illustration of how the conceptualization and treatment of young offenders, along with the allocation of resources, depends on the philosophical, economic and political factors of a particular time (Klein, 1983; Polier, 1977). Developed out of the politics of the 1960s and 1970s, when the call for alternatives was strong, diversion held the hope of offering the legal system an innovative strategy for addressing the needs of juvenile offenders. However, the ideal of making society more responsive to the individual and collective needs of young people—inherent in the alternatives including diversion in the 1970s—met with a different political reality during the 1980s. During this period resources were once again directed toward traditional treatment and punishment approaches.

Unfortunately, this reversal in justice system policy occurred at a time when rates of juvenile and adult criminal behavior have increased—and left the United States as the country with the highest percentage of its population in prison (Lacayo, 1994). Once again the US is confronted with the challenge of finding alternative approaches to the problem of crime and of examining the role of social factors and domestic social policies as possible contributors to criminal behavior. This is evidenced in the increased prominence of the crime issue on the national agenda (Lacayo, 1994) and the recent introduction of anti-crime legislation at the Federal level. While the resurgence of attention to the issue of crime is promising, many of the 'new' approaches that have been suggested reflect a return to the punitive, reactionary policies that have dominated American justice policy for the past decade.

The justice system in the United States is proof that arrest and incarceration approaches to crime do not reduce criminal behavior and that relying primarily on these punitive approaches while ignoring truly preventive strategies may actually exacerbate the crime problem. It is time to redirect policy and funding toward preventive approaches that include diversion. This chapter has presented the case that diversion remains a viable alternative that can be effective in reducing juvenile crime when implemented properly. In addition, a specific model of an effective diversion program—the ADP—has been presented. Diversion programs such as the ADP offer a humane strategy for addressing the root causes of crime using a preventive model.

The basic elements for replication of an alternative diversion program, such as the Adolescent Diversion Project, include a community that recognizes a need for juvenile intervention services, cooperation from law enforcement and juvenile officials, and accessible resources and interested individuals (Ku & Blew, 1977). Diversion programs such as the ADP offer a viable alternative to the use of secure detention and offer flexibility for an overburdened juvenile justice system.

Finally, while this chapter has focused on the United States, countries with crime problems similar to those in America could benefit from alternative programs such as diversion. The methods used in the ADP may be generalizable to other nations and cultures. By offering an alternative to the juvenile justice system that emphasizes prevention, diversion programs such as the Adolescent Diversion Project can help young people avoid further involvement with the legal system.

REFERENCES

Basta, J., & Davidson, W. S. (1988). Treatment of juvenile offenders: Study outcomes since 1980. *Behavioral Sciences and the Law*, **6**(3), 355–84.

Blakely, C. H. (1981). *The diversion of juvenile delinquents: A first step toward the dissemination of a successful innovation.* Unpublished doctoral dissertation. East Lansing, MI: Michigan State University.

Bullington, B., Sprowls, J., Katkin, D., & Phillips, M. (1990). A critique of diversionary juvenile justice. In R. A. Weischeit & R. G. Culbertson (eds), *Juvenile Delinquency: A Justice Perspective*. Prospect Heights, IL: Waveland Press, pp. 117–30.

Davidson, W. S. & Johnson, C. D. (1987). *Diversion in Michigan*. Lansing, MI: Department of Social Services, Office of Children and Youth Services.

Davidson, W. S. & Rapp, C. A. (1976). *Diversion in Michigan*, Lansing, MI: Department of Social Services, Office of Children and Youth Services.

Davidson, W. S., Snellman, K. & Koch, J. R. (1981). Current status of diversion research: Implications for policy and programming. In R. Roesch & R. Corrado (eds), *Evaluation and Criminal Justice Policy*. Beverly Hills, CA: Sage Publications, pp. 103–21.

Davidson, W. S., Seidman, E., Rappaport, J., Berck, P. L., Rapp, N. A., Rhodes, W. & Herring, J. (1977). Diversion program for juvenile offenders. *Social Work Research and Abstracts*, **13**(2), 40–9.

Davidson, W. S., Redner, R., Amdur, R. L. & Mitchell, C. M. (1990). *Alternative Treatments for Troubled Youth: The Case of Diversion from the Justice System.* New York: Plenum Press.

Dean, C. W. & Repucci, N. D. (1974). Juvenile correctional institutions. In D. Glaser (ed.), *Handbook of Criminology*. New York: Rand McNally, p. 874.

Gensheimer, L. K., Mayer, J. P., Gottschalk, R. & Davidson, W. S. (1987). Diverting youth from the juvenile justice system: A meta-analysis of intervention efficacy. In S. J. Apter & A. P. Goldstein (eds), *Youth Violence*. New York: Pergamon, pp. 39–57.

Grey, A. L. & Dermody, H. E. (1972). Reports of casework failure. *Social Casework*, **16**, 207–12.

Kahn, A. J. (1965). A case of premature claims. *Crime and Delinquency*, **20**, 233–40.

Kantrowitz, R. E. (1979). *Training nonprofessionals to work with delinquents: Differential impact of varying training/supervision/intervention strategies.* Unpublished doctoral dissertation. East Lansing, MI: Michigan State University.

Klein, M. W. (1983). When juvenile justice meets social service: Social intervention with troubled youth. In E. Seidman (ed.), *Handbook of Social Intervention*. Beverly Hills, CA: Sage Publications, pp. 362–84.

Krisberg, B. & Austin, J. F. (1993). *Reinventing Juvenile Justice*. Newbury Park: Sage Publications.

Ku, R. & Blew, C. H. (1977). *A University's Approach to Delinquency Prevention: The Adolescent Diversion Project.* Washington, DC: Office of Technology Transfer, National Institute of Law Enforcement and Criminal Justice.

Lacayo, R. (1994). Lock 'em up. *Time*, **143**(6), 28–34.

Levitt, E. L. (1971). Research on psychotherapy with children. In A. Bergin & S. L. Garfield (eds), *Handbook of Psychotherapy and Behavior Change.* New York: Wiley, pp. 474–94.

Lipsey, M. & Wilson, D. B. (1993). The efficacy of psychological, educational, and behavioral treatment. *American Psychologist*, **48**(12), 1181–209.

Lipton, D., Martinson, R. & Wilks, J. (1975). *The Effectiveness of Correctional Treatment.* New York: Praeger.

Mennel, R. M. (1972). Origins of the juvenile court: Changing perspective on the legal rights of juvenile delinquents. *Crime and Delinquency*, **18**, 68–78.

Polier, J. W. (1977). External and internal roadblocks to effective child advocacy. *Child Welfare*, **56**(8), 497–509.

President's Commission on Law Enforcement and Crime. (1967, February). *The Challenge of Crime in a Free Society.* Washington, DC: US Government Printing Office.

Rappaport, J., Laimell, J. T. & Seidman, E. (1980). Ethical issues for psychologists in the juvenile justice system: Know and tell. In J. Monahan (ed.), *Who is the client? The Ethics of Psychological Intervention in the Criminal Justice System.* Washington, DC: American Psychological Association, pp. 93–125.

Romig, D. A. (1978). *Justice for our Children.* Lexington, MA: Lexington Books.

US Department of Justice (1992a). *National Juvenile Custody Trends 1978–1989.* Washington, DC: Office of Juvenile Justice and Delinquency Prevention.

US Department of Justice (1992b). *Arrests of Youth 1990.* Washington, DC: Office of Juvenile Justice and Delinquency Prevention.

Whitehead, J. T. & Lab, S. P. (1990). *Juvenile Justice: An Introduction.* Cincinnati, OH: Anderson.

Part 3
Working with Offenders

6

Sociomoral Group Treatment for Young Offenders

JOHN C. GIBBS
The Ohio State University, Columbus, USA

Sociomoral group treatment for young offenders rests upon two theses: (a) young offenders can be motivated to help other such adolescents lead more positive and responsible lives; and (b) the helpers must become equipped with appropriate skills if their help is to be effective. Effective sociomoral group treatment programs, in other words, must not only motivate but also remedy the limitations of offending youth who would help one another change. Following a review of pertinent literature, this chapter will discuss a multi-component sociomoral group treatment program for young offenders. Included will be a discussion of practical aspects of program implementation, an illustrative case study, outcome evidence, and a plea for program evaluation.

MUTUAL HELP PROGRAMS: DESCRIPTION AND CRITIQUE

Mutual Help Group Programs for Young Offenders

For the past several decades, self-help—or more properly *mutual* help—group programs in schools and residential facilities have sought to actualize the prosocial potential of antisocial juveniles, in particular to encourage them to help one another. In a psychiatric hospital setting, Maxwell Jones (1953) innovated techniques for cultivating a 'therapeutic community' among sociopathic patients. At about the same time, Lloyd McCorkle, F. Lowell Bixby and others applied McCorkle's 'guided group interaction' techniques to delinquent boys (McCorkle, Elias & Bixby, 1958). These techniques were subsequently refined by Vorrath

Clinical Approaches to Working with Young Offenders. Edited by C. R. Hollin and K. Howells.
© 1996 John Wiley & Sons Ltd.

and Brendtro (1985), who characterized the guided group interaction approach as 'Positive Peer Culture' (PPC).

PPC and other guided group programs for antisocial youth explicitly address the need to redirect their orientation from opposition to rules or authorities and physical or verbal intimidation to caring or providing help for one another. Carducci (1980) asserted that PPC 'delivers the teacher from an embattled "me against them" position' (p. 157), and encourages the teacher to respect the positive potential for helping others of otherwise antisocial students. Harstad (1976) described PPC as a 'humane' (p. 119) and optimistic approach positing that antisocial (like other) youths: (a) have a strong desire to feel good about themselves; (b) will seek to help others if challenged and given sufficient support for doing so; and (c) will improve their own behavior and come to feel genuinely good about themselves as they help others to change. In PPC and similar programs at juvenile correctional facilities, youths are even empowered to recommend an eligible group membs as suitable for release (cf. Kohlbergian 'just community' empowerment; Hickey & Scharf, 1980).

The Mutual Help Meeting

The heart of any guided peer group program is the mutual help meeting. In Guided Group Interaction or PPC programs, these meetings are adult-guided but youth-run, last from one hour to 90 minutes, and take place five times a week (typically weekdays). A key feature of mutual help meetings is the use of 12 names or labels for typical problems of antisocial adolescents. Three of the twelve names are general and can be used as catch-all terms: inconsiderate of others, inconsiderate of self and low self-image. For more precise identification and clear communication of common problems, nine specific labels are also learned: authority problem, misleads others, easily misled, aggravates others, easily angered, stealing, alcohol or drug problem, lying and fronting (Vorrath & Brendtro, 1985, p. 28).

In a typical peer group meeting, each group member reports a recurring problem; the group then 'awards' the meeting to a particular group member for discussion of his or her problem. The groups use the problem names throughout the meeting. For example, use of the problem vocabulary in reporting problems helps to keep the group's attention appropriately directed to members' behaviors that have harmed others or themselves, and may itself stimulate youths' awareness of the extent and breadth of their antisocial behavior.

Techniques for Dealing with Resistance

Unlike most mutual help groups that are initiated voluntarily by their participants, mutual help groups for antisocial youths are initiated by adults and typically meet with initial resistance. Hence, juveniles who are at the outset antisocial must become motivated to help one another. Perhaps the most formidable impediment to change encountered in working with antisocial youth is their tendency to project blame for their victimizing behavior onto others (referred to later as a

Blaming Others cognitive distortion). As long as projecting blame allows violent and other antisocial youth not to feel accountable for their behavior, little can be accomplished in any treatment program. Hence, Vorrath and Brendtro stress the importance of 'shifting the responsibility back ... on those who must do the changing,' a technique they refer to as 'reversing' (p. 39). To the adolescent who says, 'I got in trouble because both of my parents are alcoholics and don't care about me,' Vorrath and Brendtro suggest a rejoinder such as: 'Do you mean that all people with parents who have problems get in trouble?' (p. 39).

Also critical to inducing accountability is a technique called *confronting*, defined as 'making the student aware of the effect of his actions on others' (p. 109). In this spirit, Yochelson and Samenow (1977) recommended that change agents challenge antisocial individuals to put themselves in another's position and to understand the 'chain of injuries' (p. 223) resulting from every crime. Agee and McWilliams (1984) contrasted confronting with therapeutic styles emphasizing unconditional affirmation or support for the youths:

> If by some miracle you could provide for every need and desire of the youths at all times, they would still attempt to escape. ... They prefer criminal excitement to the stress and pressure of critically examining their behavior and changing it. The reality of the situation is that if the program is not making life fairly uncomfortable for the youth, it is unlikely to be successful in changing his behavior. (Agee and McWilliams, 1984, p. 290)

In situations where full-fledged confronting may not be necessary or feasible (such as a classroom), *checking* may be used. Whereas reversing and constructive confronting usually require extensive modelling by the group leader, group members typically begin quickly to learn and use checking.

> As a student begins to show a problem, the group gives him a cue or reminder to control himself. For example, if a person becomes angry and it appears that he may lose his temper, the group simply says to him, 'Check yourself.' This provides instant feedback on the unacceptability of the behavior and calls on the youth to control himself. In situations when verbal checking is inappropriate, students can give nonverbal cues to one another. (Vorrath & Brendtro, 1985, p. 107)

As the group leader's modeled and direct influence continues, the group should begin to develop a positive culture. For example, the group leader should witness increasing frequencies of use by the group of reversing, confronting and checking (as well as certain other techniques; see Vorrath & Brendtro, 1985). All of these techniques are critical for counteracting resistance and negativity among the youths, inducing personal responsibility, and encouraging them to help and care about one another.

Evaluation Studies

Research on the effectiveness of mutual help programs has yielded a promising but mixed picture. A number of studies of PPC and related programs have been conducted in schools (public and alternative), juvenile correctional facilities or detention centers, private residential treatment facilities and community group homes. The programs have been found to be effective in many but not all cases.

Numerous studies found mutual help programs to be effective in improving self-concept and amenability to treatment, and in reducing recidivism (Martin & Osgood, 1985; Vorrath & Brendtro, 1985, pp. 151–168; Wasmund, 1988), consistent with the thesis that helping others provides a basis for self-esteem. On the other hand, the trustworthiness of the results was generally undermined by serious methodological flaws such as the absence of a control group. Significant reduction in recidivism was less likely to be found among the more rigorously controlled studies (Garrett, 1985; Gottfredson, 1987). Gottfredson did note in connection with a controlled study of PPC in Chicago that those schools in which mutual help programs operated 'became [relative to control schools] safer over time, schoolwide reports of negative peer influence went down, and schoolwide belief in conventional rules went up' (p. 710).

Limitations of Antisocial Youth

In an important critique of PPC, Carducci (1980) concluded that the effectiveness of PPC is limited precisely because of the limitations of its participants. The limitations Carducci identified might be summarized as the 'three Ds' in social functioning: social skill *deficiencies*, social developmental *delays* and social cognitive *distortions*.

Social skill deficiencies

Carducci asserted that, while antisocial youth can identify a problem, 'they do not know what specific steps, on their part or the part of the owner of the problem, will result in its being solved' (p. 158). This observation is consistent with Goldstein and Glick's (1987) research review-based conclusion that 'delinquent and other aggressive children and teenagers display widespread interpersonal, planning, aggression management, and other psychological skill deficiencies' (p. 22). Using the Inventory of Adolescent Problems—Short Form (IAP-SF), Simonian, Tarnowski and Gibbs (1991) found that social skills deficiencies were related to offense severity, alcohol abuse history, and AWOL activity of incarcerated juvenile delinquents.

Sociomoral developmental delay and primary cognitive distortion

Second, Carducci referred to the problem of social or moral developmental delay, writing that the antisocial juvenile is 'frequently at a stage of arrested moral/ethical/social/emotional development in which he is fixated at a level of concern about getting his own throbbing needs met, regardless of effects on others' (p. 157). Carducci refers, then, to both aspects of sociomoral developmental delay as identified in cognitive-developmental theory (see review by Gibbs, 1993), namely, the persistence beyond early childhood of (a) immature or superficial moral judgment; and (b) pronounced egocentric bias ('me-centeredness,' Lickona, 1983, p. 152; or in Carducci's words, 'getting our own throbbing needs met, regardless of effects on others'). Controlled comparisons of delinquent or conduct-disordered youth with normal children or adolescents (Bear & Richards, 1981; Blasi, 1980; Campagna & Harter, 1975; Chandler & Moran, 1990; Gavaghan, Arnold & Gibbs, 1983; Gregg, Gibbs & Basinger, 1994; Jennings, Kilkenny & Kohlberg, 1983; Trevethan & Walker, 1989) indicate that, at least on production measures, significantly higher percentages of delinquent or conduct-disordered youth are at Kohlberg's opportunistic and pragmatic stage 2 of moral judgment (Gibbs, Basinger & Fuller, 1992; Kohlberg, 1984) Similarly, the perspective-taking scores of recidivist delinquents resemble the performance of 7 to 8-year-old children (Chandler, 1973). Damon (1977) found that young children tend to confuse fair distribution with egocentric, momentary desires, e.g. 'I should get it because I want to have it,' (p. 75) or 'Whatever I want is what's fair'.

If the child's egocentric bias does not decline with age (for any number of reasons), it tends to become consolidated as a primary *cognitive distortion*, i.e. a self-serving, rationalizing, or otherwise non-veridical attitude or belief (Gibbs, 1993). Primary cognitive distortions are defined in Gibbs and Potter's (1991) recent typology as: 'According status to one's own immediate views, expectations, needs, feelings and desires, to such a degree that the legitimate views, etc. of others (or even one's own long-term best interests) are scarcely considered or are disregarded altogether.' For example, Samenow (1984) quoted a 14-year-old delinquent: 'I was born with the idea that I'd do what I wanted. I always felt that rules and regulations were not for me' (p. 160).

Secondary social cognitive distortions

In addition to indicating the primary bias of 'getting our own throbbing needs met, regardless of the effects on others,' Carducci also observed that antisocial juveniles typically evidence 'the defense mechanism of projection ... in which they blame others for their misbehavior' (p. 157). Gibbs and Potter (1991) characterize this distinction as one between primary and secondary cognitive distortions. Primary cognitive distortions comprise the first category ('Self-Centered') in Gibbs and Potter's (1991) typological model (see Table 6.2 later in the chapter). The remaining three categories constitute secondary social cognitive distortions, which serve to support the primary (self-centered) distortions (Gibbs, 1991). Gibbs and Potter defined the secondary distortion categories— Minimizing/Mislabeling, Assuming the Worst, Blaming Others (cf. Carducci)— as follows:

Minimizing/mislabeling.   Depicting antisocial behavior as causing no real harm, or as being acceptable or even admirable; or referring to others with belittling or dehumanizing labels.

Assuming the worst.   Gratuitously attributing hostile intentions to others; considering a worst-case scenario for a social situation as if it were inevitable; or assuming that improvement is impossible in one's own or others' behavior.

Blaming others. Misattributing blame for one's harmful actions to outside sources, especially: another person, a group or a momentary aberration (one was drunk, high, in a bad mood, etc.); or misattributing blame for one's victimization or other misfortune to innocent others.

Secondary cognitive distortions have been characterized as pre- or post-transgression rationalizations that serve to 'neutralize' conscience or guilt and thereby to prevent damage to the self-image following antisocial behavior (Sykes & Matza, 1957). Similarly, Gibbs (1991) suggested that secondary distortions reduce the stresses from the consequences of the primary distortions. Two such stresses that can stem from one's harm to others are: empathic distress (and possibly empathy-based guilt), and cognitive dissonance between harmful actions and a self-definition as one who does not unjustifiably harm others.

The Need for a Multi-Component Approach

Given these delays, deficiencies and distortions among antisocial youths—as either receivers or givers of help—the best intentions of these newly motivated juveniles to help group members can quickly meet with resistance and turn to frustration. Once frustrated, antisocial juveniles all too quickly resort to established behavioral habits, i.e. to coercive or vindictive forms of 'helping'. Brendtro and Ness (1982) surveyed 10 schools and facilities using guided group programs, in order to explore problems and program needs as seen by participants. Cited as a problem at nine out of 10 centers—the highest proportion of any problem—was 'abuse of confrontation,' e.g. 'harassment, name-calling, screaming in someone's face, hostile profanity, and physical intimidation' (p. 322). Although Vorrath and Brendtro (1985) railed against such abuses in PPC programs, one can argue that the abuses are to some extent inevitable when insufficient attention is accorded to the limitations of the help providers (Gibbs, Potter & Goldstein, 1995).

EQUIPPING MUTUAL HELP GROUPS: A MULTI-COMPONENT PROGRAM

Despite Vorrath and Brendtro's (1985) warning against 'hybrid' (p. 162) programs, both Carducci (1980) and Agee and McWilliams (1984) advocate combining PPC with a training or teaching—we would say 'equipping'—component. One such multi-component program is called EQUIP (Gibbs, Potter & Goldstein, 1995). EQUIP complements mutual help group motivational techniques with psychoeducational material designed to redress the above-described deficiencies, distortions and delays of antisocial youth. These materials are used in the context of both mutual help group meetings and alternative meetings called equipment meetings. The EQUIP program shares with Goldstein and Glick's (1987) Aggression Replacement Training a curriculum entailing moral judgment development (cf. Gibbs et al., 1984), anger management, and social skills development. The EQUIP curriculum (summarized in Table 6.1) draws upon, reworks, and supplements all three of these facets of the Aggression Replacement Training curriculum.

Equipment meetings are held once or twice each week, and provide not only psychological resources but also some variety in the daily group sessions. However, EQUIP curriculum material is not introduced until the group is genuinely receptive. Whereas EQUIP provides the group with tools for correcting group members' cognitive distortions mainly in mutual help meetings, EQUIP tools for remediating group members' social skill/anger management deficiencies and sociomoral developmental delays are provided mainly in 'equipment' meetings. Although both mutual help meeting and equipment meeting group leaders use Socratic questioning and other indirect techniques, the group leader's role is much more salient in equipment meetings (Gibbs, Potter & Goldstein, 1995).

Remediating Cognitive Distortions in Mutual Help and Equipment Meetings

As noted, the typical mutual help group session lasts between 60 and 90 minutes, and features problem reporting by all group members, awarding the meeting to the member most in need of help that day, problem solving for the group member awarded the meeting, and the summary of the meeting by the group leader. Also noted was the innovation that in EQUIP, the problem names used during the group session include not only terms for antisocial behavior (lying problem, aggravates others, stealing, etc.), but also terms for antisocial, distorted cognitions or 'thinking errors' (Yochelson & Samenow, 1976, in the Gibbs & Potter typology, Self-Centered, Minimizing/Mislabeling, Assuming the Worst, and Blaming Others, as described earlier). Hence, in problem reporting, group members describe and label not only a behavior problem but also the underlying cognitive distortion. Requiring a deeper level of problem reporting reduces the misuse of problem reporting to externalize blame (a problem acknowledged by Vorrath and Brendtro themselves), or to engage in 'mechanical verbalizations', the second most frequently cited problem with PPC (Brendtro & Ness, 1982, p. 313).

Accordingly, we teach EQUIP groups not only the PPC problem list but also descriptions of the four categories of 'thinking errors' (the term for cognitive distortion used by Yochelson and Samenow, 1976, 1977). Youths entering an EQUIP group are administered the How I Think (HIT) questionnaire (Barriga & Gibbs, in press; Gibbs, Barriga & Potter, 1994), which can serve as a vehicle for teaching these thinking error categories. Sample items from the How I Think questionnaire illustrating each category are listed in Table 6.2. Subjects are told: 'Each statement in this questionnaire may describe how you usually think about things in life. Ask yourself: "Is it fair to say that this statement describes how I usually think about things?"' Following each item, respondents indicate agreement or disagreement along a five-point scale. The HIT and other tools are used for teaching the thinking errors vocabulary (unless the HIT is being used in

Table 6.1   The 10-week EQUIP course: agenda and main features

Week	Anger management	Social skills	Social decision-making (moral education)
1	*Evaluating anger/aggression* 1. Re-evaluating, relabeling 2. Anger management, not elimination	*Expressing a complaint constructively* 1. Think ahead what you'll say, etc. 2. Say how you contributed to problem 3. Make constructive suggestion	*Martian's adviser* 1. Planet A self-centered 2. Planet B labeled truly strong 3. Making the group Planet B
2	*Anatomy of anger (AMBC)* 1. Self-talk (Mind) makes you angry 2. Notice Early Warning Signs (Body) 3. Anger-reducing self-talk	*Caring for someone sad or upset* 1. Notice and think ahead 2. Listen, don't interrupt 3. 'Be there'	*Jerry, Mark* 1. Loyalty, commitment 2. Value of close friendships 3. Breaking up in a considerate way 4. Getting even is immature
3	*Monitoring/correcting thinking errors* 1. 'Gary's Thinking Errors' 2. Daily logs	*Dealing constructively with negative peer pressure* 1. Think 'why' 2. Think ahead to consequences 3. Suggest something else (less harmful)	*Jim* 1. Can't trust 'friend' with a stealing problem 2. Stealing wrong even if from stranger
4	*More anger reducers* 1. Deep breathing, counting backwards, peaceful imaginary 2. Anger reducers 'buy time'	*Keeping out of fights* 1. Stop and think 2. Think ahead to consequences 3. Handle the situation another way	*Larry, Sarah* 1. Shouldn't let friend steal (car, store items) 2. Harm from stealing 3. True friend wouldn't put you on the spot 4. Closing gap between judgment and behaviour (relabeling, using social skill)
5	*Think ahead to consequences* 1. Thinking ahead of if-then thinking 2. Types of consequences (especially for others) 3. Inducing awareness	*Helping others* 1. Think—Is there a need? 2. Think ahead how to help, when, etc. 3. Offer to help	*George, Leon* 1. Should tell (on drug-dealing brother, friend planning to go AWOL) 2. Others could get killed 3. Important to send drug dealers to jail

6	*Use I statements for constructive consequences* 1. You statements (put-downs, threats) 2. Use I statements instead of You statements	*Preparing for a stressful conversation* 1. Imagine ahead your feelings, the other person's feelings 2. Think ahead what to say 3. Think ahead how the other person might reply	*Dave* 1. Dave shouldn't deliver drugs for friend 2. Sister's life may be at stake 3. Closing gap between judgement and behavior (relabeling, correcting thinking errors, exhorting)
7	*Self-evaluation* 1. Self-evaluation, self-reflection 2. Talk back to thinking errors 3. Stay constructive	*Dealing constructively with someone angry at you* 1. Listen openly and patiently 2. Think of something you can agree with, say he's right about that 3. Apologize or explain, make constructive suggestion	*Ned* 1. Should tell on suicidal friend 2. Suicide is self-centered thinking error 3. Existential/spiritual concerns
8	*Reversing* 1. Things *you* do that make *other* people angry 2. Practise reversing (correcting Blaming Others error)	*Expressing care and appreciation* 1. Think if the person would like to know you care 2. Think ahead what you'll say, when, etc. 3. Tell the person how you feel	*Sam* 1. Should tell on friend who shoplifted 2. Important to prosecute shoplifters 3. Store owner is not to blame (Blaming Others)
9	*Self as victimizer* 1. Victims and victimizers 2. Consequences for victims 3. That you were a victim is no excuse for victimizing others	*Dealing with someone accusing you* 1. Think how you feel, tell yourself to calm down 2. Think if the accuser is right 3. If the accuser right, apologize/make restitution; if wrong, say it isn't true, wrong impression, etc.	*Reggie* 1. Should reveal violent dad's drinking 2. Should do what's best for family 3. Wouldn't want someone to lie to you 4. But mother wrong to put Reggie on spot
10	*Victimizer and grand review* 1. Mind of the victimizer 2. Conclusion of consciousness-raising	*Responding constructively to failure* 1. Ask yourself if you did fail 2. Think what you could do differently 3. Decide, plan to try again	*Howard* 1. Shouldn't help friend cheat 2. Can't trust 'friend' with cheating problem 3. Correcting thinking errors

Reprinted, by permission, from Gibbs, Potter and Goldstein (1995)

Table 6.2   How I think questionnaire items: four categories of cognitive distortion

---

1. Self-centered

If I desire something, it should be mine.
If I lie to people, that's nobody's business but my own.
If I want to do something, I don't care if it's legal or not.
When I get mad, I don't care who gets hurt.

2. Minimizing or Mislabeling

If you can get away with it, only a fool wouldn't steal.
Everybody lies. It's no big deal.
Taking a car doesn't really hurt anyone if nothing happens to the car and the owner gets it back.
Hitting someone can really knock some sense into them.

3. Assuming the Worst

You might as well steal. If you don't steal it, somebody else will.
I might as well lie—if I tell the truth, people aren't going to believe me anyway.
Adults are always trying to hassle young people.
You should hurt people first, before they hurt you.

4. Blaming Others

If someone is careless enough to lose a wallet, they deserve to have it stolen.
People force me to lie when they ask me too many questions.
If I tell someone off, it's their fault for trying to tell me what to do.
If people don't cooperate with me, it's not my fault if someone gets hurt.

From *The How I Think Questionnaire* by J. C. Gibbs, A. G. Barriga and G. Potter (1995). Unpublished manuscript, The Ohio State University, Columbus. Copyright 1995 by the authors. Reprinted by permission.

program evaluation; see final chapter section). Thus equipped, the group member's reporting (with the group's help if needed) the thinking error underlying the behavior problem often thereby enhances group insight into the basis for the youth's behavior problems.

Case Illustration

One youth in an EQUIP group, Mac, reported resisting and yelling profanities at a staff member who, in accordance with institutional policy, attempted to inspect his carrying bag. The designation of the incident as 'Authority Problem' was easy enough. Identification of the underlying cognitive distortion required some discussion, but provided a problem analysis which the group later used once Mac was awarded the meeting. The youth explained that the bag contained something very special and irreplaceable—photos of his grandmother—and he was not going to let anyone take them from him. In seeking to identify underlying thinking errors, the group learned important further information: Mac thought only of having his photos every moment. He did not for a moment consider where the staff member was coming from (she was only carrying out institutional policy concerning inspection for contraband). Nor did he consider that this staff member was not abusive, and hence that he had no reason to assume the photos would be confiscated. Generating the Authority behavior problem, then, were Self-Centered and Assuming the Worst thinking errors. Furthermore, Mac's anger at staff for his subsequent disciplinary write-up was identified as an Easily Angered problem and attributed to a Blaming Others thinking error (Mac, not staff, was responsible for the write-up).

As Mac came to achieve these awarenesses—and to acquire certain social and anger management skills—with the help of his peers, his anger dissipated considerably. Perhaps most important, he began to regret his verbal assault on the staff member. We believe that Mac's remorse was therapeutically crucial: He could now see the unfairness of his behavior toward her, empathize with her, and attribute blame to himself. Through this and other sessions, the youth's Authority and Easily Angered problems came to be seldom rather than frequently reported. We surmise that the conduct improvement was partly attributable to the attenuation of cognitive distortion and consequent activation of inhibitory factors such as empathy-based guilt and dissonance with self-concept.

Besides cognitive distortion, other contributing factors to Mac's outburst included the other two 'Ds': social skill deficiencies and delay in moral judgment stage. Hence, we believe that Mac's conduct improvement was also attributable to tools he had learned—and of which the group reminded him—during the equipment meetings. A relevant social skill, 'Expressing a Complaint Constructively,' had been learned and practised during previous equipment meetings. The group (with some prompting from the group leader) reminded Mac of the four steps involved in this social skill (see Table 6.3), especially Step One, requiring the recognition of how one has 'contributed to the problem' (e.g. Mac's Self-Centered and Assuming the Worst thinking errors). Finally, it should be noted that in addition to the social skill equipment, certain anger management tools were helpful with Mac, e.g. taking deep breaths, counting backward, and thinking ahead to the undesirable consequences of aggression (see Table 6.1).

Because the group was equipped to help Mac with all three 'Ds' (distortions, deficiencies, delays), the group members administered *effective* help, and prognosis for subsequent conduct gains was better than if the group had been equipped only with motivational techniques. Indeed, Mac's social skill and conduct gains illustrate systematic group gains found in a recent controlled evaluation study of an EQUIP program (see later section).

Implementation

This section discusses principles, procedures and techniques for implementing a sociomoral group treatment program such as EQUIP. We discuss: (1) the importance of preparing the staff to become a unified team; (2) introducing EQUIP to the youth; (3) the use of 'seeding' and assessment in starting a youth group; and (4) strategies for dealing with the negative leader as well as with various types of resisting or disruptive behavior. In general, critical to the success of a sociomoral group treatment program is the cultivation of a positive, caring youth culture.

1. Staff Preparation: the unified treatment team

To prepare for and establish an EQUIP program, staff must establish a team approach. In correctional facilities, the staff team spans traditional departments (classroom, clinical, dormitory) to encompass all staff having regular significant contact with the youth group members. Vicki Agee and Bruce McWilliams (1984)

Table 6.3   Social Skill 1: Expressing a Complaint Constructively; four steps (with discussion notes)

[In group, describe the situation for group members.]

Step One: **Identify the problem**. How are you feeling? What is the problem? Who is responsible for it? Did you contribute—or are you contributing—to the problem in any way?

Note Discuss how you can recognize a problem (by how someone treats you or what they say to you; by the way you act toward someone or what you say to them; by the way you feel inside).

Step Two: **Plan and think ahead**: To whom should you express your complaint? When? Where? **What will you say** (see **Step Three**)?

Notes What is a good time to tell that person (when the person isn't involved with something else, when the person is alone, seems calm)? Wait until you have calmed down before approaching the person.

[For Steps Three and Four, you will need a partner.]

Step Three: **State your complaint**. In a calm, straightforward way, tell the person the problem and how you feel about it. If you've contributed to the problem, mention how you may be partly at fault, what you are willing to do.

Note If the person gets angry, suggest that you talk about the problem some other time. The person is less likely to get angry if you are strong enough to apologize for your role in the problem.

Step Four: **Make a constructive suggestion**: Tell the person what you would like done about the problem. Ask the other person if he or she thinks your suggestion is fair. If the *other* person makes a constructive suggestion, tell him or her that you appreciate the suggestion, or that it sounds fair.

Notes You can mention how your suggestion would help the other person, too. To help clear up any remaining hard feelings, you may wish to ask the person how he or she feels about what you've said.

Reprinted, by permission, from Gibbs, Potter & Goldstein (1995).

present the rationale for the team approach as used at the Closed Adolescent Treatment Center, a maximum security correctional facility for violent juvenile offenders in Denver, Colorado:

> The [team] concept requires that staff work so closely together as to appear almost to be a gestalt organism. For one thing, they must role model cooperative interpersonal relationships to the peer group, and for another, the violent juveniles are obviously dangerous, and safety is achieved through cohesion. ... In an ideal family, the parents present a united front to their offspring. In the therapeutic community the same thing must occur. Violent juvenile offenders usually have much experience at being able to split staff (and their own parents) and set them up against each other in an effort to divert attention from their negative behaviors. Ideally, in a team setting, there are very strong values against allowing this to happen, and attempts to do so are promptly confronted. (p. 289)

Working closely together and presenting a unified front consolidate staff into a team with a positive 'culture'. Just as sharing, cooperating and having a direct role in treatment develop a positive youth culture, such a mode of group activity develops a positive *staff* culture. A team spirit among staff is crucial if a positive youth culture is to develop and last.

2. Introducing EQUIP to the youths

Introducing to the youths the EQUIP program is the responsibility of the administrator (superintendent, principal) as well as the EQUIP treatment team staff, who should plan for a several-hour orientation meeting with prospective youths (selection strategies are discussed in the next section). Given the importance of presenting a united front to the youths (previous section), it is vitally important that the administrator be present along with the treatment staff during this orientation meeting. The presence of the administrator will demonstrate that commitment to EQUIP exists at all levels, i.e. that staff are working closely with administration and have administration's full support (Gibbs, Potter & Goldstein, 1995).

In preparing the introduction, staff should think of adolescent offenders as currently negative but potentially positive. Accordingly, the introduction should stress to the youths that they will have an opportunity, through group meetings with peers, to help their peers identify and resolve problems; and that as they help others they will also be helping themselves.

Beyond the opening comments by administrator and staff, the introduction should provide a comprehensive explanation of the program, with concrete illustrations of the major features and with ample opportunity for the youths to ask questions. Many of the illustrations can be adapted from the EQUIP curriculum (the material can be used more fully later during the group's equipment meetings). Staff may also 'walk the group through' the phases of a mutual-help meeting (introduction, awarding a problem, problem reporting, problem-solving, summary), and have several youth role-play a sample social skill (e.g. 'Keeping out of Fights'). Although staff should attribute to the youths themselves the desire for positive change, the youths should also be made aware that the staff will communicate regularly with pertinent authorities (e.g. a juvenile justice judge) on each peer's participation and progress (Gibbs, Potter & Goldstein, 1995).

3. Starting a youth group: 'seeding' and intake assessment

'Seeding' is the term used by Vorrath and Brendtro for the transfer of several youths from an ongoing group program to membership in a newly created group; ideally, a new positive group culture will develop as the experienced youths in effect socialize the new members. One is reminded of the time-honored strategy for extending the life of bread dough by transplanting samples ('starters') into new batches.

The essential spirit of 'seeding' can be used for starting a youth group where there is no pre-existing mutual-help group. Specifically, one can 'seed' a new group with adolescents in the facility or school who are: (a) at least relatively non-oppositional and positive, i.e. relatively high-functioning; and (b) popular or at least not disliked by the other institutional youths. We (Gibbs, Potter & Goldstein, 1995) recommend selecting five or six relatively high-functioning individuals with whom to start a preliminary mutual-help group. This core group should be taught the PPC problem list and the thinking errors, and how to use them in a mutual-help meeting. As the core group expands to the standard seven to nine members, the initial members are responsible for teaching EQUIP's basic operational features to new members (the new members should be 'next best' available juveniles and ideally should be added one at a time, several weeks apart). Once a 'climate of change' (Vorrath & Brendtro, 1985, p. 11) grows and the positive group culture is sufficiently strong and equipped, seeding ends; at that point, the group can absorb and help new, initially negative members without suffering serious deterioration.

To help identify promising youths with whom to begin the group, the staff team at a facility may decide to implement the use of one or more standard measures, e.g. the HIT (Table 6.2; Gibbs, Barriga & Potter, 1995; reliability and validity presented in Barriga & Gibbs, in press), the Social Reflection Questionnaire—Short Form (SRM—SF; Gibbs, Basinger & Fuller, 1992; reliability and validity reported in Basinger, Gibbs & Fuller, 1995) and the Inventory of Adolescent Problems—Short Form (IAP—SF; Gibbs, Potter & Goldstein, 1995; reliability and validity reported in Simonian, Tarnowski & Gibbs, 1991). These instruments assess, respectively, moral judgment maturity and social skills competence. If the EQUIP setting is a juvenile correctional facility, the SRM—SF, IAP—SF and/or HIT may be administrable during each youth's intake period. Selecting youths who are relatively high-functioning on these measures should ensure at least some positive potential for the starting group. Even where the youth population of a facility appears to be uniformly low-functioning, it is likely that some youths are in some if not all respects 'positive', and it is worthwhile to begin a group with these youths. If administration of assessment measures for determining level of social functioning is not feasible, informal treatment team judgments may suffice.

4. Redirect the negative leader

A major threat to the development of a positive youth culture is the influence of a negative leader. Even a seeded group is likely to have at least one member whose offense history is so extensive that it reflects a long-standing, entrenched, pervasively criminal way of living and thinking. This type of youth:

> ... has considerable ability to con and to manipulate and views himself as slick and sly. In his home situation, he is able to control his parents or at least to avoid their control. He is highly status conscious and is successful at climbing to a position of power among his peers. He usually has average or above-average intelligence that may not be shown in testing, and he may be seriously underachieving in school. Even though he may not be physically strong, he carries himself in a confident manner and has the capacity to enlist others if force is required. ... Usually [he] operates with assistants referred to as *lieutenants* (Vorrath & Brendtro, 1985, p. 109).

Vorrath and Brendtro suggest that the negative leader be viewed as a potential asset because the group would also be amenable to his strong influence in a positive direction. In the relabeling technique, 'caring' is depicted as showing strength and redirected toward positive values. Similarly, the strength and influence of the negative leader must be redirected toward positive group leadership.

To redirect the negative leader, the most effective strategy is to attack his support by confronting the lieutenants. The assistants must be held accountable for the leader's hurtful behavior. For example, the coach should relabel their 'loyalty' as an Easily Misled problem. The coach should make clear that true caring about the negative leader would mean showing the strength to stand up to his manipulation of them and to insist on positive behavior. The lieutenants should be reminded that EQUIP separates the problem from the person, that the negative leader is still someone who is worthy of their help.

In the EQUIP program, where group members have learned the thinking errors, using the cognitive distortion vocabulary can strengthen the appeals to the lieutenants: Are they *minimizing* the harm his behavior is having on the group, *mislabeling* it as smart or cool or strong? Are they *assuming the worst*, that they are helpless to confront the leader's *self-centered* attitude?; that they cannot check his *blaming others* instead of accepting responsibility for his problems? Again, their 'loyalty' should be identified as a thinking error (Minimizing/Mislabeling); it should be relabeled not only as an Easily Misled problem but more broadly an Inconsiderate of Self problem (insofar as their 'loyalty' amounts to a failure to identify and correct thinking errors) and an Inconsiderate of Others problem (insofar as the negative leader is not being helped to identify and correct *his* thinking errors). The lieutenants and other group members can in turn use the cognitive distortion vocabulary in the appeals to the negative leader. The vocabulary tools gained in EQUIP, then, equip the assistants to be effective in redirecting the negative leader. (Even so, the lieutenants should be forewarned that the effort to redirect the negative leader will not be quick or easy; he will be unlikely to give up his cognitive distortions and negative behavior without a fight.)

Outcome effectiveness

The effectiveness of the EQUIP program was recently evaluated in an outcome study (Leeman, Gibbs & Fuller, 1993). The study was conducted at a medium-security correctional facility maintained by the juvenile corrections department of a midwestern state. The subjects were 57 male juvenile offenders aged 15–18 who were incarcerated at the facility. The subjects were randomly assigned either to the EQUIP experimental unit or to one of two control groups. The experimental treatment initiative was introduced by the authors to institutional staff; the EQUIP staff (youth leaders, social workers, supervisors and a teacher) was then formed and trained from interested institutional staff members. The EQUIP treatment program took place at a living unit located in one wing of the facility building. The unit had the same design as other units in the institution, providing a dormitory, a living area, a 'quiet room' (for studying etc.), and a staff office. The quiet room was used as the meeting room for the experimental group. EQUIP groups met daily during weekdays for 60 to 90 minutes. In addition to regular mutual help meetings, two of the five meetings each week were Equipment meetings.

Outcome measures for the study addressed both institutional and post-release conduct. Institutional misconduct was assessed through both self-report and archival measures. Experimental as well as control group subjects completed both pre-test and post-test self-report questionnaires. The questionnaire asked whether or how often in the past month the subject had damaged something, was involved in a fight, defied staff, or took drugs (adapted from Gold, 1970). Archival measures of institutional misconduct were based on disciplinary incident reports and unexcused school absences. The post-release archival measure consisted of parole revocation and/or institutional recommitment.

EQUIP was found to stimulate substantial institutional and post-release conduct gains. Institutional conduct gains were highly significant for the EQUIP group relative to the control groups in terms of self-reported misconduct, staff-filed incident reports, and unexcused absences from school. These results corroborated informal observations and comments by institutional staff that the EQUIP unit was dramatically easier to manage than other units, in that there were substantially fewer instances of fighting, verbal abuse, staff defiance and AWOL attempts. Interestingly, the control subjects approached the low frequency levels of the EQUIP groups on incident reports and unexcused absences during the final month of incarceration (see Figures 6.1 and 6.2). Possibly, the control group boys were

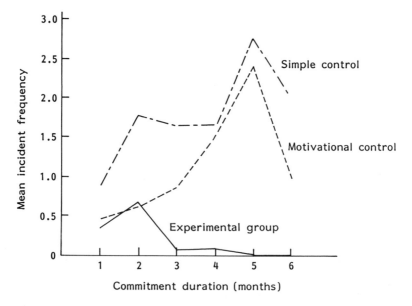

Figure 6.1   Mean incident report frequencies by month for the experimental and control groups

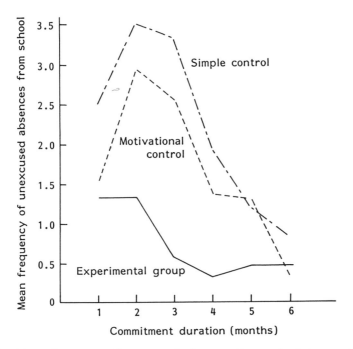

Figure 6.2 Mean frequency of unexcused absences from school by month for the experimental and control groups

on their best behavior just before their release dates to avoid risking a disciplinary action and delay in their release.

The most notable finding was that the EQUIP program's impact was evident 12 months after subjects' release. The recidivism rate remained low and stable while the likelihood of recidivism for the untreated subjects climbed. Specifically, the EQUIP group's recidivism rate was 15% at both 6 months and 12 months after release. In contrast, the mean recidivism rate for the control groups was 29.7% at 6 months and 40.5% at 12 months; the latter difference, between 15 and 40.5%, was statistically significant. Overall, the study by Leeman, Gibbs and Fuller showed that a multi-component sociomoral group treatment program can be highly effective: young offenders' conduct significantly improved during incarceration and their conduct gains were maintained during the year following release from the institution.

PROGRAM EVALUATION

Years ago, people thought that 'good intentions' were sufficient—that if a child were surrounded by good people, the benefits would flow to him and be self-evident. However, the ballooning expense of both education and treatment, along with the obvious and frightening failures of education, has made a pained public suspicious. Their sensitivity has resulted in a sensitivity to the need to be accountable: What *are* we doing for children? What works? What doesn't? How can we prove it? (Carducci & Carducci, 1984, p. 180).

Gibbs, Potter and Goldstein (1995) discuss the applicability of the EQUIP intervention program to a variety of persons with antisocial behavior problems (not only male adolescents but females, preadolescents, young adults, associated families), in a variety of settings (school, short-term center, day treatment, individual therapy), and even in conjunction with certain compatible programs (cooperative learning, substance abuse, severe-offender). Regardless of how a particular sociomoral group treatment program such as EQUIP is adapted or expanded, however, its effectiveness and the accuracy of its implementation should be monitored and evaluated with an eye toward examination and improvement. The public has a right to expect that programs for antisocial youth be accountable for evaluating and demonstrating the effectiveness of their treatment procedures. Indeed, development and use of valid methods for assessing the effectiveness of one's therapeutic services should be considered a professional responsibility.

Although the specifics will vary, evaluation procedures should satisfy certain basic requirements. The first requirement is to ensure that the actual beginning and continued implementation do not depart substantially from the agreed-upon plan. To enhance the prospect for fidelity to the plan or 'program integrity', it is important to specify as precisely as possible just what the plan is. Kazdin (1987) recommends that treatment 'be delineated in *manual* form that includes written materials to guide the therapist in attaining the specific goals of treatment, and in the procedures, techniques, topics, themes, therapeutic maneuvers, and activities' (p. 92; cf. Luborsky & DeRubeis, 1984). Explicit and specific procedural materials, however, are insufficient by themselves to ensure program integrity. As Goldstein (1991b) points out:

> A wide and usually unpredictable variety of 'emergencies,' 'exigencies,' 'realities,' and the like may arise. Caseloads may expand. Workers may grow tired, lazy, or overburdened. ... Even if appropriately described, detailed, and exemplified in an intervention procedures manual, the intervention plan may fail to anticipate an array of crucial circumstances. Whatever the bases for diminished intervention integrity, program efficacy is likely to suffer. (Goldstein, 1991b, p. 483).

Because of such possibilities, Kazdin (1987) recommends that 'some monitoring of the [treatment] sessions [be] conducted to ensure that the treatment [is] actually [being] carried out' (p. 92).

The second requirement is for standard measurement of the presenting problems of the treatment population. As Kazdin (1987) points out: 'the failure to use standard diagnostic criteria or widely used assessment devices makes it difficult to identify the severity of child dysfunction relative to other samples and to normal (nonreferred) peers' (p. 93). Furthermore, establishing a means for measuring problem severity is a prerequisite for assessing whether a program has been successful in *reducing* severity. In our implementations of EQUIP, we have found the IAP—SF, the SRM—SF, and the HIT to be very helpful pre–post assessment devices for this purpose. Goldstein (1991a) refers to such measures as 'proximal', i.e. 'directly tied to the content of the intervention' (p. 29). Proximal-outcome evaluations are especially helpful as constructive feedback to staff on the strengths and weaknesses of the program components. For example, in our own preliminary implementation, weak changes in moral judgment as measured by the SRM—SF led to scrutiny of—and certain improvements in—the moral education curriculum. That major gains in social skills were highly correlated with degree of self-reported institutional change improvement (Leeman, Gibbs & Fuller, 1993) suggested that the social skills component as then formulated was already effective. Presumably dependent upon 'proximal' effectiveness are more 'distal' or derivative changes such as a resultant decline in a group's recidivism rate.

Ideally, assessing treatment effectiveness would entail comparisons of a treatment group's pre–post changes with those of a matched or randomly assigned control group (e.g. Leeman, Gibbs & Fuller, 1993). Kazdin (1988) acknowledges, however, that a scientifically optimal design may not be feasible in many field settings where staff and financial resources may be limited. Kazdin argues that where large-scale studies are not feasible, detailed case studies entailing pre–post assessment would represent an improvement over anecdotal reports or impressions.

A democratically agreed-upon plan is also a democratically revisable plan. Carducci and Carducci (1984) recommend that plan revisions (whether for the individual student or the youth group) be expected and that periodic meetings expressly for this purpose be incorporated into staff operations. After all, EQUIP is in most essentials an intervention strategy and program, and the growth of EQUIP will entail some unique features in accordance with the particular setting for its adaptation, partial application or expansion. 'Interventions cannot, nor should they be, automated or implemented unswervingly and unresponsively in a manner dictated by program manuals, and we are not championing such literalness of application here' (Goldstein, 1991b, p. 483). None the less, we believe that once EQUIP takes the form of a specific program with explicit directives, such a program deserves to be accurately implemented, faithfully maintained, and rigorously evaluated.

REFERENCES

Agee, V. L. & McWilliams, B. (1984). The role of group therapy and the therapeutic community in treating the violent juvenile offender. In R. Mathais (ed.), *Violent Juvenile Offenders*. San Francisco, CA: National Council on Crime and Delinquency, pp. 283–96.

Barriga, A. Q. & Gibbs, J. C. (in press). *Measuring cognitive distortion in antisocial youth: Preliminary development and validation of the How I Think questionnaire. Aggressive Behavior.*

Basinger, K. S., Gibbs, J. C. & Fuller, D. (1995). Context and the measurement of moral judgement. *International Journal of Behavioral Development*, **18**, 537–556.

Bear, G. G. & Richards, H. C. (1981). Moral reasoning and conduct problems in the classroom. *Journal of Educational Psychology*, **73**, 644–70.

Blasi, A. (1980). Bridging moral cognition and moral action: A critical review of the literature. *Psychological Bulletin*, **88**, 1–45.

Brendtro, L. K. & Ness, A. E. (1982). Perspectives on peer group treatment: The use and abuse of Guided Group Interaction/Positive Peer Culture. *Children and Youth Services Review*, **4**, 307–24.

Campagna, A. F. & Harter, S. (1975). Moral judgment in sociopathic and normal children. *Journal of Personality and Social Psychology*, **31**, 199–205.

Carducci, D. J. (1980). Positive Peer Culture and assertiveness training: Complementary modalities for dealing with disturbed and disturbing adolescents in the classroom. *Behavioral Disorders*, **5**, 156–62.

Carducci, D. J. & Carducci, J. B. (1984). *The Caring Classroom: A Guide for Teachers Troubled by the Difficult Student and Classroom Disruption*. New York: Bull Publishing.

Chandler, M. (1973). Egocentrism and antisocial behavior: The assessment and training of social perspective-talking skills. *Developmental Psychology*, **9**, 326–32.

Chandler, M. & Moran, T. (1990). Psychopathy and moral development: A comparative study of delinquent and nondelinquent youth. *Development & Psychopathology*, **2**, 227–46.

Damon, W. (1977). *The Social World of the Child*. San Francisco, CA: Jossey-Bass.

Damon, W. (1988). *The Moral Child: Nurturing Children's Natural Moral Growth*. New York: The Free Press.

Garrett, C. (1985). Effects of residential treatment on adjudicated delinquents: A meta-analysis. *Journal of Research in Crime and Delinquency*, **22**, 287–308.

Gavaghan, M. P., Arnold, K. D. & Gibbs, J. C. (1983). Moral judgment in delinquents and nondelinquents: Recognition versus production measures. *Journal of Psychology*, **114**, 267–74.

Gibbs, J. C. (1991). Sociomoral developmental delay and cognitive distortion: Implications for the treatment of antisocial youth. In W. M. Kurtines & J. L. Gewirtz (eds), *Handbook of Moral Behavior and Development: Vol 3. Application*. Hillsdale, NJ: Lawrence Erlbaum Associates, pp. 95–110.

Gibbs, J. C. (1993). Moral-cognitive interventions. In A. P. Goldstein & C. R. Huff (eds), *The Gang Intervention Handbook*. Champaign, IL: Research Press.

Gibbs, J. C., Arnold, K. D., Ahlborn, H. H. & Cheesman, F. L. (1984). Facilitation of sociomoral reasoning in delinquents. *Journal of Consulting and Clinical Psychology*, **52**, 37–45.

Gibbs, J. C., Barriga, A. Q. & Potter, G. (1995). *The How I Think Questionnaire*. Unpublished manuscript. Columbus, OH: The Ohio State University.

Gibbs, J. C., Basinger, K. S. & Fuller, D. (1992). *Moral Maturity: Measuring the Development of Sociomoral Reflection*. Hillsdale, NJ: Lawrence Erlbaum Associates.

Gibbs, J. C. & Potter, G. (1991) *Aggression Replacement Training in the Context of Positive Peer Culture*. Paper presented at the meeting of the Ohio Council for Children with Behavioral Disorders, Columbus, OH.

Gibbs, J. C., Potter, G. B. & Goldstein, A. P. (1995). *The EQUIP Program: Teaching Youth to Think and Act Responsibly Through a Peer-helping Approach*. Champaign, IL: Research Press.

Gold, M. (1970). *Delinquent Behavior in an American City*. Belmont, CA: Brooks/Cole.

Goldstein, A. P. (1991a). Gang intervention: A historical review. In A. P. Goldstein & C. R. Huff (eds), *Delinquent Gangs: A Psychological Perspective*. Champaign, IL: Research Press, pp. 21–51.

Goldstein, A. P. (1991b). Gang intervention: Issues and opportunities. In A. P. Goldstein & C. R. Huff (eds), *Delinquent Gangs: A Psychological Perspective*. Champaign, IL: Research Press, pp. 477–93.

Goldstein, A. P. & Glick, B. (1987). *Aggression Replacement Training: A Comprehensive Intervention for Aggressive Youth*. Champaign, IL: Research Press.

Goldstein, A. P., Sprafkin, R. P., Gershaw, N. J. & Klein, P. (1980). *Skill-streaming the Adolescent: A Structured Learning Approach to Teaching Prosocial Skills*. Champaign, IL: Research Press.

Gottfredson, G. D. (1987). Peer group interventions to reduce the risk of delinquent behavior: A selective review and a new evaluation. *Criminology*, **25**, 671–714.

Gregg, V., Gibbs, J. C. & Basinger, K. S. (1994). Patterns of delay in moral judgment by male and female delinquents. *Merrill-Palmer Quarterly*, **40**, 538–53.

Harstad, C. D. (1976). Guided group interaction: Positive Peer Culture. *Child Care Quarterly*, **5**, 109–20.

Hickey, J. E. & Scharf, P. L. (1980). *Toward a Just Correctional System: Experiments in Implementing Democracy in Prisons*. San Francisco, CA: Jossey-Bass.

Jennings, W. S., Kilkenny, R. & Kohlberg, L. (1983). Moral development theory and practice for youthful and adult offenders. In W. S. Laufer & J. M. Day (eds), *Personality Theory. Moral Development and Criminal Behavior*. Lexington, MA: Lexington Books.

Jones, M. (1953). *The Therapeutic Community*. New York: Basic Books.

Kazdin, A. E. (1987). *Conduct Disorders in Childhood and Adolescence*. Newbury Park: Sage.

Kazdin, A. E. (1988). *Child Psychotherapy: Developing and Identifying Effective Treatments*. New York: Pergamon.

Kohlberg, L. (1984). *The Psychology of Moral Development: Essays on Moral Development* Vol. 2. San Francisco, CA: Harper & Row.

Leeman, L. W., Gibbs, J. C. & Fuller, D. (1993). Evaluation of a multi-component group treatment program for juvenile delinquents. *Aggressive Behavior*, **19**, 281–92.

Lickona, T. (1983). *Raising Good Children*. Toronto: Bantam Books.

Luborsky, L. & DeRubeis, R. J. (1984). The use of psychotherapy treatment manuals: A small revolution in psychotherapy research style. *Clinical Psychology Review*, **4**, 5–14.

Martin, F. P. & Osgood, D. W. (1987). Autonomy as a source of prosocial influence among incarcerated adolescents. *Journal of Applied Social Psychology*, **17**, 97–108.

McCorkle, L., Elias, A. & Bixby, F. L. (1958). *The Highfields Story*. New York: Henry Holt.

Samenow, S. E. (1984). *Inside the Criminal Mind*. New York: Random House.

Simonian, S. J., Tarnowski, K. J. & Gibbs, J. C. (1991). Social skills and antisocial conduct of delinquents. *Child Psychiatry and Human Development*, **22**, 17–22.

Sykes, G. M. & Matza, D. (1957). Techniques of neutralization: A theory of delinquency. *American Sociological Review*, **22**, 664–70.

Trevethan, S. D. & Walker, L. J. (1989). Hypothetical versus real-life moral reasoning among psychopathic and delinquent youth. *Development and Psychopathology*, **1**, 91–103.

Vorrath, H. H. & Brendtro, L. K. (1985). *Positive Peer Culture*, 2nd edn. New York: Aldine.

Wasmund, W. C. (1988). The social climates of peer group and other residential programs. *Child and Youth Care Quarterly*, **17**, 146–55.

Yochelson, S. & Samenow, S. E. (1976). *The Criminal Personality: A Profile for Change*, Vol. 1. New York: Jason Aronson.

Yochelson, S. & Samenow, S. E. (1977). *The Criminal Personality: The Change Process*, Vol. 2. New York: Jason Aronson.

7

Aggression Replacement Training: Methods and Outcomes

ARNOLD P. GOLDSTEIN
Syracuse University, New York, USA

BARRY GLICK
New York State Division for Youth, New York, USA

A substantial number of investigators have demonstrated that chronically aggressive or delinquent youth are very frequently weak or lacking in constructive, prosocial behaviors for dealing with provocative, challenging or problematic interpersonal situations (Freedman et al., 1978; Patterson et al., 1975; Spence, 1981). Many of these young people are skilled in fighting, bullying, intimidating, harassing or manipulating others; however, they are frequently inadequate in more socially desirable behaviors such as negotiating differences, dealing appropriately with accusations, and responding effectively to failure, teasing, rejection or anger.

For the past 10 years, we have been developing and evaluating Aggression Replacement Training (ART), our response to this behavior deficit perspective. It is a multimodal, psychoeducational intervention. The primary ART trainers for clients are teachers, counselors, social workers, child-care workers, and others who have direct responsibility for youngsters who frequently behave aggressively. The intervention is made up of the following three components, each of which the youngster attends on a weekly basis.

THE CURRICULUM

Skillstreaming

Skillstreaming is an intervention in which a 50-skill curriculum of prosocial behaviors is systematically taught to chronically aggressive adolescents

---

Clinical Approaches to Working with Young Offenders. Edited by C. R. Hollin and K. Howells.
© 1996 John Wiley & Sons Ltd.

(Goldstein et al., 1980) and younger children (McGinnis & Goldstein, 1984, 1990). The Skillstreaming curriculum is implemented with small groups of youngsters (preferably six to eight) by (a) *modeling* that is, showing several examples of expert use of behaviors constituting the skills in which they are weak or lacking; (b) *role playing*, providing several guided opportunities to practise and rehearse these competent interpersonal behaviors; (c) *performance feedback* or providing praise, reinstruction, and related feedback on how well the youth's role playing of the skill matched the expert model's portrayal of it; and (d) *transfer training*, or encouraging the youth to engage in a series of activities designed to increase the chances that the skills learned in the training setting will endure and be available for use when needed in the youth's real-life environment, whether it be the institution, home, school, community or other real-world setting.

The skills that students learn from these procedures fall into one of six families that compose the entire curriculum and include the following.

1. Beginning social skills (e.g. Starting a conversation, Introducing yourself, Giving a compliment).
2. Advanced social skills (e.g. Asking for help, Apologizing, Giving instructions).
3. Skills for dealing with feelings (e.g. Dealing with someone's anger, Expressing affection, Dealing with fear).
4. Alternatives to aggression (e.g. Responding to teasing, Negotiation, Helping others).
5. Skills for dealing with stress (e.g. Dealing with being left out, Dealing with an accusation, Preparing for a stressful conversation).
6. Planning skills (e.g. Goal setting, Decision making, Setting priorities for solving problems).

Anger Control Training

Anger Control Training (ACT) was first developed by Feindler, Marriott and Iwata (1984). It was partially based on the earlier anger control and stress inoculation research of Novaco (1975) and Meichenbaum (1977). Its goal is to teach youngsters the self-control of anger. In ACT, each young person is required to bring to each session a description of a recent anger-arousing experience (a hassle), which they record in a binder ('hassle log'). For 10 weeks the youngsters are trained to respond to their hassles with a chain of behaviors that include the following.

1. Identifying triggers, (i.e. those external events and internal self-statement that provoke an anger response).
2. Identifying cues (i.e. those individual physical events, such as tightened muscles, flushed faces and clenched fists that let the young person know that the emotion he or she is experiencing is anger).
3. Using reminders (i.e. self-statements, such as 'stay calm', 'chill out', and 'cool down', or non-hostile explanations of others' behavior).
4. Using reducers (i.e. a series of techniques that, like the use of reminders, is designed expressly to lower the individual's level of anger, such as deep

breathing, counting backward, imagining a peaceful scene, or imagining the long-term consequences of one's behavior).

5. Using self-evaluation (i.e. reflecting on how well the hassle was responded to by identifying triggers, identifying cues, using reminders, and using reducers and then praising or rewarding oneself for effective performance).

The trainee, having participated in both Skillstreaming and Anger Control Training, is thus knowledgeable about what to do and what not to do in circumstances that instigate aggression. Because aggressive behavior is so consistently, immediately and richly rewarded in many of the real-world settings in which youngsters live, work, go to school and interact, they may still consciously choose to behave aggressively. Thus, we believed that it was important to add a values-oriented component to this intervention approach. The final component of ART, therefore, is moral education.

Moral Education

Moral education is a set of procedures designed to raise the young person's level of fairness, justice and concern with the needs and rights of others. In a long and pioneering series of investigations, Kohlberg (1969, 1973) demonstrated that exposing youngsters to a series of moral dilemmas (in a discussion group context in which youngsters reason at differing levels of morality) arouses an experience of cognitive conflict whose resolution will frequently advance a youngster's moral reasoning to that of peers in the group who reason at a higher level. Such advancement of moral reasoning is a reliable finding, but, as with other single-component interventions, efforts to use it alone as a means of enhancing actual, overt moral behavior have resulted in mixed success (Arbuthnot & Gordon, 1983; Zimmerman, 1983). We suggest a need for increasing youngsters' levels of moral reasoning because such youngsters did not have in their behavioral repertoires either the actual skills for acting prosocially or for successfully inhibiting antisocial or more aggressive behaviors. We thus reasoned that Kohlberg's moral education has marked potential for providing constructive direction toward sociability and away from antisocial behavior. We have offered the ART curriculum in a variety of lengths, but a 10-week sequence has emerged as a 'core' curriculum, as detailed in Table 7.1.

EVALUATION

Annsville Youth Center

Our first evaluation was conducted at a New York State Division for Youth facility in central New York State (Goldstein et al., 1986). Sixty youth at Annsville were included, most having been incarcerated at this limited-secure institution for such crimes as burglary, unarmed robbery and various drug offenses. Twenty-four youngsters received the 10-week ART program outlined in Table 7.1. As noted earlier, this required them to attend three sessions per week,

Table 7.1 Aggression Replacement Training core curriculum

Week	Skillstreaming	Moral reasoning	Anger control
1	*Expressing a Complaint* 1. Define what the problem is, and who is responsible for it. 2. Decide how the problem might be solved. 3. Tell that person what the problem is and how it might be solved. 4. Ask for a response. 5. Show that you understand his or her feelings. 6. Come to an agreement on the steps to be taken by each of you.	1. The Used Car 2. The Dope Pusher 3. Riots in Public Places	*Introduction* 1. Rationale: Presentation and discussion 2. Rules: Presentation and discussion 3. Training procedures: Presentation and discussion 4. Contracting for ACT participation 5. Initial history taking regarding antecedent provocations–behavioral response–consequences (A–B–C)
2	*Responding to the Feelings of Others (Empathy)* 1. Observe the other person's words and actions. 2. Decide what the other person might be feeling, and how strong the feelings are. 3. Decide whether it would be helpful to let the other person know you understand his or her feelings. 4. Tell the other person, in a warm and sincere manner, how you think he or she is feeling.	1. The Passenger Ship 2. The Case of Charles Manson 3. LSD	*Assessment* 1. Hassle Log: purposes and mechanics 2. Anger self-assessment: physiological cues 3. Anger Reducers: Reducer 1: Deep breathing training Reducer 2: Refocusing: backward counting Reducer 3: Peaceful imagery
3	*Preparing for a Stressful Conversation* 1. Imagine yourself in the stressful provoking situation. 2. Think about how you will feel and why you will feel that way. 3. Imagine that other person in the stressful situation. Think about how that person will feel and why. 4. Imagine yourself telling the other person what you want to say. 5. Imagine what he or she will say. 6. Repeat the above steps using as many approaches as you can think of. 7. Choose the best approach.	1. Shoplifting 2. Booby Trap 3. Plagiarism	*Triggers* 1. Identification of stimuli (a) Direct triggers (from others) (b) Indirect triggers (from self) 2. Role Play: Triggers + cues + anger reducer 3. Review of Hassle Logs
4	*Responding to Anger* 1. Listen openly to what the other person has to say. 2. Show that you understand what the other person is feeling. 3. Ask the other person to explain anything you don't understand. 4. Show that you understand why the other person feels angry. 5. If it is appropriate, express your thoughts and feelings about the situation.	1. Toy Revolver 2. Robin Hood Case 3. Drugs	*Reminders (Anger Reducer 4)* 1. Introduction to self-instruction training 2. Modeling use of reminders under pressure 3. Role play: Triggers + cues + reminders + anger reducer 4. Homework assignments and review of Hassle Log
5	*Keeping Out of Fights* 1. Stop and think about why you want to fight. 2. Decide what you want to happen in the long run. 3. Think about other ways to handle the situation besides fighting. 4. Decide on the best way to handle the situation and do it.	1. Private Country Road 2. New York vs. Gerald Young 3. Saving a Life	*Self-evaluation* 1. Review of reminder homework assignment 2. Self-evaluation of post-conflict reminders (a) Self-reinforcement techniques (b) Self-coaching techniques 3. Review of Hassle Log post-conflict reminders 4. Role play: Triggers + cues + reminders + anger reducer + self-evaluation

6	**Helping Others** 1. Decide if the other person might need and want your help. 2. Think of the ways you could be helpful. 3. Ask the other person if he/she needs and wants your help. 4. Help the other person.	1. The Kidney Transplant 2. Bomb Shelter 3. Misrepresentation	*Thinking Ahead (Anger Reducer 5)* 1. Estimating future negative consequences for current acting out 2. Short-term *vs.* long-term consequences 3. Worst to least consequences 4. Role play: 'If …then …' thinking ahead 5. Role play: Triggers + cues + reminders + anger reducers + self-evaluation + Skillstreaming skill
7	*Dealing with an Accusation* 1. Think about what the other person has accused you of. 2. Think about why the person might have accused you. 3. Think about ways to answer the person's accusation. 4. Choose the best way and do it.	1. Lt. Berg 2. Perjury 3. Doctor's Responsibility	*The Angry Behavior Cycle* 1. Review of Hassle Logs 2. Identification of own anger-provoking behavior 3. Modification of own anger-provoking behavior 4. Role play: Triggers + cues + reminders + anger reducers + self-evaluation + Skillstreaming skill
8	*Dealing with Group Pressure* 1. Thinking about what the other people want you to do and why. 2. Decide what you want to do. 3. Decide how to tell the other people what you want to do. 4. Tell the group what you have decided.	1. Noisy Child 2. The Stolen Car 3. Discrimination	*Full Sequence Rehearsal* 1. Review of Hassle Logs 2. Role play: Triggers + cues + reminders + anger reducers + self-evaluation + Skillstreaming skill
9	*Expressing Affection* 1. Decide if you have good feelings about the other person. 2. Decide whether the other person would like to know about your feelings. 3. Decide how you might best express your feelings. 4. Choose the right time and place to express your feelings. 5. Express affection in a warm and caring manner.	1. Defense of Other Persons 2. Lying in Order to Help Someone 3. Rockfeller's Suggestion	*Full Sequence Rehearsal* 1. Review of Hassle Logs 2. Role play: Triggers + cues + reminders + anger reducer + self-evaluation + Skillstreaming skill
10	*Responding to Failure* 1. Decide if you have failed. 2. Think about both the personal reasons and the circumstances that have caused you to fail. 3. Decide how you might do things differently if you tried again. 4. Decide if you want to try again. 5. If it is appropriate, try again, using your revised approach.	1. The Desert 2. The Threat 3. Drunken Driving	*Full Sequence Rehearsal* 1. Review of Hassle Logs 2. Role play: Triggers + cues + reminders + anger reducer + self-evaluation + Skillstreaming skill

one each of Skillstreaming, Anger Control Training and Moral Education. An additional 24 youths were assigned to a no-ART, Brief Instruction Control group. This condition controlled for the possibility that any apparent ART-derived gains in skill performance were not due to ART *per se*, but, in case youngsters already possess the skills but are not using them, simply to enhanced motivation to display already possessed skills. A third group, the No Treatment Control Group, consisted of 12 youths not participating in ART or Brief Instructions procedures.

The overall evaluation goal of this project was to examine the effectiveness of ART for the purposes of:

1. *Skill acquisition*, i.e. do the youngsters *learn* the 10 prosocial Skillstreaming skills in the ART curriculum?
2. *Minimal skill transfer*, i.e. can the youngsters *perform* the skills in response to new situations, similar in format to those on which they were trained?
3. *Extended skill transfer*, i.e. can the youngsters *perform* the skills in response to a new situation, dissimilar in format and more real-life-like than those on which they were trained?
4. *Anger control enhancement*, i.e. does the youngster actually demonstrate fewer altercations or other acting-out behavior as reflected in weekly Behavior Incidents Reports completed on all participating youth by Center staff?
5. *Impulsiveness reduction*, i.e. is the youngster rated to be less impulsive and more reflective and self-controlled in his interpersonal behavior?

Analyses of study data revealed, first, that youths undergoing ART, compared with both control groups, significantly acquired and transferred (minimal and extended), four of the 10 Skillstreaming skills: Expressing a complaint, Preparing for a stressful conversation, Responding to anger, and Dealing with group pressure. Similarly significant ART versus control groups comparisons emerged on both the number and intensity of in-facility acting out (Behavior incidents measure), as well as on staff-rated impulsiveness.

Following completion of the project's post-testing, in week 11, new ART groups were constituted for the 36 youths in the three control group units. As before, these sessions were held three times per week for 10 weeks, and duplicated in all major respects (curriculum, group size, materials, etc.) the first-phase ART sessions. Our goal in this second phase was an own-control test of the efficacy of ART, with particular attention to discerning possible reductions in acting-out behaviors by comparing, for these 36 youths, their Incident Reports during weeks 11–20 (while in ART) with their Incident Reports from the period (weeks 1–10) when they had served as control group members. Both of the statistical comparisons—the number and severity—conducted to test for replication effects yielded positive results.

For reasons primarily associated with the frequent indifference or even hostility of such real-world significant figures as family and peers to newly performed prosocial skills, there is often very considerable difficulty apparent in intervention efforts with incarcerated delinquents of successfully effecting the transfer to community settings of gains acquired in the more protective and benign training setting. Family and peers frequently serve as reinforcers of anti-social behaviors, ignoring or even punishing constructive alternative actions. Our hope was that ART might serve as a sufficiently powerful inoculation that at least moderate carryover of in-facility ART gains to the community would occur. In order to test for such possible transfer effects, we constructed a global rating measure of community functioning.

During the one-year period following initiation of ART at Annsville, 54 youths were released from this facility. Seventeen had received ART, 37 had not. We contacted the Division for Youth Service Team members (analogous to parole officers) around New York to whom the 54 released youth reported regularly and, without informing the worker whether the youth had or had not received ART, asked the worker to complete the global rating measure on each of the Annsville dischargees. In four of the six areas rated—namely home and family, peer, legal and overall, but not school or work—ART youth were significantly superior in rated in-community functioning than were youth who had not received ART.

MacCormick Youth Center

Our second evaluation of the efficacy of Aggression Replacement Training was conducted at MacCormick Youth Center, a New York State Division for Youth maximum secure facility for male juvenile delinquents between the ages of 13 and 21 (Goldstein et al., 1986). In essence this second evaluation project sought to replicate the exact procedures and findings of the Annsville project, as well as extend them to youth incarcerated for substantially more serious felonies. Fifty-one youth were in residence at MacCormick at the time the evaluation was conducted. Crimes committed by these youths included murder, manslaughter, rape, sodomy, attempted murder, assault and robbery. In all its procedural and experimental particulars, the MacCormick evaluation project replicated the effort at Annsville. It employed the same preparatory activities, materials, ART curriculum, testing, staff training, resident training, supervision and data analysis procedures.

On five of the 10 Skillstreaming skills, significant acquisition and/or transfer results emerge. These findings, as well as for which particular skills it does and does not hold, essentially replicate the Annsville Skillstreaming results. In contrast to the Annsville results, however, the MacCormick data also yielded a significant result on the Sociomoral Reflections Measure. At MacCormick, but not at Annsville, youths participating in moral education sessions grew significantly in moral reasoning stage over the 10-week intervention period.

Regarding overt, in-facility behavior, youth receiving ART, compared with those who did not, increased significantly over their base rate levels ln the constructive, prosocial behaviors they utilize, (e.g. offering or accepting criticism appropriately, employing self-control when provoked) and decreased significantly in their rated levels of impulsiveness. In contrast to the Annsville findings, however, MacCormick youth receiving ART did not differ from controls in either the number or intensity of acting-out behaviors. These latter findings appear to be largely explained by the substantial difference in potential for such behaviors between the two facilities. Annsville, internally, is not a locked facility. The 60 youths live in one dormitory, in contrast to the locked, single room arrangement at MacCormick. The latter's staff is twice the size of that at Annsville and MacCormick operates under a considerably tighter system of sanctions and control than does Annsville. Thus, the opportunity for acting-out behaviors—for these several contextual reasons—are lower *across all conditions* at MacCormick than at Annsville, and thus a 'floor effect' seems to be operating which makes the possibility of decreases in acting-out as a result of ART participation at MacCormick numerically a good bit more difficult than Annsville. At Annsville, such behaviors were contextually more possible at base rate, and this could (and did) decrease over the intervention period. At MacCormick, all youth started low and, probably for these same contextual reasons (e.g. sanctions, controls, rich staffing, etc.), remained low. Their use of prosocial behaviors, in regard to which no floor or ceiling effect influences are relevant, did increase differentially as a function of the ART intervention.

Community-Based Evaluation ART

The findings of our first two investigations reveal Aggression Replacement Training to be a multimodal, habilitation intervention of considerable potency with incarcerated juvenile delinquents. It enhances prosocial skill competency and overt prosocial behavior, it reduces the level of rated impulsiveness, and, in one of the two samples studied, both decreases (where possible) the frequency and intensity of acting-out behaviors and enhances the participants' levels of moral reasoning.

Furthermore, some moderately substantial evidence provided independently reveals it to lead to valuable changes in community functioning. This latter suggestion—combined with the general movement away from residential-based and toward community-based programming for delinquent youth—led to our third evaluation of the efficacy of ART, seeking to discern its value when provided to youths ($n = 84$) on a post-release, living in the community basis (Goldstein et al., 1989). We were aware of the potent contribution to functioning in the community which parents and others may make in the lives of delinquent youth. This belief led to our attempt to discern the effects of offering ART not only to youth but, for training in delivery of reinforcement and in skills reciprocal to those the youths were learning, also to their parents and other family members. Our experimental design is depicted in Table 7.2.

The community-based project is essentially a three-way comparison of ART provided directly to youth plus ART provided to youth's parents or other family members, versus ART for youth only, versus a no ART control group. For the most part, participating youth were assigned to project conditions on a random basis, with departures from randomization becoming necessary on occasion as a function of the five-city, multi-site, time-extended nature of the project. Largely as a result of how long the New York State Division for Youth has aftercare responsibility for youth discharged from their facilities, the ART program offered to project participants was designed to last three months, meeting twice per week, for a planned total of approximately 25 sessions. Each session, 90 minutes to two

Table 7.2 Evaluation design for ART in the community

	Trainee Evaluation Condition		
	I	II	III
ART for delinquent youths	X	X	—
ART for parents and family	X	—	—

hours long, was spent in (1) brief discussion of current life events and difficulties, (2) Skillstreaming skills training (of a skill relevant to the life events/difficulties discussed) and, on an alternating basis, (3) Anger Control Training or Moral Education. Once weekly, an ART session was held for the parents and other family members of a sample of participating youth. Those parents selected to participate, but who did not appear, were provided with ART in a modified form via a weekly home visit or phone visit.

Since the different ART groups that constitute the project's two treatment conditions each chose, in collaboration with their respective trainers, which of the 50 skills that comprise the full Skillstreaming curriculum they wished to learn, different groups learned different (if overlapping) sets of skills. We did not, therefore, examine in our statistical analyses participant change on *individual* skills. Instead, analyses focused upon total skill change for the ART participating youth (Conditions 1 and 2) versus both each other and non-ART control group youth (Condition 3). Results indicated that while they did not differ significantly from one another, the two ART conditions each increased significantly in their overall interpersonal skill competence compared to Condition 3 (no-ART) youth. A similarly significant outcome emerged (both ART groups versus no-ART) for decrease in self-reported anger levels in response to mild (e.g. seeing others abused, minor nuisance, unfair treatment) but not severe (e.g. betrayal of trust, control/coercion, physical abuse) anger-provoking situations.

A particularly important evaluation criterion in delinquency intervention work is recidivism. The very large majority of previously incarcerated youth who recidivate do so within the first six months following release (Maltz, 1984). Thus, the recidivism criterion employed in the current project, rearrest, was tracked for that time period. For Conditions 1 and 2 youth, the six-month tracking period consisted of the first three months during which they received ART, and three subsequent no-ART months. Condition 3 youth, of course, received no ART during the entire tracking period. Analyses examining the frequency of rearrest by condition showed a significant effect for ART participation. Both Condition 1 and Condition 2 youth were rearrested significantly less than were youth not receiving ART. Table 7.3 represents the actual frequency and percentage arrest data by condition.

Comparison of the percentage rearrested rate for the two ART conditions in Table 7.3 reveals a substantial decrement in rearrest when the youth's family (i.e. parent and sibling) are also participating simultaneously in their own ART groups. These latter groups, teaching needed and reciprocal (to what the delinquent youth was learning) interpersonal skills, as well as anger control techniques, may well

Table 7.3   Frequency of rearrest by condition

Condition	Total (*n*)	Rearrested (*n*)	Rearrested (%)
Youth ART + Parent/Sibling ART	13	2	15
Youth ART Only	20	6	30
No ART (control)	32	14	44

have provided for the delinquent youths a more responsive and prosocially reinforcing real-world environment. Perhaps a context was provided in which negotiating instead of hitting in conflict situations was praised, not castigated, or perhaps one supportive of, encouraging of, reinforcing of prosocial, not antisocial, ways of being and doing.

Gang Intervention Project

Our research group's final ART evaluation, in which trainees were all gang members, grew from precisely the same spirit. If our community-based effort 'captured', as seems likely, that part of the delinquent youths' actual interpersonal world made up of family members, and turned it, at least in part, to prosocial reinforcing directions, can the same be done with delinquent gang youth—this time seeking to 'capture' and turn his or her peer group (the gang) in prosocial directions? Can we, our project asked, not only use ART to teach youths to be more prosocial but, when they indeed do behave in such a manner in their real-life peer environment, can they more frequently be met with acceptance, support and even praise for such behaviors by fellow gang members?

This project was conducted in two Brooklyn, New York youth care agencies, the Brownsville Neighborhood Community Youth Action Center, and Youth DARES of Coney Island. Each agency conducted three four-month sequences of ART. Within each sequence, the trainees were all members of the same gang. Also for each sequence, we constituted a control group all of whose members were also from the same gang as one another—though from a different gang from the ART trainees. Thus, across both agencies, 12 different gangs participated in the program, six receiving ART, six as no-ART controls. All the youths, ART and controls, also received the diverse educational, vocational and recreational services offered by the two participating agencies.

Repeated measures analysis of variance crossing project condition (ART versus control) with time of measurement (pre versus post) revealed a significant interaction effect favoring ART participants for each of the seven skills categories, Beginning Social Skills, Advanced Social Skills, Feelings-Relevant Skills, Aggression-Management Skills, Stress-Management Skills and Planning Skills, as well as Total Skills score.

None of the ANOVA comparisons of ART with control group scores for Anger Control yielded significant differences. Of the five community domains, only Work Adjustment yielded a significant difference. This result accords well (and no doubt largely reflects) the real-world employment pattern for project participants. For example, in the months immediately following their ART sequence, the majority of the participating Lo-Lives left their gang and took jobs in one or another retail business. At an analogous point in time, following their own ART participation, a substantial minority of the participating Baby Wolfpack members obtained employment in the construction trades.

Arrest data were available for the youth participating in our first two ART sequences and their respective control groups. Five of the 38 ART participants (13%) and 14 of the 27 control group members (52%) were rearrested during the 8-month tracking period ($\chi^2 = 6.08$, $p < 0.01$). It will be recalled that our primary rationale for working with intact gangs in this project was the opportunity afforded by such a strategy to attempt to 'capture' a major feature of the youths' environment and 'turn it' in prosocial directions. Once having learned the given prosocial behaviors, the transfer and maintenance of them may be facilitated or discouraged by the persons with whom the youth interacts regularly in his or her real-world environment. Our favorable outcome *vis à vis* rearrest implies the possibility that such a more harmonious and prosocially promotive post-ART peer environment may have been created. While it is important that future research examines this possibility more directly, it is of considerable interest to note that very similar rearrest outcomes were obtained in our earlier attempt to create a prosocially reinforcing post-ART environment for delinquent youths by employing this intervention with both them and their families. For these youth (ART for self and family), the rearrest rate on follow-up was 15%. For control group youths, the comparable figure was 43%. Both outcomes parallel closely that found here (13% and 52%) for the presence or absence of a rather different type of 'family'—the youth's fellow gang members.

Other Efficacy Evaluations

Our own four studies of the effectiveness of ART yielded a series of promising findings, both proximal to the ART procedures (i.e. skill acquisition, anger control, enhanced moral reasoning) and distal to it but central to its ultimate purposes (i.e. reduced rearrest, enhanced community functioning). We will now examine the independent findings of other investigators.

Coleman, Pfeiffer and Oakland (in press) evaluated the effectiveness of a 10-week ART program used with behavior disordered adolescents in a Texas residential treatment center. Study results indicated improved participant skill *knowledge* but not actual overt skill behaviors. These authors comment:

> The current study thus provides additional support for the contention that although cognitive gains can be demonstrated, the link to actual behavior is tenuous, especially with disturbed populations. (p. 17).

As our own discussion above would suggest, however, we believe that the likelihood of overt behavioral expression (performance) of newly acquired skills is less a function of the degree of trainee emotional disturbance, and more a matter of both trainee motivation to perform, and staff or other significant persons' perceived receptivity to and likely reward for such overt behaviors.

Coleman, Pfeiffer and Oakland (in press) continue:

Of the ten social skills that were taught, three accounted for the improvement in social skills knowledge: keeping out of fights, dealing with group pressure, and expressing a complaint. The fact that Goldstein *et al.* (1986) also found these same skills to be improved in two separate studies suggests that these skills may be the most responsive to intervention. One plausible explanation is that these three skills may be construed as contributing to self-preservation, especially within the context of residential or institutional living. (p. 15).

Curulla (in press) evaluated (1) a 14-week ART program versus (2) ART without the moral education component, versus (3) a no-ART control condition. Her trainees were 67 young adult offenders being seen in a community intervention setting in Seattle. She reports:

Tendency toward recidivism and actual recidivism were compared among the three groups. Tendency towards recidivism as measured by the Weekly Activity Record, was significantly reduced in the dilemma group [Condition 1 above]. The nondilemma [Condition 2] and control [Condition 3] groups showed no significant reduction. The dilemma group also had the lowest frequency of subsequent offense ... However, the differences in actual recidivism among the three groups did not reach statistical significance due to the low incidence of recorded charges during the six month follow-up. (pp 1–2).

Unlike the result of Coleman, Pfeiffer and Oakland (in press), in Curulla's (in press) study—as in our own—overt acting-out behaviors were significantly reduced via ART participation. However, unlike our own results, post-ART recidivism was not.

Jones (in press) compared ART to moral education and a no-treatment control using a sample of high-aggressive male students in a Brisbane, Australia high school. Her results were consistent and positive:

Compared to the two control conditions, students completing the ART program: showed a significant decrease in aggressive incidences, a significant increase in coping incidences, and acquired more social skills. Students in condition 1 [also] improved on ... self-control and impulsivity ... ART appears to be an effective intervention for aggressive youth within a high school setting. (p. 1).

A final investigation, also affirming of the efficacy of ART, takes this intervention in a new direction. Gibbs and his co-workers in the Ohio Department of Youth Services had for some years employed and evaluated a Positive Peer Culture approach in their work with delinquent youth (see Chapter 6). This technique, described as an 'adult-guided but youth-run small group approach', places major responsibility upon the youth group itself for the management of their living environment, as well as change in youth behavior. Feeling that while youths were successfully motivated to conduct much of their own governance and direction, but that they too frequently lacked the skills and anger-control to do so, Gibbs and his group combined the Positive Peer Culture approach with ART to yield a motivation plus skills-oriented intervention they term EQUIP. Leeman et al. (in press) note:

In EQUIP, moral discussion, anger management, or social skills sessions are designated as 'equipment meetings,' i.e., meetings wherein the group gains 'equipment' for helping group members. (pp 5–6).

Table 7.4 Recidivism (rearrest) outcomes for Aggression Replacement Training for delinquent youths plus significant others

Study	Months Following	Recidivism (%)	
		ART +	No-ART control
1. Youth + family (Goldstein et al., 1986)	4	15	43
2. Youth + peers (gang) (Goldstein et al., 1986)	8	13	53
3. Youth + peers (PPC) (Leeman et al. (in press))	12	15	40

These investigators conducted an efficacy evaluation of EQUIP at a medium-security institution for juvenile felony offenders, the Buckeye Youth Center in Ohio. Three conditions were constituted, EQUIP, a motivational control group, and a no-treatment group. Outcome results were significant and supportive of the EQUIP intervention on both proximal and distal criteria. The investigators comment:

> Institutional conduct improvements were highly significant for the EQUIP relative to the control groups in terms of self-reported misconduct, staff-filed incident reports, and unexcused absences from school. (p. 18).
> Interestingly, whereas the recidivism rate of EQUIP subjects was low (15 percent) at both 6 and 12 months following release, the control group rates worsened from 6–12 months (25 to 35 percent for the motivational control, 30 to 40 percent for the simple passage-of-time control). This pattern suggests that the treatment result is maintained as a stable effect. (p. 19).

Table 7.4 shows the combined results of this investigation (Leeman et al., 1991) and both our family and gang (Goldstein et al., 1986) ART evaluations. In all three studies, each of which yielded significant comparisons of the treatment versus control conditions, ART was offered both to the delinquent youths themselves *and* to those other persons in his or her real-world (parents, fellow gang members or fellow unit members) who serve as arbitrators, reinforcers or punishers of the youths' behavior. As change agents of all types have noted for decades, the client's system is as crucial a treatment target as the client him or herself. These three investigations strongly confirm this assertion.

CONCLUSION

The efficacy evaluations we have presented combine to suggest that ART is an impactful intervention. With considerable reliability it appears to promote skills acquisition and performance, improve anger control, decrease the frequency of acting-out behaviors and increase the frequency of constuctive, prosocial behaviors. Beyond institutional walls, its effects persist, less fully perhaps than when the youth is in the controlled institutional environment, but persist none the less, especially when significant others in the youth's real world environment are simultaneously also recipients of ART. In general, its potency appears to us to be sufficiently adequate that its continued implementation and evaluation with chronically aggressive youngsters is clearly warranted.

REFERENCES

Arbuthnot, J. & Gordon, D. A. (1983). Moral reasoning development in correctional intervention. *Journal of Correctional Education*, **34**, 133–8.

Coleman, M., Pfeiffer, S. & Oakland, T. (in press). Aggression replacement training with behavior disordered adolescents. (Preprints available from M. Coleman, Special Education, University of Texas.)

Curulla, V. L. (in press). Aggression replacement training in the community for adult learning disabled offenders. (Preprints available from V. L. Curulla, Special Education, University of Washington.)

Feindler, E. L., Marriott, S. A. & Iwata, M. (1984). Group anger control training for junior high school delinquents. *Cognitive Therapy and Research*, **8**, 299–311.

Freedman, B. J., Rosenthal, L., Donahoe, C. P., Schlundt, D. G. & McFall, R. M. (1978). A social behavioral analysis of skill deficits in delinquent and non-delinquent adolescent boys. *Journal of Consulting and Clinical Psychology*, **46**, 1448–62.

Goldstein, A. P., Sprafkin, R., Gershaw, N. J. & Klein, P. (1980). *Skillstreaming the Adolescent*. Champaign, IL: Research Press.

Goldstein, A. P., Glick, B., Reiner, S., Zimmerman, D. & Coultry, T. (1986). *Aggression Replacement Training*. Champaign, IL: Research Press.

Goldstein A. P., Glick, B., Irwin, M. J., McCartney, C. & Rubama, I. (1989). *Reducing Delinquency: Intervention in the Community*. New York: Pergamon Press.

Jones, Y. (in press). Aggression replacement training in a high school setting. (Preprints available from Center for Learning & Adjustment Difficulties, 242 Gladstone Road, Dutton Park 4102, Brisbane, Australia.)

Kohlberg, L. (1969). Stage and sequence: The cognitive-developmental approach to socialization. In D. A. Goslin (ed.), *Handbook of Socialization Theory and Research*. Chicago, IL: Rand McNally, pp. 347–480.

Kohlberg, L. (ed.) (1973). *Collected Papers on Moral Development and Moral Education*. Cambridge, MA: Harvard University, Center for Moral Education.

Leeman, L. W., Gibbs, J. C., Fuller, D. & Potter, G. (in press). Evaluation of multi-component treatment program for juvenile delinquents. (Preprints available from J. C. Gibbs, Psychology Dept, Ohio State University, Columbus, OH.)

Maltz, D. (1984). *Recidivism*. New York: Academic Press.

McGinnis, E. & Goldstein, A. P. (1984). *Skillstreaming the Elementary School Child*. Champaign, IL: Research Press.

McGinnis, E. & Goldstein, A. P. (1990). *Skillstreaming in Early Childhood*. Champaign, IL: Research Press.

Meichenbaum, D. H. (1977). *Cognitive-behavior Modification: An Integrative Approach*. New York: Plenum.

Novaco, R. W. (1975). *Anger Control: The Development and Evaluation of an Experimental Treatment*. Lexington, MA: Lexington.

Patterson, G. R., Reid, J. G., Jones, R. R. & Conger, R. E. (1975). *A Social Learning Approach to Family Intervention*. Eugene, OR: Castilia.

Spence, S. H. (1981). Differences in social skills performance between institutionalized juvenile male offenders and a comparable group of boys without offence records. *British Journal of Clinical Psychology*, **20**, 163–71.

Zimmerman, D. (1983). Moral education. In Center for Research on Aggression, *Prevention and Control of Aggression*. New York: Pergamon Press, pp. 210–40.

8

Empirically Based Behavioral Treatment Programs for Families with Adolescents who are at Risk for Failure

LORETTA A. SERNA
University of New Mexico, Albuquerque, USA

JAMES A. SHERMAN AND
JAN B. SHELDON
University of Kansas, Kansas USA

Traditionally, the adolescent years have been identified as a transitional period between childhood and adulthood when adolescents: (a) search for their identity; (b) act impulsively; and (c) attempt to establish independence and autonomy within home and community environments (e.g. Mussen et al. 1984). Although establishing one's identity, independence and autonomy can be admirable goals to seek, many youths exhibit behaviors that are quite disturbing to adults when the youths are attempting to attain their identity and independence or when acting impulsively. These disturbing behaviors can include deviations from state laws, national mores and family rules. Owing to these disturbing deviant exhibitions, many youths have been labeled as adolescents who are at risk for failure within our society.

Technically, the problem behaviors exhibited by these adolescents are countless and vary in severity. For this chapter, though, adolescents who are at risk for failure are defined as youths between 12 and 18 years of age (i.e. the normal age range of the adolescent period) who are referred to the juvenile court but are allowed to remain with their families (i.e. they have committed crimes that the juvenile court judge does not believe are serious enough to warrant placement outside the home) or who are referred to counseling by their parents or teachers. Additionally, although these youths have not committed violent and injurious acts (e.g. murder, rape,

Clinical Approaches to Working with Young Offenders. Edited by C. R. Hollin and K. Howells.
© 1996 John Wiley & Sons Ltd.

suicide attempts, drug abuse, or arson) or been diagnosed as severely disturbed (e.g. schizophrenic), their behavior and interactions with family members, peers or individuals in the community are quite inappropriate (e.g. running away from home, non-compliance in the home and at school). Finally, youths who are at risk for failure are often described as being sources of secondary level disturbances such as familial problems (e.g. arguments between parents) and familial stress (e.g. when parents have to deal with the youth's court involvement).

Because many youths in the United States may exhibit some or all of the above characteristics, the exact number of adolescents who are at risk for failure is unknown. Statistics taken from the *FBI Uniform Crime Reports* (1990) show that 81 000 status offense cases were handled through the juvenile courts in 1987. Additionally, 20.3% of all juvenile crimes were property crimes. Dryfoos (1990) and Schorr (1988) indicate that: (a) 25% of US youth drop out of high school before the age of 18; (b) many urban areas report their dropout rates are more that 50% of their adolescents; (c) increasing numbers of children under the age of 16 are becoming sexually active and few are likely to use contraceptives; and (d) a quarter of sexually active youth will be infected with a sexually transmitted disease before they graduate from high school. Finally, these prevalence reports are most disheartening when one realizes that many of the offenses committed by juveniles go undetected by legal authorities and that many unidentified families are experiencing distress due to the incorrigible behaviors of their adolescent children (McWhirter et al., 1993; Trojanowicz & Morash, 1992).

Even more disheartening than the prevalence reports on offenses committed by adolescents are the outcome reports that many youth who are at risk for failure continue to engage in inappropriate behaviors throughout their adult lives. For example, Glueck and Glueck (1940) reported that many youths with juvenile court records had several contacts with the adult court system after the age of 18 years. Many of these youths had: (a) increased numbers of offenses against persons (e.g. assault of person or family violence); (b) increased numbers of alcohol and drug offenses; (c) received dishonorable discharges from the army or navy; and (d) increased numbers of offenses against property and public welfare (e.g. vagrancy). Since the Gluecks' study was published, several investigators have reported similar outcome results regarding the later lives of many adolescents who exhibited problem behaviors (e.g. Garmezy, 1976). Thus, the issue of adolescents who are at risk for school and community failure is a growing vexation with long-term social repercussions; it is an issue that human service professionals must address.

In reality, human service professionals and researchers have been attending to the issue of adolescents who are at risk for failure for more than 30 years in a variety of service-delivery systems. For example, investigators have initiated treatment programs within institutions (places of incarceration), in clinical settings (e.g. in individual and group psychotherapy), in community social programs (e.g. employment settings and group homes) and in prevention programs (e.g. community diversion programs). Unfortunately, most of the attempts of these professionals have met with limited success in changing these adolescent behaviors (e.g. Trojanowicz & Morash, 1992).

Also, investigators of the 1970s and 1980s have been criticized for providing little new information concerning the treatment programs and the nature and functioning of the social systems within which behavior-problem adolescents interact (Graziano & Mooney, 1984). One of the primary social systems for adolescents is the family and yet very little is known about the families of adolescents who are at risk for failure. Few behavioral investigators have explored, experimentally, the issues of family interactions, family relationships and family social systems. Additionally, few investigators have developed or validated experimentally treatment programs focusing on familial factors related to the problems of adolescents. It seems, therefore, that investigators have faltered in two areas regarding the adolescent who is at risk. First, they have often failed in their attempts to ameliorate the behavior problems of adolescents. Second, they have failed to seek out new and potentially important treatment options concerning the family social system of the adolescent. If success could be achieved in ameliorating problems within the family social system, perhaps success would follow the attempts to ameliorate behavior problems of adolescents who are at risk for failure.

The idea that changes in the family social system might help ameliorate an adolescent's problems seems logical for several reasons. First, the family unit is the only social system that a child will experience for his or her entire childhood and often throughout his or her adulthood. Its importance cannot be minimized when addressing personal and social issues. Second, the amount of social learning taking place within the family unit is an ever changing and ongoing process (Bandura, 1977). Because the possibility of an adolescent learning new and more socially adaptive behaviors within the family structure is great, therapists may be able to change some of the maladaptive behavior patterns (within the family) that are contributing to the behavior problems of the adolescent. Third, the learned social behaviors among family members may be viewed as mutual control systems with each family member's behavior being controlled or maintained by certain contingencies and reinforcement schedules supplied by other family members (Conger, 1977). A positive control system among family members may prove to be an element that is needed if an adolescent's behavior is to change and maintenance is to occur. Finally, family treatment may prove to have long-term personal and behavioral value for the youth, the parents and society as a whole. If youths who are at risk for failure can be treated effectively at home (i.e. the members of the familial social system can facilitate prosocial skills that are adaptive to school, job and family-related situations), the youth may be able to establish a positive long-term relationship with family members, with individuals in the community, and with a future spouse and children of his or her own. Being able to establish a positive network of people may influence a person's social, emotional and professional well-being.

Unfortunately, little empirically based behavioral research has been done in the area of families of adolescents who are at risk for failure. Little is known about the implementation of treatment methods, the reinforcement value of familial relationships, the interaction patterns of adolescents who are at risk and their parents, and the overall treatment costs for families with adolescents who are at risk for failure. Because of the paucity of empirical research in the area of treatment programs for such families, the purpose of this chapter is two-fold in nature: (a) to review briefly and evaluate empirically based behavioral interventions for families with adolescents who are at risk for failure; and (b) to provide recommendations for future investigations in the field of behavioral interventions for such families.

EMPIRICALLY BASED INTERVENTIONS

For the purposes of this chapter, empirically based behavioral interventions for families with adolescents who are at risk for failure in society will refer to behavioral treatment procedures that have been experimentally evaluated for their effectiveness. These procedures may be categorized into three primary intervention areas: (a) behavioral contracting; (b) communication training; and (c) combined treatment interventions. In an attempt to compare and evaluate these different treatment procedures in these three areas, the following will be done: (1) the characteristics of each intervention area will be defined and identified; (2) the rationales for using the specified intervention area will be outlined; (3) the programs employed in the empirical studies under each intervention area will be described and evaluated; and (4) the research efforts and recommendations within each intervention area will be discussed.

BEHAVIOURAL CONTRACTING

Characteristics of Behavioural Contracting

Behavioral contracting is a technique or therapeutic intervention that is used to structure an arbitrated, written agreement between two or more family members whereby the parties agree to provide reinforcement to one another contingent on the performance of certain desired behaviors (DeRizi & Butz, 1975; Stuart, 1971a). This written agreement usually contains five components that outline the *responsibilities* one family member must have for another family member, the *privileges* that are received in return for performing each responsibility, the *bonuses* that are received by meeting long-term contingencies of the contracting conditions, the *sanctions* that are received for not abiding by the conditions of the contract, and the *monitoring* of the contract (Stuart, 1971a). The contract development should include the following steps: (a) selecting and defining the behaviors; (b) identifying rewards; (c) developing an understandable written contract; (d) collecting data on the behaviors being performed and the privileges being given; (e) revising the contract if necessary; (f) continuing the revision and monitoring steps; (g) selecting another set of behaviors (DeRizi & Butz, 1975); and (h) involving each family member in the contract signing (Martin & Pear, 1978). Thus, a therapist can initiate a behavior contract, through the above steps, as a formal written agreement that family members must abide by in order that therapeutic changes take place.

Rationales for Using Behavioral Contracts

There are several reasons why behavioral contracting may be beneficial for families of adolescents who are at risk. One advantage is that well defined behaviors establish clear expectations and predictable consequences for the youth (he/she knows what to expect). A second advantage is that a behavior-monitoring system may be established to determine how much progress the family is making in reaching therapeutic goals. Additionally, the continuous monitoring of family behaviors deters contract violations. A third advantage of implementing a behavior contract is that the contract represents a public commitment to change for family members. When family members make a commitment to the agreement through a ceremoniously drafted and signed contract, they allow the therapist to become a public monitor of their behavior. This commitment, to a non-family member, signifies that all parties consent to being held accountable for their behavior (Martin & Pear, 1978). Finally, a fourth advantage for using behavior contracts with families is based on the idea that the positive reinforcement one family member receives from another family member is a privilege rather than a right. The more positive reinforcement family members receive on a reciprocal basis, the more each person will come to value the relationship (Stuart, 1971a).

Empirical Research on Behavioral Contracting

Four groups of researchers contributed to the initial and most significant research on behavioral contracting (Emshoff & Blakely, 1983; Schumaker, Hovell & Sherman, 1977; Stuart 1971a; Stuart & Lott, 1972; Stuart & Tripodi, 1973, Stuart, Jayaratne & Tripodi, 1976; Stuart et al., 1976; Tharp & Wetzel, 1969). These early researchers conducted investigations whereby contracts were implemented with single families as well as large groups of families. Consistent use of selecting and defining behaviors, identifying rewards and developing written contracts was seen among all investigators. Not all investigators, however, employed sanctions, monitoring systems and contract signatures. Because of the inconsistencies in implementation, a comparison of the studies cannot be attempted. A critique of individual investigations, however, shows that uniform procedures across families were lacking (Tharp & Wetzel, 1969) and no baseline measures were taken in some instances (Stuart, 1971a). Lack of random assignment of subjects occurred in investigations that employed a control-group design (Stuart & Lott, 1972; Stuart & Tripodi, 1973) and primarily subjective measures were used to show differences (Stuart & Tribodi, 1973).

Aside from the noted methodological flaws, these researchers made considerable contributions to the area of behavioral treatment of families with at-risk adolescents. For example, Tharp and Wetzel's pioneer study (1969) indicated the importance of behavioral contracts as an effective treatment program. Stuart (1971a) exemplified the importance of the reciprocity that must occur during the family's negotiation of a behavioral contract. Stuart and Lott, (1972) and Stuart & Tripodi, (1973) introduced the use of teachers as collaborators with families.

These teachers monitored daily school behaviors for parents and indicated that the adolescents' school attendance improved during the contract period. Stuart also indicated that behavioral contracts may contribute to initial improved attitudes of adolescents, but cautioned that these attitudes may dissipate over time. The data of Stuart et al. also indicated that when the number of privileges and bonuses exceeded the number of sanctions and responsibilities, school attendance seemed to increase and court recidivism may be impacted. Finally, Schumaker, Hovell and Sherman (1977) implemented the first methodologically sound study, in which they introduced one of the first home–school contract programs. Their experimental evaluation (a multiple-baseline design) indicated significant change in youth school behaviors.

Because of these reported successes, the use of behavioral contracts seems to merit some attention as a possible option when considering treatment programs for families with adolescents who are at risk. If a behavioral contract is to be considered as a treatment option from families with at risk adolescents, one may wish to identify factors that seem to contribute to the effectiveness of the contract. Six factors that possibly contribute to contract effectiveness, are: (a) specification of behaviors; (b) high ratios of privileges and bonuses as compared to the number of youth responsibilities met; (c) identification of desirable privileges and bonuses; (d) parent and teacher instruction in monitoring behaviors; (e) implementation of effective monitoring systems; and (f) implementation of a system to monitor adult compliance with the contracts schedule of rewards and bonuses.

Recommendation for Further Investigations

Because of the paucity of empirically based behavioral studies that target behavioral contracts for families of adolescents who are at risk for failure, several recommendations for further investigations may be noted. First, one issue of concern involves the programming of maintenance or generalization of changed behaviors. Except for Tharp and Wetzel (1969) and the study of Schumaker, Hovell and Sherman (1977), the maintenance of the attained behavior changes was not measured. Whether youths need continuous contractual monitoring and reinforcement of school behaviors or whether this intervention can be gradually faded out is an important question for school personnel and parents.

A second recommendation concerns parents' ability to implement contract agreements. The parents' inability effectively to implement contract agreements may prove to be a limiting factor in the exchange of responsibilities for privileges. If a contracting system includes a difficult exchange process, parents may find the monitoring of points and privileges difficult. These difficulties could be causal factors in parental negligence in carrying through with agreements. Procedures to simplify the exchange process or to teach parents how to monitor points and point exchanges may need to be developed.

A final recommendation for the use of contracts involves the role of the therapist. Stuart and Lott (1972) indicated that the therapist's ability to arbitrate and to work with each family may have an impact on the success of a behavioral contracting program. Thus, methods for training effective therapists may be researched as well as monitoring a therapist's arbitration skills, the amount of time spent working with families, and the problem areas that are most affected by the therapist's ability.

FAMILY COMMUNICATION TRAINING

Another area of investigation with the families under discussion involves the use of communication programs to ameliorate maladaptive communication patterns among adolescents and their parents.

Characteristics of Communication and Communication Training within Families

Communication among people may be categorized as spoken behaviors and non-spoken behaviors (e.g. Weintraub, 1981). Many communication theorists (e.g. Davis, 1972; Hall, 1966) describe spoken behaviors as being either paralanguage behaviors or verbal behaviors. Paralanguage behaviors are the non-verbal aspects of speech that include voice quality, intonation, pitch, volume and rhythm. Theorists (Davitz & Davitz, 1959) assert that the communication of affect is accomplished through these paralanguage behaviors. In contrast, verbal behaviors are the behaviors that communicate the lexical meaning of a message: its syntax and semantic variables (Skinner, 1957; Walsh, 1983).

The second category of communication, non-spoken behaviors, can also be divided into two subcategories: body language and spatial behaviors (Weintraub, 1981). Body language is often described in terms of a person's gait, posture, gestures, eye contact and facial expressions. These behaviors are said to transmit both intended and non-intended messages. Spatial behavior, on the other hand, involves the way people use the space around them (Sommer, 1965).

As can be seen from the above definition of communication, the investigation of general communication patterns in an individual or among dyads must necessarily be a complex process. This task becomes more complex as one begins to investigate the communication patterns of groups of people such as families. Approaches to studying communication patterns among families have included the investigation of communication patterns in optimally functioning families and in problem families. Clinicians (e.g. Haley, 1976; Minuchin, 1974; Westley & Epstein, 1969) have observed and reported that optimally functioning families exhibit problem-solving abilities, negotiation skills and affectionate behaviors when communicating with one another. Problem families are described differently; for instance, negotiation skills are seldom observed in these families (Minuchin, 1974). Additionally, when problem families do try to problem solve, their attempts are often futile in that problem-solving steps are left out or the problem is never fully resolved (Haley, 1976). Finally, many families that are experiencing problems do not give many affectionate messages such as praise, support, encouragement and empathy (Walsh, 1983).

Rationales for Implementing Communication Training

There are several advantages of incorporating Communication Training into a treatment program for families with adolescents who are at-risk failure. First, increasing positive familial interactions may accelerate the probability that parent–youth relationships will be valued more (Clore & Baldridge, 1968). A second advantage concerns the notion that many families may engage in coercive interactions because of skill deficits or inappropriate attitudinal responses (e.g. Alexander, 1973). If family members are taught how to solve problems, negotiate, appropriately give and accept criticism, and have constructive conversations, they may be more likely to develop skills that alleviate the stress and resentment caused by interpersonal conflicts. A third reason for concentrating on familial communication patterns involves the idea of a democratic environment. Because adolescents are constantly searching for independence from familial ties (Conger, 1977), parents often respond to this behavior by wanting to maintain control. Teaching skills such as negotiation require that each member partake in the bargaining process. Parents may be more likely to allow youths to take part in the decision-making process if youths can communicate well with the parents. Additionally, because youths and parents are involved in the decision-making or negotiation process, they may be more likely to comply with agreed-upon resolutions to problems. The teaching of communication skills among family members, therefore, may increase positive familial interactions, enhance familial relationships, and decrease deviant youth behaviors.

Empirical Research in Communication Training

Behavioral investigators have evaluated two training approaches toward the amelioration of communication problems among adolescents and their parents. The first approach is the delivery of feedback from the therapist or other family members, in which praise is given for improvements that occur in the communication process and criticism and suggestions are given for areas that need improvement (Lysaght & Burchard, 1975, Stuart 1971b). The second approach involves a therapist teaching the parent and youth (verbally or through written materials) how to resolve familial problems through an interaction process (Kifer et al., 1974; Serna et al., 1986). Lysaght and Burchard (1975) and Stuart (1971b) used automated feedback devices (signal lights and tape recorders) to provide feedback to family members. Kifer et al. (1974) focused their inquiries on developing a skill-oriented communication program whereby family dyads were taught the negotiation process so that reciprocal conflict-resolution behaviors could take place. Serna and colleagues (1986) extended Kifer's work by teaching family dyads eight reciprocal communication skills (e.g. giving and accepting positive feedback, giving and accepting negative feedback) to improve the communication process of families involved in the juvenile court system.

A critique of these investigations finds that generalization to larger populations and generalization of treatment procedures to naturally occurring situations were problematic among all studies. In some cases, the experimental evaluation of the treatment was problematic. For example, Stuart (1971b) showed no control for extraneous variables when he implemented an A–B–C experimental design with single family units.

Recommendations for Future Investigations

Of the above studies, only those by Kifer et al. (1974) and Serna et al. (1986) lead to firm conclusions on the effectiveness of communication training for these families. Both studies were able to teach communication skills to parent–adolescent dyads in specific laboratory situations and their use of these skills was generalized to specific follow-up probed conditions in the home.

Although the conclusions drawn from the Kifer et al. and Serna et al. studies do contribute to the body of knowledge regarding the communication between parents and their adolescent who is at risk for failure, several recommendations may be made for future studies in the area: (a) more evaluative measures need to be utilized to assess treatment effects; (b) investigative procedures need to be expanded to examine more complex parent–youth interaction patterns; and (c) generalization and maintenance of treatment procedures need to be investigated further.

COMBINED-TREATMENT PROGRAMS

Although behavioral investigators interested in behavioral contracting and communication training have contributed a substantial body of knowledge in the area of empirically based behavioral treatment programs for families with adolescents who are at risk for failure, the amelioration of problems within these families appears to be quite difficult and complex. Because this difficulty and the complexity of the familial interactions have been recognized by several researchers and clinicians, investigators have combined two or more treatment components in their programs in attempts to accommodate the varied needs of these parents and adolescents.

Characteristics of Combined-Treatment Programs

The most obvious characteristic of combined-treatment programs is the numerous treatment components used to ameliorate the many problems that have been identified among families with adolescents who are at risk. These combined-treatment programs may be categorized according to the use or non-use of a particular treatment component: (a) behavioral contracting in combination with other treatment approaches; and (b) combined-treatment programs without the use of behavioral contracting. In their totality, these combined-treatment programs were developed to address the following familial, parental and adolescent target behaviors: (1) youth behavior problems; (2) youth development problems; (3) youth academic problems; (4) family communication problems; (5) parenting skills deficits; (6) parent–youth relationship problems; and (7) problems concerning the verbalization of negative self-statements among family members.

Rationales for Using Combined-Treatment Programs

There are two primary reasons why combined-treatment programs may be beneficial. One is that combined-treatment programs may be able to address the many skill deficits that seem to be exhibited by members of these families. If various skill deficits are contributing to parent–youth interaction problems as well as youth behavior problems, researchers may be able to provide a treatment program that addresses each deficit area.

A second reason is that investigators can use several treatment components to address extraneous variables (in different settings) that might be counterproductive to those behaviors being treated. A classic example is Wahler's (1980) suggestion that an insular mother's extra-family social contacts may influence her child interaction patterns at home. Wahler stated that the aversive nature of a mother's social contacts with other adults may influence her interactions with her child despite the successful completion of a parent-training program. Employing additional treatment procedures that address the mother's aversive social contacts as well as treatment procedures that address the mother–child interactions may lessen the existing familial problems.

Empirical Research on Combined-Treatment Programs

Behavioral contracting in combination with other treatment programs

There are several studies that use behavioral contracting in combination with other treatment programs that are considered classic studies in the area of behavioral family therapy (Alexander & Parsons, 1973; Barton et al., 1985; Besalel & Azrin, 1981; Blechman, Olson & Hellman, 1976; Blechman et al., 1976; Gordon et al. 1988; Jayaratne, 1978; Klein, Alexander & Parsons, 1977; Parsons & Alexander, 1973; Weathers & Liberman, 1975). Researchers combined the use of behavioral contracts with other novel treatment approaches such as: (a) positive interruption; (b) negotiation; (c) electronic devices for feedback; (d) family contract games; (e) decision-making skills, problem-solving skills; (f) behavior management techniques that include self-correction, overcorrection, and positive practice; and (g) communication training that includes happy talk, positive requests and no-blame procedures. Additionally, these researchers identified and developed their interventions for several familial and adolescent problems. The many problem behaviors included: (1) parent–child relationships; (2) verbal abuse; (3) parent off-task behavior; and (4) conversation. Of most importance is the contribution of Besalel and Azrin (1981) for introducing the notion of reciprocal interactions among parents and their youth. Although the behavioral contract and the skill of negotiation foster reciprocity among family members, Besalel and Azrin actually labeled and attempted to teach reciprocal communication skills among family members. This approach gives responsibility to both parent and youth and recognizes the role of reciprocal interactions in the communication patterns of family members.

Combined-treatment programs without the use of behavioral contracts

The number of researchers (Bright & Robin, 1981; Burdsal & Buel, 1980; Druckman, 1979; Foster, Prinz & O'Leary, 1983; Gant et al. 1981; McPherson, McDonald & Ryer, 1983; Patterson, Cobb & Ray, 1973; Patterson & Reid, 1973; Reid & Patterson, 1976, Robin, 1981; Robin et al., 1977; Serna et al., 1991) using a combination of other treatment programs without the major component of behavioral contracting is growing. These investigators have relied on communication skills as well as behavior management techniques as their primary components. For example, problem solving, communication training, didactic dialogue, giving rationales, negotiation and cognitive restructuring have been used in order to change the interaction patterns of these families. Behavior management techniques such as defining behaviors, observing and recording behaviors, praise, tokens, self-management, and time-out from positive reinforcement have been part of various treatment packages. Only two studies (Gant et al., 1981 and Serna et al., 1991) took place in the home. The study of Serna et al. is of particular interest because it featured a Family Conference session that taught family members to use communication skills to resolve family conflicts. Additionally, this study actually measured the communication skills in natural occurring situations within the home. This procedure has been lacking in many of the family studies, but is of importance for the purpose of determining the generalization of treatment effects to the home environment.

Recommendation for Future Investigations

Although the positive aspects of these empirically based investigations into combined-treatment programs for families with at-risk adolescents are of great importance, several deficit areas may be found in the above studies. Several recommendations may, therefore, be made for future investigators into these treatment programs: (a) measuring specific behaviors targeted for change in the treatment program; (b) specifying treatment procedures for the purposes of replication; (c) obtaining reliability measures; (d) conducting component analyses of the treatment programs; (e) utilizing additional objective measures and direct measures of naturally occurring situations; (f) utilizing experimental procedures that control for extraneous variables; and (g) obtaining consumer satisfaction and social validation measures.

DISCUSSION

This brief review of the literature associated with the research on treatment programs for families with adolescents who are at-risk for failure indicates that these programs have progressed from single-component interventions to multi-component treatment efforts. Additionally, Druckman (1979), McPherson et al. (1981), and Sema et al (1986; 1991) were among the first investigators to specifically develop and use group training programs as well as individual family treatment procedures for parents and adolescents, as opposed to using individual family treatment procedures alone. Also, a few investigators (i.e. Gant et al., 1981; Lysaght & Burchard, 1975; Serna et al., 1991; Stuart, 1971a; Weathers & Liberman, 1975) conducted their treatment programs within the home environment where the problems were actually occurring. Finally, although one investigator indicated that siblings were involved in their treatment program, one should note that Besalel and Azrin did involve the parents, youth and relevant persons (e.g. policemen, victims of a crime, teachers) in their negotiation of behavioral contracts.

Contributions Made to the Field

From the above overview, two major contributions are seen to have been made to empirically based treatment programs for families with adolescents who are at risk for failure. One involves the many ideas concerning treatment efforts that have been provided for clinicians and researchers. Over 25 treatment components have been suggested for the treatment of such families.

Additionally, three groups of investigators (Kifer et al., 1974; Schumaker, Hovell & Sherman, 1977; Serna et al., 1986; 1991) contributed to the literature concerning treatment programs for families with behavior-problem adolescents by choosing experimental designs that directly controlled for extraneous variables. Because of the chosen experimental designs (i.e. multiple baseline designs across families/subjects), these investigators demonstrated that their treatment intervention(s) were solely responsible for the change in the targeted behaviors. Thus one may conclude that parent–adolescent dyads can learn specific negotiation statements (Kifer et al., 1974), that behavioral contracts (implemented in the home and school) can aid in improving adolescent school behaviors and school grades (Schumaker, Hovell & Sherman 1977), and that reciprocal communication skills coupled with a family-conference procedure in the home can serve as an effective conflict resolution procedure in the home environment (Serna et al. 1991).

Future Treatment Programs

Building on the knowledge that the above researchers have provided, we have learned that home-based multi-component treatment components can serve as vital tools when working with families with adolescents who are at risk for failure. We also know that the problems of these families are quite complex and need the work of many service providers. It is, therefore, recommended that researchers look toward the use of several programs when working with these families. Developing comprehensive assessment instruments such as a Functional Analysis Assessment (Robin, Koepke & Moye, 1990) may prove to be effective in developing meaningful treatment procedures. Incorporating Individual Family Treatment Plans (Sheldon et al., in preparation) for the purpose of coordinating services as well as meeting the individual needs of the family may be explored. Finally, teaching the family new skills to meet the demands of today's world must also be addressed. These skills may vary, yet the family must work together through Family Action plans (Serna & Lau-Smith, 1995) that will help them focus on the skills they need to develop and on how other family members can support the adolescent toward appropriate independence, functional dependence, and productivity in the community.

REFERENCES

Alexander, J. F. (1973). Defensive and supportive communication in normal and deviant families. *Journal of Consulting and Clinical Psychology*, **40**, 223–31.

Alexander, J. F. & Parsons, B. V. (1973). Short-term behavioral intervention with delinquent families: Impact on family process and recidivism. *Journal of Abnormal Psychology*, **81**, 219–25.

Bandura, A. (1977). *Social Learning Theory*. New York: General Learning Press.

Barton, C., Alexander, J. F., Waldron, H., Turner, C. W. & Warburton, J. (1985). Generalizing treatment effects of functional family therapy: Three replications. *American Journal of Family Therapy*, **13**, 16–26.

Besalel, V. A. & Azrin, N. H. (1981). The reduction of parent–youth problems by reciprocity counseling. *Behavior Research and Therapy*, **19**, 297–301.

Blechman, E. A., Olson, D. H. L. & Hellman, I. D. (1976). Stimulus control over family problem-solving behavior: The family contract game. *Behavior Therapy*, **7**, 686–92.

Blechman, E. A., Olson, D. H. L., Schornagel, C. Y., Halsdorf, M. J. & Turner, A. J. (1976). The family contract game: Technique and case study. *Journal of Consulting and Clinical Psychology*, **44** 449–55.

Bright, P. D. & Robin, A. L. (1981). Ameliorating parent–adolescent conflict and problem-solving communication training. *Journal of Behavior Therapy and Experimental Psychiatry*, **12**, 275–80.

Burdsal, C. & Buel, C. L. (1980). A short-term community based early stage intervention program for behavior-problem youth. *Journal of Clinical Psychology*, **36**, 226–41.

Clore, L. G. & Baldridge, B. (1968). Interpersonal attraction: The role of agreement and topic interest. *Journal of Personality and Social Psychology*, **9**, 340–6.

Conger, J. J. (1977). *Adolescence and Youth: Psychological Development in a Changing World*. (2nd edn). New York: Harper and Row.

Davis, M. (1972). *Understanding Body Movement: An Annotated Bibliography*. New York: Arno Press.

Davitz, J. R. & Davitz, L. J. (1959). The communication of feelings by content-free speech. *The Journal of Communication*, **9**, 6–13.

DeRizi, W. & Butz, G. (1975). *Writing Behavioral Contracts*. Champaign, IL: Research Press.

Druckman, J. M. (1979). Program for female status offenders. *Journal of Marriage and the Family*, **August**, 627–35.

Dryfoos, J. G. (1990). *Adolescents at Risk: Prevalence and Prevention*. New York: Oxford Press.

Emshoff, J. G. & Blakely, C. H. (1983). The diversion of delinquent youth: Family-focused intervention. *Children and Youth Review*, **5**, 343–56.

FBI Uniform Crime Report. (1990). *Crime in the United States, 1989*. Washington, DC: US Government Printing Office.

Foster, S. L., Prinz, R. J. & O'Leary, K. D. (1983). Impact of problem-solving communication training and generalization procedures on family conflict. *Child and Family Behavior Therapy*, **5**, 1–23.

Gant, B. L., Barnard, J. D., Kuehn, F. E., Jones, H. H. & Christophersen, E. R. (1981). A behaviorally based approach to improving intrafamilial communication patterns. *Journal of Clinical Child Psychology*, **Summer**, 102–6.

Garmezy, N. (1976). The experimental study of children vulnerable to psychopathology. In A. Davids (eds), *Child Personality and Psychopathology*, Vol. 2. New York: Wiley.

Glueck S. & Glueck, E. (1940). *Juvenile Delinquents Grown Up*. New York: Oxford University Press.

Gordon, D. A., Arbuthnot, J., Gustafson, K. E. & McGreen, P. (1988). Home-based behavioral-systems family therapy with disadvantaged juvenile delinquents. *American Journal of Family Therapy*, **16**, 243–54.

Graziano, A. M. & Mooney, K. C. (1984). *Children and Behavior Therapy*. New York: Aldine Publishing.

Haley, J. (1976). *Problem-solving Therapy. New Strategies for Effective Family Therapy*. San Francisco, CA: Jossey-Bass.

Hall, E. T. (1966). *The Hidden Dimension*. New York: Doubleday.

Jayaratne, S. (1978). Behavioral intervention and family decision-making. *Social Work* **23**, 20–5.

Kifer, R. E., Lewis, M. A., Green, D. R. & Phillips, E. L. (1974). Training predelinquent youths and their parents to negotiate conflict situations. *Journal of Applied Behavior Analysis*, **7**, 357–64.

Klein, N. C., Alexander, J. F. & Parsons, B. V. (1977). Impact of family systems intervention on recidivism and sibling delinquency: A model of primary prevention and program evaluation. *Journal of Consulting and Clinical Psychology*, **43**, 469–74.

Lysaght, T. V. & Burchard, J. B. (1975). The analysis and modification of a deviant parent–youth communication pattern. *Journal of Behavior Therapy and Experimental Psychiatry*, **6**, 339–42.

Martin, G. & Pear, J. (1978). *Behavior Modification: What it is and How to Do it*. Englewood Cliffs, NJ: Prentice Hall.

McPherson, S. J., McDonald, L. E. & Ryer, C. W. (1983). Intensive counseling with families of juvenile offenders. *Juvenile and Family Court Journal*, **February**, 27–33.

McWhirter, J. J., McWhirter, B. T., McWhirter, A. M. & McWhirter, E. H. (1993). *At-risk Youth: A Comprehensive Response*. Pacific Grove, CA: Brooks/Cole.

Minuchin, S. (1974). *Families and Family Therapy*. Cambridge. MA: Harvard University Press.

Mussen, P. H., Conger, J. J., Kagan, J. & Huston, A. C. (1984). *Child Development and Personality*. New York: Harper and Row.

Parsons, B. V. & Alexander, J. F. (1973). Short-term family intervention: A therapy outcome study. *Journal of Consulting and Clinical Psychology*, **41**, 195–201.

Patterson, G. R. & Reid, J. B. (1973). Intervention for families of aggressive boys: A replication study. *Behavior Research and Therapy*, **11**, 1–12.

Patterson, G. R., Cobb, J. A. & Ray, R. S. (1973). A social engineering technology for retraining the families of aggressive boys. In H. E. Adams and I. P. Unikel (eds), *Issues and Trends in Behavior Therapy*. Springfield, IL: Charles C. Thomas, pp. 139–224.

Reid, J. B. & Patterson, G. R. (1976). The modification of aggression and stealing behavior of boys in the home setting. In A. Bandura & E. Ribes (eds), *Behavior Modification: Experimental Analyses of Aggression and Delinquency*. Hillsdale, NJ: Lawrence Erlbaum, pp.l 123–45.

Robin, A. L. (1981). A controlled evaluation of problem-solving communication training with parent–adolescent conflict. *Behavior Therapy*, **12**, 593–609.

Robin, A. L., Koepke, T. & Moye, A. (1990). Multidimensional assessment of parent–adolescent relations. *Psychological Assessment*, **3**(4), 451–9.

Robin, A. L., Kent, R., O'Leary, K. D., Foster, S. L. & Prinz, R. (1977). An approach to teaching parents and adolescents problem-solving communication skills. A preliminary report. *Behavior Therapy*, **8**, 639–43.

Schumaker, J. B., Hovell, M. F. & Sherman, J. A. (1977). An analysis of daily report cards and parent-managed privileges in the improvement of adolescent classroom performance. *Journal of Applied Behavior Analysis*, **10**, 449–64.

Serna, L. A. & Lau-Smith, J. N. (1995). Learning with PURPOSE: Self-determination skills for students who are at-risk for school and community failure. *Intervention in School and Clinic*, **30**(3), 142–6.

Serna, L. A., Schumaker, J. B., Hazel, J. S. & Sheldon, J. B. (1986). Teaching reciprocal social skills to parents and their delinquent adolescents. *Journal of Clinical Child Psychology*, **15**, 64–77.

Serna, L. A., Schumaker, J. B., Sherman, J. A. Sheldon, J. B. (1991). In-home generalization of social interactions in families of adolescents with behavior problems. *Journal of Applied Behavior Analysis*, **24**(4), 733–46.

Sheldon, J. B., Sherman, J. A., Keeling, C., Gauna, T. & Elwell, A. (in preparation). Family enhancement: An intensive in-home family treatment program for families with adolescents with behavior problems.

Schorr, L. B. (1988). *Within our Reach: Breaking the Cycle of Disadvantage*. New York: Doubleday.

Skinner, B. F. (1957). *Verbal Behavior*. New York: Appleton-Century-Crofts.

Sommer, R. (1965). Further studies of small group ecology. *Sociometry*, **28**, 337–48.

Stuart, R. B. (1971a). Behavioral Contracting within the families of delinquents. *Journal of Behavior Therapy and Experimental Psychiatry*, **2**, 1–11.

Stuart, R. B. (1971b). Assessment and change of the communicational patterns of juvenile delinquents and their parents. In R. D. Rubin, H. Fensterheim, A. A. Lazarus & C. M. Franks (eds), *Advances in Behavior Therapy: Proceedings of the Third Conference of the Association for Advancement of Behavior Therapy*. New York: Academic Press.

Stuart, R. B. & Lott, L. (1972). Behavioral contracting with delinquents: A cautionary note. *Journal of Behavior Therapy and Experimental Psychiatry*, **3**, 161–9.

Stuart, R. B. & Tripodi, T. (1973). Experimental evaluation of three time-constrained behavioral treatments for predelinquents and delinquents. In R. D. Rubin, J. P. Brady & J. D. Henderson (eds), *Advances in Behavior Therapy*, Vol. 4. New York: Academic Press.

Stuart, R. B., Jayaratne, S. & Tripodi, T. (1976). Changing adolescent deviant behavior through reprogramming the behaviour of parents and teachers: An experimental evaluation. *Canadian Journal of Behavior Science*, **8**, 132–44.

Stuart, R. B., Tripodi, T., Jayaratne, S. & Camburn, D. (1976). An experiment in social engineering in serving the family of predelinquents. *Journal of Abnormal Child Psychology*, **4**, 243–61.

Tharp, R. G. & Wetzel, R. J. (1969). *Behavior Modification in the Natural Environment*. New York: Academic Press.

Trojanowicz, R. C. & Morash, M. (1992). *Juvenile Delinquency: Concepts and Control*. Englewood Cliffs, NJ: Prentice Hall.

Wahler, R. G. (1980). The insular mother: Her problems in parent–child treatment. *Journal of Applied Behavior Analysis*, **13**, 207–19.

Walsh, F. (1983). *Normal Family Process*. New York: The Guilford Press.

Weathers, L. & Liberman, R. P. (1975). Contingency contracting with families of delinquent adolescents. *Behavior Therapy*, **6**, 356–66.

Weintraub, W. (1981). *Verbal Behavior: Adaptation and Psychopathology*. New York: Springer.

Westley, W. A. & Epstein, N. B. (1969). *The Silent Majority*. San Francisco, CA: Jossey-Bass.

Part 4
Working with Offences

9

Adolescent Sex Offenders

JUDITH V. BECKER, BRADLEY R. JOHNSON AND JOHN A. HUNTER JR
University of Arizona, Tucson, USA

INTRODUCTION

Over the past decade there has been increased attention paid to youth who commit sexual offenses. In the United States it has been estimated that 20% of all rapes and 30–50% of cases of child molestation are perpetrated by adolescent males (Becker et al., 1986). Sexual offenses committed by juveniles are not limited to adolescent or postpubescent males. An increasing number of juvenile females have been identified as perpetrating offenses against children of both genders. There has also been growing awareness in the United States that prepubescent children have also committed offenses involving molestation and at times sexual aggression (Hunter, 1993), although little in the way of systematic data collection on these populations has appeared in the literature to date.

There has, however, been an increasing data base on adolescent male sexual offenders, which this paper will address. Prior to 1980 there were only 19 major papers published on the topic of youthful sexual offenders (Barbaree, Hudson & Seto, 1993). A recent literature review found 73 citations in the psychological literature referencing youthful sexual offenders (Becker, Harris & Sales, 1993). As greater attention has been focused on youth who commit sex offenses, there has been an increasing number of mental health professionals specializing in the assessment and treatment of this population. There are at present approximately 1000 mental health professionals in the US who provide services to this population.

As a result of the need for a forum among these professionals in the United States, the National Adolescent Perpetrator Network was founded. Members of that network supported the formation of a National Task Force. That task force

---

Clinical Approaches to Working with Young Offenders. Edited by C. R. Hollin and K. Howells.
© 1996 John Wiley & Sons Ltd.

published its Preliminary Report in 1988 (National Adolescent Perpetrator Network, 1988) and recently published its Revised Report (National Task Force Report, 1993). This report describes basic principles and guidelines for evaluating and treating youthful sexual offenders and is highly recommended reading for any clinician who is considering working with this population.

Brief Literature Review

For reasons of space, a comprehensive review of the literature is not possible, and only a brief synopsis will be presented. Those readers interested in a more detailed review are referred to Barbaree, Hudson and Seto, 1993; Becker, Harris and Sales, 1993; and Morenz and Becker (in press).

To date there are no generally accepted theories or models that explain the etiology of youthful sexual offending. Currently two models can be found in the published literature which address this issue. Ryan et al. (1987) described a 'sexual assault cycle' and identified six steps leading to escalating dysfunction in juveniles.

Becker and Kaplan (1988), working from a cognitive-behavioral framework, have identified three potential pathways a juvenile may take after having engaged in inappropriate sexual behavior: (a) the 'dead end path', where he no longer commits any further sexual offenses; (b) the 'delinquency path', where the youth continues to commit sexual as well as non-sexual offenses, and (c) the 'sexual interest path', where the adolescent continues to commit sex crimes and often develops a paraphiliac arousal pattern. It is important to note that none of these models has been empirically validated.

Recently, a conceptual model was proposed by Figueredo and McCloskey (in press, a). This model, which has received partial empirical support (Kobayashi et al., in press), proposes a graded continuum of sexual tactics used by males ranging from the coerciveness of subtle pressure to overtly violent assault. Violence is seen as instrumental in the pursuit of sexual gratification, rather than as a behavioral end in itself. A preliminary test of the theory revealed that there are multiple causal pathways to a sexual offense being committed and that psychosocial deficiency was a strong predictor of non-criminal sexuality (sexual variations). Non-criminal sexuality was predictive of non-sexual criminality. Non-sexual criminality was the strongest predictor of sexual criminality. Further research is warranted to investigate the etiology and identify the multiple causal pathways to youthful sexual offending.

Adolescent sexual offenders form a heterogeneous group and come from all socio-economic and ethnic backgrounds. They often display many of the same variations in sexually abusive behaviors that are seen in adult offenders. Their offenses range from 'hands off offenses' such as voyeurism and exhibitionism to 'hands on offenses' such as molestation, fondling and penetration (oral, anal, vaginal).

Several characteristics have been found to be associated with juvenile sexual offending. These include: a history of delinquency or conduct-disordered behavior (Kavoussi, Kaplan & Becker, 1988; Saunders, Awad & White, 1986);

familial dysfunction and histories of prior physical and sexual maltreatment (Awad, Saunders & Levene, 1984, Becker et al., 1986, Blaske et al., 1989); and academic dysfunction, including lower achievement and school-related behavioral problems (Awad & Saunders, 1989). A high incidence of psychiatric co-morbidity has also been found in this clinical population, with over 40% showing signs of significant depressive symptomatology (Becker et al., 1991). Further research needs to be conducted to determine the frequency of the above characteristics in juvenile sexual offenders relative to other youthful clinical populations.

Two taxonomic systems for the categorization of youthful sex offenders have been proposed (Knight & Prentky, 1993; O'Brien & Bera, 1986), but neither has been experimentally validated to date. O'Brien and Bera (1986) describe seven types: Naive experimenter, Group influenced, Disturbed impulsive, Low social competence, Early childhood abuse, Impulsive life-style, and Sexual pre-occupation and compulsivity.

The second taxonomic system (Knight & Prentky, 1993) was observed from work with adult sexual offenders (Knight & Prentky, 1990). The subjects used to develop the system were 564 adult male sex offenders. These subjects were categorized into three groups: those who had committed sex offenses as juveniles and had been charged or committed; those who had committed offenses as adolescents but were never apprehended; and those who had not been charged with a sex crime during adolescence. They were further classified as to whether they had engaged in rape or child molestation. Results indicated that those who had committed offenses prior to age 19 were defined by low social competence and higher life-style impulsivity and criminal activity.

Treatment of adolescent offenders should be based on the needs of each youth as determined by a comprehensive assessment of the youth and his/her family. There is only one controlled therapy outcome study in the literature to date. Borduin et al. (1990) compared 'multisystemic' therapy with individual therapy. The multisystemic therapy consisted of a focus on personal, family and academic issues and was multi-modal. Follow-up was from 21 to 49 months. For those receiving the multisystemic therapy, 12.5% recidivized compared with 75% for those receiving only individual therapy.

Practical Issues in Working with Adolescent Sex Offenders

There are many important practical issues that must be mentioned briefly in this discussion, including problems with denial, methods of assessment, issues of treatment, and aftercare.

Before embarking on actual assessment and treatment, one must realize that a major obstacle likely to be encountered is denial and minimization on the part of both the adolescent offender and his/her family (Becker, 1988; Bethea-Jackson & Brissett-Chapman, 1989; French, 1989a; French 1989b; Margolin, 1984; McConaghy et al., 1989; Rowe, 1988; Ryan et al., 1987; Shoor, Speed & Bertelt, 1966). Denial may stem from issues of shame, embarrassment, difficulty in discussing sexual issues, fear of consequences or difficulty divulging family secrets.

Offenders may completely deny or may simply minimize their sexual offenses. Scully and Marolla (1984) found that adult rapists often distorted the nature of their offense(s) so that they did not have to accept full responsibility for their behaviors. Denial or distortion can impede assessment and treatment, thus leading many treatment programs to refuse adolescents who deny their offenses (Lombardo & DiGiorgio-Miller, 1988; Stenson & Anderson, 1987). While some programs will not accept juveniles who are in denial, others will accept them for a limited period of time. In these programs, if the juvenile does not acknowledge responsibility for the sexual misbehavior after a specified period of time he is terminated from treatment and referred back to the Juvenile Court.

The timing and methods of assessment are critical. Clinical evaluations of adolescent offenders are recommended to be conducted post-adjudication and pre-sentencing (Hunter, 1993). Prior to clinical interviews, it is important to review juvenile court and police records, psychiatric or psychological reports, pertinent medical records, and victim statements. Victim statements are especially important when the offender denies or minimizes his/her offense(s) (Becker & Hunter, 1992).

The most valuable part of the assessment process is the clinical interview with both the juvenile and his/her family (Becker & Kaplan, 1993). It is helpful to meet with the parents and with the youth, but it is imperative that the adolescent be interviewed privately. The clinical interview should start with a complete evaluation including: demographic information, history of presenting problem(s), psychiatric history, family history, social history (including developmental history, peer relationships, academic history, history of maltreatment, drug and alcohol history), medical history, and a comprehensive mental status examination. However, the clinical assessment of a sexual offender must also include a detailed psychosexual history, including: sexual behaviors, fantasies, and exposure to the sexual behaviors of others and to pornography. It is also important to obtain a detailed legal history including non-sexual delinquent behaviors.

A general psychiatric history is especially important given the high incidence of co-morbidity seen in this population. Clinicians should be especially sensitive to the presence of learning disabilities, affective disorders, post-traumatic stress disorder, attention deficit hyperactivity disorder, conduct disorders, substance abuse, and personality disorders in these youth (Awad & Saunders, 1989; Becker et al., 1991; Hunter et al., 1993; Hunter & Goodwin, 1992).

Owing to the high presence of co-morbid conditions, when there are psychiatric diagnostic dilemmas, one may want to consider the use of generalized psychological testing. Although a good clinical examination is often sufficient, in some cases intelligence and personality assessment can be helpful. It is important to note that there are no specific psychological tests or instruments that identify whether a juvenile is a sexual offender, has a specific sexual disturbance, or is at high risk for reoffending. However, one may gain useful information from such paper-and-pencil tests as: the MMPI-A; the Adolescent Sexual Interest Cardsort (Becker & Kaplan, 1988), a 64-item self-report measure to determine the presence of deviant sexual interests; the Adolescent Cognition Scale (Hunter, Becker & Goodwin, 1991), a 32-item test to measure false beliefs regarding sexual behavior; and the Multi-Phasic Sex Inventory (Nichols & Molinder, 1984), an instrument with 21 clinical scales including those that differentiate types of sexual offenders and assess sexual attitudes and cognitions.

Finally, phallometric assessment (psychophysiological measurement of penile tumescence) of sexual arousal can be used with some pubescent youth who demonstrate repeated age-appropriate sexual acting out or sustained deviant sexual interest. This assessment could be helpful in diagnosis, treatment planning and evaluation of treatment efficacy, but should be used in accordance with established guidelines (ATSA, 1993). Unfortunately there are few studies in the literature addressing issues of reliability and validity with this population. Furthermore, this form of assessment should not be used to determine whether an individual actually committed a sexual offense, especially in the sense of determining legal guilt or innocence.

Treatment of adolescent sex offenders should be highly structured (Groth et al., 1981; Margolin, 1984; Ryan et al., 1987), and should be based on the needs of the individual offender as determined through comprehensive assessment. Common modalities found to be successful include individual and group cognitive-behavioral therapies, family therapy, psychoeducational interventions, relapse prevention therapies, and psychopharmacological interventions. Support for the effectiveness of psychodynamic therapies has not appeared in the research literature. Groups can be especially helpful because offenders learn to establish trusting relationships with peers, can be confronted by peers regarding inappropriate sexual behaviors or beliefs, and learn from each other in regards to social skills and anger control. Small groups (six to ten members) are generally preferable, and one should separate pubescent adolescents from prepubescent offenders. Groups that have members with different types of offenses or paraphilias can help with the group dynamics and subjects covered.

Although disposition of juvenile offenders is a legal matter, clinicians are often asked to make recommendations to the court regarding their treatment needs. In doing so, one must be cognizant of family and community safety issues. Some offenders may require intensive residential services, for example, those individuals who have numerous offenses with more than one victim, used force or aggression, have difficulty with impulse control, have engaged in more invasive forms of perpetration, have strong deviant sexual arousal and interest patterns, have pervasive psychiatric problems, and those with poor motivation for change. Youth who are less disturbed and have strong family support may only require outpatient treatment. Those who manifest moderate levels of psychopathology and familial dysfunction may benefit from in-home support services, after-school programs, or group home/foster home placements.

Given that treatment is often mandated by the court and that sexual offenses are a matter of legal concern, one will benefit from working in conjunction with the Juvenile Probation Department and, when necessary, Child Protective Services. The therapist can especially benefit from getting informed consent from the guardian and adolescent to speak openly with the youth's probation officer. The offender should not remain in the home in cases of incestuous sexual abuse, but may receive treatment while temporarily living in a foster, group or relative's home until it is felt appropriate by both the offender's therapist and the victim's therapist for the offender to return home. Risk assessment on an ongoing regular basis during treatment can help the clinician evaluate the attainment of treatment goals and determine when and if it is safe and appropriate for his/her family and society at large.

As treatment begins and denial is reduced, the offender should be encouraged to develop empathy for the victim and learn self-control. There are a few specific cognitive-behavioral techniques that have been found to be helpful in treating youthful offenders. One technique, verbal satiation (Becker & Kaplan, 1993) requires the adolescent to verbalize deviant thoughts in a repetitive manner to the point of fatiguing or boring themselves with the stimulus that had previously caused sexual arousal. Another technique, covert sensitization, provides the adolescent with skills to disrupt the behaviors that are antecedent to the offender's actual coming into contact with his/her victim. The offender identifies the precursors of their inappropriate behavior, then associates negative consequences with these precursors. In this pattern, it is hoped that the youth can learn to connect consequences to their behaviors. Other areas that are recommended to be covered in treatment include: sex education with discussion of values and morals, social skills, anger management, and relapse prevention. Finally, sex offenders often have distorted or false beliefs regarding sexuality in general, as well as their own sexual thoughts and behaviors (Abel et al., 1984). These cognitive distortions, as they are often called, can be effectively addressed in therapy, especially in a group setting, by allowing the offender to relearn or restructure their beliefs or thoughts.

Pharmacological interventions are presently used and can be helpful in treating concomitant psychiatric illnesses often diagnosed in sexual offenders. In these cases Ritalin, for example, can be used in the treatment of attention deficit hyperactivity disorder, antidepressants (or others) for treatment of affective disorders, and antipsychotics for psychosis and related problems. Additionally, there is a growing literature on adult sex offenders demonstrating the usefulness of antiandrogens, antidepressants, and other psychotropic medications in decreasing sexual drive, paraphiliac thoughts and sexual offending behaviors (Bradford, 1988; Coleman et al., 1992; Condron & Nutter, 1987; Emory, Cole & Meyer, 1992; Federoff & Federoff, 1992; Federoff et al., 1992; Gottesman & Schubert, 1993; Rousseau et al., 1988). Antiandrogen medications can interfere with the normal process of physical pubertal development and therefore are usually restricted to postpubertal males of at least 16 years of age (Bradford, 1993).

If the youth is ever to return home, family therapy is essential so that family system and family dysfunction issues can be addressed. As necessary, other adjunctive treatments may also be important, including treatment for alcohol and drug abuse, remedial educational services, and vocational training. Special populations of concern for treatment include the developmentally disabled, female sex offenders, prepubescent youth, the seriously mentally ill, and adolescents with extensive histories of maltreatment (Gray & Pithers, 1993; Hunter et al., 1993; Knopp & Lackey, 1987; Matthews, 1987; Stermac & Sheridan, 1993).

Aftercare is critical and may entail periodic follow-up contact with the therapist via booster sessions, the court and community support monitoring. There are no specific guidelines in the literature, but it is likely that the longer the period of follow-up, the lower the chances of recidivism. The minimum length of time suggested for frequent follow-up after completion of intensive treatment is 1 year. Less frequent follow-up may need then to occur for many years to prevent chances for recidivism. The goal of relapse prevention is to assist the offender in developing awareness of high-risk situations and decisions that lead to reoffending.

Two Illustrative Cases

Case A

R. was a 14-year-old Hispanic boy who was referred for a juvenile court presentencing evaluation secondary to sexual assault of a 13-year-old girl.

Having had a normal childhood, R. was raised in a small rural community. His parents divorced when he was 6 years old; R.'s father gained legal custody and never remarried. Past medical, psychiatric and family history was reported to be unremarkable. R. achieved above-average grades in elementary school, but began having academic difficulty in middle school. He was increasingly truant and involved with a gang. R.'s legal history included shoplifting, trespassing and disorderly conduct. Since his arrest for sexual assault, he had broken curfew on three occasions. He smoked cigarettes, but denied any alcohol or illicit drug use.

On the day prior to his arrest for sexual assault, R. reported having gone to a convenience store to 'hang around'. While there, he met a 13-year-old girl and began to talk about school. Within 30 minutes, he claimed that they consensually held each others hands' and walked to the back of the store in order to talk further. However, the evaluation continued and after further discussion, R. admitted to having forcibly taken the 13-year-old girl to the back of the store saying 'if she hadn't wanted to go back there with me, she would have left on her own'. Having forced her to kneel on the ground, he instructed her to perform fellatio and have intercourse with him. She refused and ran, hiding behind a nearby tree. Catching up with her, he again grabbed her and forced her down. He laid on top of her and forced his hand under her blouse, fondling her breasts. The victim reported that R. had also forced his hands down her pants, touching her genitals. He denied that this had happened. The victim once again attempted to leave and R. grabbed her and cut her hand with a piece of broken glass. As she began to bleed, R. reported feeling sorrow for his actions. He denied any sexual arousal before or during the assault.

R.'s sexual history revealed that he had begun looking at sexually explicit magazines and movies at the age of 10. He 'learned about sex from (his) friends' and denied ever having discussed issues of sexuality with his father. He bragged about having had multiple girlfriends whom he had kissed, but denied ever having had intercourse. He also denied sexual abuse. Having entered puberty at 13 years old, he denied masturbation or having any sexual fantasies whatsoever. Furthermore, he denied all paraphilias. However, he indicated on the Adolescent Rape Myths Test that he believed that girls report rapes that actually did not occur in order to get attention, that attractive girls can fight off a rapist if they really wanted to, and that girls often pretend that they do not want sex but are really hoping the guy will force sex upon them.

Despite his son's confessions, R.'s father completely denied that any of the allegations could have occurred, claiming that although he was certain his son was sexually active, there was no possible way that his son had committed the offenses as described.

It was recommended that he be placed on intensive probation and referred to a residential treatment center where he would receive both family and individual therapy from therapists trained to work with sexual offenders. R. may have denied parts of his actual offense for a variety of reasons, including his awareness that a presentencing report would be prepared for the court based on the information obtained. Despite this, it was hoped that he would eventually develop a trusting relationship with his therapist, lowering his denial and becoming increasingly amenable to therapeutic intervention.

Case B

N. is a 16-year-old Caucasian male, who was referred for psychiatric evaluation for a history of torturing and killing animals. He lived with his father, a police officer, his mother, a medical technician, and his younger brother. He was an average student in school and had been a volunteer at a local hospital. Although denying the use of alcohol, he abused over-the-counter sleeping pills, used marijuana once or twice a month, and had experimented with LSD and cocaine. He had run away from home on one occasion and had a history of frequent shoplifting. Recent psychological evaluation had demonstrated a Full Scale IQ of 125.

N. gained an interest in dissecting animals following a worm dissection exercise in his sixth-grade science class. He stole a fetal pig from his eighth-grade science teacher and decided to dissect it on his own. He sliced it open and recalls being curious about the textures of the animal tissues, and eventually tasted parts of the dissected fetus including the skin out of curiosity. This incident led to him becoming sexually excited.

N. began a fascination with killing animals about two years later when he and a friend caught a cat and jointly decided that it might be fun to kill it. They threw a large rock on it, but the cat bit them and got away. During this, N. felt a feeling of 'power' for the first time in his life. A week later, N. took a pellet gun and attempted unsuccessfully to kill another cat. However, that same day he caught another cat and tied a rope around its neck, swinging it by the rope and hitting it to the ground until it died. This first actual killing reportedly made him feel good, in control, and powerful. He cut the head of the cat off and took it home, disposing of the remains by throwing it onto an old girlfriend's front porch.

N. explained to his parents that the cat's head was from a 'road kill'. He cleaned the skull by removing the skin with a scalpel, boiling the bone portion, and then soaking it in peroxide. The only parts kept were the skull, the tongue and the eyeballs. He mounted the skull on his headboard in his bedroom.

Over the following couple of weeks, he used a pellet gun to kill about 20 birds, keeping the skulls of the three largest and mounting them on his headboard. He commented that by keeping the skulls, the animals could continue to live on. Next, a few months later, he abducted a goose, and killed it by stabbing it many times with a knife. The action of stabbing caused him to feel good and emotionally excited. Again, the skull was prepared and mounted.

All in all, he killed an additional 20 cats (two by setting live cats on fire), two rabbits and one dog over the next few months. On one occasion, N. cut open the chest of one of the dead cats to observe and remove the internal organs. He enjoyed putting his hands in to feel the viscera and, on one occasion, placed his penis inside the viscera. He then masturbated to ejaculation in front of the carcass. The last prior animal killed was his family's cat, which he initially but unsuccessfully tried to kill by placing it in a microwave oven. However, he later successfully killed the cat by strangling it with a chain in his bathroom shower. He claimed that many of the killings made him scared and sexually excited at the same time.

N. thought about killing animals on a daily basis. Upon further questioning, N. admitted to frequent fantasies of killing humans. One particular fantasy started with capturing an adult woman, tying her up, and having intercourse with her until she screamed. He would then kill her by strangulation, having intercourse with the corpse, then cutting off and saving the nipples and her skull. The remains would be chopped up and disposed of. This recurrent fantasy would cause N. to become sexually aroused. He felt he had commonalities with the infamous serial killer, Jeffrey Dahmer, saying that both were obviously lonely and unwanted.

Review of psychiatric symptoms revealed that N. had been depressed for about a year and had been treated with antidepressant medications. He reported having a paranoid feeling at times and occasionally felt that someone was following him or calling out his name. There were even a few instances when he believed that there were cameras behind mirrors watching him. He denied any specific medical problems.

N. was questioned in detail about his sexual history. He began having consensual sexual intercourse with his same-age girlfriend at the age of 15. Although continuing to attempt intercourse weekly since that time, he had only achieved orgasm on two occasions with her. He enjoyed hearing her scream during sexual activity. However, he usually achieved orgasm when he masturbated, which occurred a maximum of eight to ten times a day. Masturbatory fantasies included sexual thoughts about same-age or prepubescent girls. Many of his fantasies involved force or rape, beating of a sexual partner and strangulation. Another specific fantasy including tying up his girlfriend, whipping her, cutting off her ears and nipples, and setting her hair on fire. Such fantasies would cause him to experience anger and sexual excitement simultaneously.

A detailed review of paraphilias revealed a history of voyeurism of a girl neighbor undressing, rubbing up against unsuspecting individuals while swimming at a water park, dressing up in female clothing when masturbating, and placing food on his penis so as to get a dog to lick it off. Paraphiliac fantasies included voyeurism, exhibitionism and urophilia.

He saw his first pornographic movie when in grade school. One of them was an animated cartoon feature showing cats walking around naked and having sexual intercourse. He had many pornographic magazines showing homosexual and heterosexual activities. However, he denied any homosexual fantasies.

Based on the clinical interview, N. was diagnosed with depression, marijuana abuse, multiple paraphilias including necrophilic fantasies, and inhibited male orgasm. A diagnosis of psychotic disorder was still to be ruled out. He was continued on antidepressant medication, increasing the dose, and was referred for immediate residential treatment specializing in sexual disorders.

CONCLUSION

Juvenile sexual offending is a phenomenon which has received increased professional attention over the past decade. It is now recognized that juveniles account for nearly one-half of the sexual assaults against children and a quarter of the rapes that are committed in this country each year. Increased cognizance of the problem of juvenile offending has led to a proliferation of treatment programs and a significant rise in the number of descriptive articles in the clinical and research literatures. However, the field still lacks an empirically derived typology which defines subtypes of juvenile sexual offenders and delineates etiological pathways associated with each. The absence of a clear understanding of the etiologies of juvenile sexual offending has hampered the development of early identification and prevention programming for high-risk youth. Likewise, the lack of an empirically derived method for profiling juvenile sexual offenders has complicated the tasks of ascertaining amenability to treatment, determining type and level of services required, and defining risk of recidivism and made them less than scientific endeavors. Additional research in the above areas is vitally needed.

Practitioners working with juvenile sexual offenders are advised to conduct comprehensive psychosocial, psychosexual and psychiatric assessments prior to the initiation of treatment. Juvenile sexual offenders are a heterogeneous clinical population with varied treatment needs. Effective treatment planning requires an understanding of the overall personality and environmental context in which the sexual acting out occurred. Treatment plans need to address all of the emotional and behavioral needs of the youth, not just the psychosexual problems.

It is imperative that clinicians working with juvenile sexual offenders maintain ongoing communication with other professionals and agencies involved in providing services to the youth and family. For those youths who have legal involvement, it is critically important that the mental health professional works in close coordination with the court in ensuring that both the treatment needs of the youth and community safety needs are being adequately addressed. Similarly, it is vital that the family of the youth be involved in his treatment. In cases of sibling incest, it is especially important that the therapist take into consideration the needs of the victim in making decisions about family reunification.

Specialized approaches to the treatment of this clinical population have been developed. Juvenile sexual offenders have been observed as benefiting from focused, didactic approaches to correcting cognitive distortions and increasing client accountability, improving social and self-control skills, enhancing empathy for the victim, and developing relapse prevention strategies. These skills are typically taught in a group format which also offers opportunities for peer support and encouragement. Psychopharmacological therapies have been found to be helpful as adjuncts to psychological therapies in the treatment of those youths who manifest co-existing psychiatric disorders.

Although currently there is a dearth of carefully controlled outcome studies in the literature, preliminary data and clinical observation suggest that juveniles who receive sex offender-specific treatment generally fare well. A positive long-term outcome appears to be contingent not only on the delivery of specialized treatment services, but also on the availability of effective after-care and community monitoring programs.

REFERENCES

Abel, G. G., Becker, J. V., Cunningham-Rathner, J., Rouleau, J., Kaplan, M. & Reich, J. (1984). *Treatment Manual: The Treatment of Child Molesters*. Tuscaloosa, AL: Energy University Clinic, Department of Psychiatry.

American Association for the Treatment of Sexual Abusers (ATSA). (1993). *The ATSA Practitioners Handbook*. Lake Oswego, OR: American Association for the Treatment of Sexual Abusers.

Awad, G. A. & Saunders, E. (1989). Adolescent child molesters: clinical observations. *Child Psychiatry and Human Development*, **19**, 195–206.

Awad, G. A., Saunders, E. & Levene, J. (1984). A clinical study of male adolescent sex offenders. *International Journal of Offender Therapy and Comparative Criminology*, **28**, 105–16.

Barbaree, H. E., Hudson, S. M. & Seto, M. C. (1993). Sexual assault in society: the role of the juvenile offender. In H. E. Barbaree, W. L. Marshall & S. M. Hudson (eds), *The Juvenile Sex Offender*. New York: Guilford Press, pp. 10–11.

Becker, J. V. (1988). Adolescent sex offenders. *Behavior Therapist*, **11**, 1985–7.

Becker, J. V. & Hunter, J. A. (1992). Evaluation of treatment outcome for adult perpetrators of child sexual abuse. *Criminal Justice and Behavior*, **19**(1), 74–92.

Becker, J. V. & Kaplan, M. S. (1988). The assessment of sexual offenders. *Advances in Behavioral Assessment of Children and Families*, **4**, 97–118.

Becker, J. V. & Kaplan, M. S. (1993). Cognitive behavioral treatment of the juvenile sex offender. In H. E. Barbaree, W. L. Marshall & S. M. Hudson (eds), *The Juvenile Sex Offender*. New York: The Guilford Press, pp. 264–77.

Becker, J. V., Cunningham-Rathner, J. & Kaplan, M. S. (1986). Adolescent sexual offenders: demographics, criminal and sexual histories, and recommendations for reducing future offenses. Special issue: the prediction and control of violent behavior: II. *Journal of Interpersonal Violence*, **1**, 431–45.

Becker, J. V., Harris, C. D. & Sales, B. D. (1993). Juveniles who commit sex offenses: a critical review of research. In G. C. N. Hall, R. Hirschman, J. Graham & M. Zaragoza (eds), *Sexual Aggression: Issues in Etiology and Assessment, Treatment, and Policy*. Washington, DC: Taylor and Francis.

Becker, J. V., Kaplan, M. S., Cunningham-Rathner, J. & Kavoussi, R. J. (1986). Characteristics of adolescent incest sexual perpetrators: preliminary findings. *Journal of Family Violence*, **1**, 85–97.

Becker, J. V., Kaplan, M. S., Tenke, C. E. & Tartaglini, A. (1991). The incidence of depressive symptomatology in juvenile sex offenders with a history of abuse. *Child Abuse and Neglect*, **15**, 531–6.

Bethea-Jackson, G. & Brissett-Chapman, S. (1989). The juvenile sexual offender: Challenges to assessment for outpatient intervention. *Child and Adolescent Social Work Journal*, **6**, 127–37.

Blaske, D. M., Borduin, C. M., Henggeler, S. W. & Mann, B. J. (1989). Individual, family, and peer characteristics of adolescent sex offenders and assaultive offenders. *Developmental Psychology*, **25**, 846–55.

Borduin, C. M., Henggeler, S. W., Blaske, D. M. & Stein, R. J. (1990). Multisystemic treatment of adolescent sexual offenders. *International Journal of Offender Therapy and Comparative Criminology*, **34**, 105–13.

Bradford, J. M. (1988). Organic treatment of the male sexual offender. *Annals of the New York Academy of Sciences*, **528**, 193–202.

Bradford, J. M. (1993). The pharmacologic treatment of the adolescent sex offender. In H. E. Barbaree, W. L. Marshall & S. M. Hudson (eds), *The Juvenile Sex Offender*. New York, Guilford Press, pp. 278–88.

Coleman, E., Cesnik, J., Moore, A. & Dwyer, S. M. (1992). An exploratory study of the role of psychotropic medications in the treatment of sex offenders. *Journal of Offender Rehabilitation*, **18**(3–4), 77–88.

Condron, M. K. & Nutter, D. E. (1987). Use of medroxy-progesterone acetate in treatment of a deaf-mute sex offender. *Journal of Sex Research*, **23**(3), 397–400.

Emory, L. E., Cole, C. M. & Meyer, W. J. (1992). The Texas experience with depoProvera: 1980–1990. *Journal of Offender Rehabilitation*, **18**(3–4), 125–39.

Fedoroff, J. P. & Fedoroff, I. C. (1992). Buspirone in paraphiliac sexual behavior. *Journal of Offender Rehabilitation*, **18**(3–4), 89–108.

Fedoroff, J. P., Wisner-Carlson, R., Dean, S. & Berlin, F. S. (1992). Medroxy-progesterone acetate in the treatment of paraphiliac sexual disorders: Rate of relapse in paraphiliac men treated in long-term group psychotherapy with or without medroxy-progesterone acetate. *Journal of Offender Rehabilitation*, **18**(3–4), 109–23.

Figueredo, A. J. & McCloskey, L. A. (in press, a). The evolutionary psychology of domestic violence. In C. T. Palmer & M. Studd (eds), *Evolutionary Perspectives on Coercive Sexuality*.

Figueredo, A. J. & McCloskey, L. A. (in press, b). Sex, money, and paternity: the evolutionary psychology of domestic violence. *Ethology and Sociobiology*.

French, D. D. (1989a). Treatment of the juvenile sex offender. *Health Visitor*, **60**, 97–8.

French, D. D. (1989b). Distortion and lying as defense processes in the adolescent child molester. *Journal of Offender Counseling, Services and Rehabilitation*, **14**, 161–7.

Gottesman, H. G. & Schubert, D. S. P. (1993). Low dose oral medroxyprogesterone debate in the management of the paraphilias. *Treatment of Clinical Psychiatry*, **56**, 182–8.

Gray, A. S. & Pithers, W. D. (1993). Relapse prevention with sexually aggressive adolescents and children: Expanding treatment and supervision. In H. E. Barbaree, W. L. Marshall & S. M. Hudson (eds), *The Juvenile Sex Offender*. New York: Guilford Press, pp. 289–321.

Groth, A. N., Hobson, W. F., Lucey, K. P. & St. Pierre, J. (1981). Juvenile sexual offenders: Guidelines for treatment. *International Journal of Offender Therapy and Comparative Criminology*, **25**, 265–75.

Hunter, J. A. (1993). The Clinical Diagnosis and Treatment of Juvenile Sex Offenders. Prepared under a grant by the National Center on Child Abuse and Neglect for use by the National Training Program on Effective Treatment Approaches in Child Sexual Abuse. (Available from author).

Hunter, J. A. & Goodwin, D. W. (1992). The utility of satiation therapy in the treatment of juvenile sexual offenders: Variations and efficacy. *Annals of Sex Research*, **5**, 71–80.

Hunter, J. A., Becker, J. V. & Goodwin, D. W. (1991). The reliability and discriminative utility of the Adolescent Cognition Scale for juvenile sexual offenses. *Annals of Sex Research*, **4**, 281–6.

Hunter, J. A., Lexier, L. J., Goodwin, D. W., Browne, P. A. & Dennis, C. (1993). Psychosexual, attitudinal, and developmental characteristics of juvenile female sexual perpetrators in a residential treatment setting. *Journal of Child and Family Studies*, **2**(4), 317–26.

Kavoussi, R. J., Kaplan, M. & Becker, J. V. (1988). Psychiatric diagnoses in adolescent sex offenders. *Journal of the American Academy of Child and Adolescent Psychiatry*, **27**, 241–3.

Knight, R. A. & Prentky, R. A. (1990). Classifying sexual offenders: the development and corroboration of taxonomic models. In W. L. Marshall, D. R. Laws & H. E. Barbaree (eds), *The Handbook of Sexual Assualt: Issues, Theories, and Treatment of the Offender*. New York: Plenum Press, pp. 27–52.

Knight, R. A. & Prentky, R. A. (1993). Exploring characteristics for classifying juvenile sex offenders. In H. E. Barbaree, W. Marshall & S. M. Hudson (eds), *The Juvenile Sex Offender*. New York: The Guilford Press, pp. 45–83.

Knopp, F. H. & Lackey, L. D. (1987). *Female Sexual Abusers: A Summary of Data From 44 Treatment Providers*. New York: The Safer Society Press.

Kobayashi, J., Sales, B. D., Becker, J. V., Figueredo, A. J. & Kaplan, J. S. (in press). *Perceived Parental Deviance, Parental–child Bonding, Child Abuse, and Child Sexual Aggression* (submitted for publication).

Lombardo, R. & DiGiorgio-Miller, J. (1988). Concepts and techniques in working with juvenile sex offenders. *Journal of Offender Counseling, Services and Rehabilitation*, **13**, 39–53.

Margolin, L. (1984). Group therapy as a means of learning about the sexual assaultive adolescent. *International Journal of Offender Therapy and Comparative Criminology*, **28**, 65–72.

Mathews, R. (1987). *Female Sexual Offenders*. Workshop presented to the 3rd National Adolescent Perpetrator Network Meeting, Keystone, CO, May 1987.

McConaghy, N., Blaszcynski, A. P., Armstrong, M. S. & Kidson, W. (1989). Resistance to treatment of adolescent sex offenders. *Archives of Sexual Behavior*, **18**, 97–107.

Morenz, B. and Becker, J. V. (in press). *The Treatment of Youthful Sexual Offenders*.

National Adolescent Perpetrator Network (1988). *Juvenile and Family Court Journal*, **39**(2).

National Adolescent Perpetrator Network. (1993). The revised report from the National Task Force on juvenile sexual offending. *Juvenile and Family Court Journal*, **44**, 1–120.

Nichols, H. R., & Molinder, I. (1984). *Multiphasic Sex Inventory Manual: A Test to Assess the Psychosexual Characteristics of the Sexual Offender*. (Research Edition Form A). Tacoma, WA: Nichols & Molinder.

O'Brien, M. & Bera, W. (1986). Adolescent sexual offenders: a descriptive typology. *A News Letter of the National Family Life Education Network*, **1**, 1–5.

Rousseau, L., Dupont, A., Labrie, F. & Couture, M. (1988). Sexuality changes in prostate cancer patients receiving anti-hormonal therapy combining the anti-androgen Flutamide with medical (LHRH agonist) or surgical castration. *Archives of Sexual Behavior*, **17**(1), 87–98.

Rowe, B. (1988). Practical treatment of adolescent sexual offenders. *Journal of Child Care*, **3**, 51–8.

Ryan, G., Lane, S., Davis, J. & Isaac, C. (1987). Juvenile sex offenders: development and correction. *Child Abuse and Neglect*, **11**, 385–95.

Saunders, E. B., Awad, G. A. & White, G. (1986). Male adolescent sexual offenders: The offender and the offense. *Canadian Journal of Psychiatry*, **31**, 542–549

Scully, D. & Marolla, J. (1984). Convicted rapists vocabulary of motive: Excuses and justifications. *Social Problems*, **13**, 530–44.

Shoor, M., Speed, M. H. & Bertelt, C. (1966). Syndrome of the adolescent child molester. *American Journal of Psychiatry*, **122**, 783–9.

Stenson, P. & Anderson, C. (1987). Treating juvenile sex offenders and preventing the cycle of abuse. *Journal of Child Care*, **3**, 91–102.

Stermac, L. & Sheridan, P. (1993). The developmentally disabled adolescent sex offender. In H. E. Barbaree, W. L. Marshall & S. M. Hudson (eds), *The Juvenile Sex Offender*. New York: Guilford Press, pp. 235–42.

10

Adolescent Firesetters

CLIVE R. HOLLIN
University of Birmingham, Birmingham, UK

KEVIN J. EPPS
Glenthorne Centre, Birmingham, UK

Fire is a part of everyday life yet, with justification, there is a widespread fear of the consequences, for both people and property, of an uncontrolled fire. Indeed, Soothil! (1990) has suggested that the development of sophisticated techniques to reduce the risk of accidental fires has resulted in growing concern about intentionally set fires. Certainly, there is evidence of a recognition of the need for action at government level (Home Office, 1988; Federal Emergency Management Agency, US Fire Administration, 1983). In this light, it is not surprising that a reasonably substantial literature has amassed over time on the study of those individuals responsible for setting uncontrolled fires (Prins, 1994). Of the known firesetter population, children and adolescents constitute a significant proportion (DeSalvatore & Hornstein, 1991).

The phenomenon of the young firesetter was first alluded to in the 19th century, since when a variety of explanations have been advanced to explain this behaviour (Kolko, 1985). While early theories associated firesetting with psychosexual development, particularly amongst young women (Harris & Rice, 1984; Yarnell, 1940), contemporary theories tend to a cognitive-behavioural persuasion (Kolko & Kazdin, 1986). Further, the evidence very much suggests that firesetting is an activity predominant among young males (Kolko, 1985), although, of course, there are female firesetters (Stewart, 1993).

Clinical Approaches to Working with Young Offenders. Edited by C. R. Hollin and K. Howells.
© 1996 John Wiley & Sons Ltd.

CHARACTERISTICS OF THE YOUNG FIRESETTER

Psychological Factors

While firesetting is prevalent among child and adult psychiatric populations (Geller, 1992, Kolko & Kazdin, 1988), not all firesetters are psychiatrically disturbed and some studies have looked at the personal characteristics of non-psychiatric firesetters. Beginning with the fascination of fire, Kolko and Kazdin (1989a) reported that, compared with non-firesetters, children who set fires are characterized by a high level of curiosity about fire, but are neither less skilled in handling fire nor less aware of the dangers of fire. In terms of personal skills, Rice and Chaplin (1979) found that arsonists were shy and unassertive (although this study was carried out with an adult population, there are similarities between adult and adolescent firesetters, e.g. Bradford & Dimock 1986). Accordingly, Harris and Rice (1984) suggested that some individuals set fires as a consequence of a lack of interpersonal problem-solving skills: unable to resolve conflicts in an acceptable manner, fires are set to gain revenge or express anger. Other often cited motivations for firesetting include crime concealment, fraud, excitement, frustration, mental instability, and the desire to be a hero or heroine (Kolko, 1985; Swaffer & Hollin, 1995).

Another theme that runs through the literature is the association between firesetting and other childhood disorders. While links specifically with enuresis and cruelty to animals remain doubtful (Jacobson, 1985), there is evidence to suggest that firesetting is associated with conduct disorder, including social skills deficits, as well as high levels of delinquent and antisocial behaviour (Heath et al., 1983, Kolko, Kazdin & Meyer, 1985). However, the nature of the relationship between conduct disorder, delinquency and firesetting remains a matter for debate.

Family Factors

A number of studies have looked at both the family background and family functioning of young people who set fires (Bradford & Dimock, 1986; Kazdin & Kolko, 1986; Kolko, 1985; Kolko & Kazdin, 1988, 1989a, 1990; Strachan, 1981). The family backgrounds of juvenile firesetters are typically characterized by high levels of parental absence, family breakdown and disorganization, and parental distress and psychopathology. Patterns of family functioning are marked by low levels of affection, affiliation and marital satisfaction, erratic styles of parental monitoring and discipline (including physical child abuse), and low levels of parental involvement with their children. The nature of the relationship between family background, functioning and child firesetting is less than clear and whether background or functioning plays the greater role is uncertain: indeed, both may interact with age of onset of firesetting (Kolko & Kazdin, 1992). In addition, many young firesetters have experienced multiple placements in child care establishments and foster homes (Kolko, 1985).

While the research literature is mostly American, Strachan (1981) investigated a delinquent group of juvenile firesetters who had been referred to a Children's Hearing Panel (equivalent to a juvenile court) in Scotland. Strachan reported that these young firesetters were predominately male, often presented with multiple problems including other criminal offences, were already known to other agencies prior to referral, and had family backgrounds characterized by high levels of parental disharmony.

WORKING WITH THE YOUNG FIRESETTER

Assessment

In terms of assessment, the adolescent firesetter poses a challenge with respect to understanding the problem behaviour. As several commentators note, given the complexity of firesetting it is necessary to assess a wide range of factors in order to begin to understand any individual case (Jackson, 1994; Jackson, Glass & Hope, 1987; Kolko, 1985). It is necessary to obtain information on the sites at which the fires are set, along with any details from fire scene investigations. For obvious reasons, it is particularly important to determine whether there was any risk to life. Most juveniles set more than one fire, so information on frequency of firesetting should be gathered. Other questions about the events prior to the firesetting would include whether the individual was alone or with others, and whether there had been a significant argument prior to the incident.

Alongside a full assessment of delinquent history, psychiatric status and history, social competency, intelligence, family functioning and so on, information needs to be gathered regarding the actual firesetting. What were the young person's thoughts, emotions and actions as the fire was set? How did they feel and react when the fire was alight? What actions did they take: did they watch the fire, call the emergency services, or leave the scene? The difficulty in making this type of assessment is that it very much depends on self-report, which may or may not be reliable. However, knowledge of the accounts of any accomplices and details of the forensic evidence from the scene of the crime can help to verify or refute self-reported accounts.

Intervention Programmes

As Kolko (1985) notes, there are two main types of intervention for young firesetters: the first is a traditional treatment approach; the second comprise fire service programmes.

Treatment of adolescent firesetting

As Barnett and Spitzer (1994) note, the treatment of adolescent firesetters has run the gauntlet of models of therapy, from behavioural and family therapy to psychodynamic and group psychotherapy. However, the outcome evidence is sorely limited, Kolko (1985) makes the point:

> Regarding effectiveness, the majority of studies and clinical case reports fail to provide an objective documentation of outcomes, relying primarily upon subjective impressions of change ... The relative absence of experimental designs and follow-up assessment compounds the difficulty in making firm conclusions about the impact of different interventions. (p. 369).

However, a more recent study by DeSalvatore and Hornstein (1991) did suggest a successful outcome. The programme consisted of the three phases of assessment, teaching, and practice. The assessment incorporated many of the details noted above, including the firesetting behaviour. The didactic phase focused on teaching the young people about the potential dangers of fire along with fire safety and prevention. The practice phase was concerned with teaching the proper way to strike and use matches. The 12-month follow-up data were encouraging with regard to recidivism.

Fire service programmes

In the United States there are a substantial number of programmes, generally conducted in the community, run by fire service and allied groups (Kolko, 1988). In the UK there are similar initiatives, such as the 'Learn not to Burn' project, with a similar initiative in Australia (Adler et al., 1992). In terms of content, there is some overlap with the treatment programmes, as many fire service programmes contain a substantial educational component aimed at fire safety. As was the case with treatment programmes, there are reports of good outcomes but a lack of solid data regarding the effectiveness of fire service programmes.

CASE STUDY

Adam, a 16-year-old boy, was admitted to secure accommodation at Glenthorne Centre to serve a three-year sentence under Section 53 of the 1933 Children and Young Person's Act. He received this sentence for the offence of arson, although several other offences were also taken into consideration, including burglary and theft. Glenthorne Centre is one of two centres operating under the auspices of the Youth Treatment Service, providing secure and open accommodation for some of Britain's most difficult and delinquent young people (Bullock et al., 1990).

Before Adam was admitted, consideration was given to the risks that he may present to others as a result of setting fires within security. Reports received from other agencies indicated that he had set at least one fire within a secure unit, causing smoke damage and requiring himself and one other boy to receive hospital treatment. Particular attention was paid to the availability of fire-raising materials. Matches or cigarette lighters are occasionally smuggled into secure units, either at the point of admission or following an outside visit. Visiting family members and other friends or relatives may also pass-on forbidden items. On occasion, other young people, perhaps those under less scrutiny, have been known to give firesetters fire-raising materials, knowing that they will be used to set fires. As a precaution, therefore, Adam and his possessions were thoroughly searched before admission. His room was also searched at random intervals, and to facilitate these searches he was allowed to keep only a limited quantity of personal possessions in his room.

The first few weeks of Adam's stay at Glenthorne were spent developing a care-plan. This process involves collating information from a variety of sources with the aim of creating a structure to inform the delivery of care, management and intervention programmes, taking into account age and psychological development (Hollin, Epps & Kendrick, 1995). The care-plan also sets up a process of goal-planning, with the aim of moving the young person into an open setting at the earliest opportunity, taking into account risk to self and others.

Whereas the care-plan provides a global view of the young person's needs, the intervention programme aims to focus on the specific problems resulting in admission. The goals of intervention are to reduce the risk of reoffending and facilitate a successful return to the community. Wherever possible, the intervention programme is tailored to the needs of each individual, beginning with a period of assessment.

Assessment

Although Adam had been involved in a variety of criminal activities, the process of developing a care-plan indicated that his firesetting behaviour warranted most concern. Reports received from agencies previously involved with his care and education stated that his index offence of arson was not an isolated incident and that he had an extensive history of firesetting. The decision was therefore taken by the treatment team to target Adam's firesetting behaviour. The assessment had three main aims: first, to assess the extent to which Adam identified his firesetting behaviour as a problem with which he wanted help; second, to decide what methods of intervention were required to help reduce the risk of further episodes of firesetting; third, to evaluate the degree of risk resulting from his firesetting behaviour and to use this information to inform decision-making about his care and management.

Information about Adam's firesetting behaviour was collected from a variety of sources, using several different assessment methods.

Archival material

Before admission, and in the weeks following, written information was collated that could shed light on Adam's behaviour and psychological functioning. Reports were requested from schools that he had attended, with particular reference to his academic performance, peer relationships and antisocial behaviour. Reports were also obtained from other residential establishments and from psychologists, psychiatrists and social workers previously involved in his care and treatment. Finally, contact was made with the fire investigation officer responsible for the investigation of Adam's index offence of arson. He supplied a fire investigation report detailing the circumstances surrounding the fire, including the exact location where the fire began and evidence of the use of accelerants, such as petrol. Access to this kind of information can be crucial when interviewing young firesetters. It can help when challenging the young person's attempts to distort accounts of his or her offending behaviour. It also helps to convey the impression that the interviewer is well informed and has taken the time to collect relevant information.

Interviews

Adam was interviewed on successive occasions over a period of several weeks. Some of the interviews were carried out as part of the care-planning process, covering a variety of areas and helping to establish a constructive working relationship. During these interviews Adam was able to disclose for the first time that he had been sexually abused, along with his younger brother, over a period of several years. The perpetrator was supposedly a trusted friend of the family who was allowed to take the children out on weekly trips. Frequently, these involved going to a derelict house, where Adam and his brother were forced to take part in a variety of sexual acts, including buggery. The perpetrator had threatened to kill Adam and other members of his family if he spoke about the abuse. It was only within the safe confines of security that he felt able to disclose.

Other interviews focused specifically on Adam's firesetting behaviour. Several screening questionnaires, developed by Kolko and Kazdin (1989b), were used to help structure the interviews. The Firesetting History Screening Questionnaire (Revised)—Present, focuses on episodes of firesetting during the past year, examining the antecedents and consequences surrounding up to three separate incidents of firesetting. In contrast, the Firesetting History Screening Questionnaire (Revised)—Past, covers fires that were set more than one year ago, extending back to early childhood if necessary.

Detailed descriptive information was collected about his firesetting behaviour (i.e. time, place, frequency, social context, use of fire-setting materials, action taken to extinguish fire). Adam reported that he had set up to 20 fires in addition to his index offence, beginning when he was about 10 or 11 years old. Usually he was with friends and other young people from his neighbourhood. Typically, Adam and his friends did not plan to set fires. Rather, firesetting was just another delinquent behaviour in which they engaged, taking advantage of opportunities as they occurred. Most of the fires were small, involving waste-disposal skips and derelict property. One fire, however, was more serious, causing considerable property damage. This occurred in a builder's yard as a result of Adam and his friends experimenting by setting fire to aerosol canisters. One of the containers exploded, setting fire to a wooden shed containing paint and cleaning materials. It took the fire service some considerable time to gain control of the fire, although nobody was injured. Adam reported feeling alarmed and excited by the speed at which the fire spread, although relieved that nobody was injured. During interview he emphasized that he had no intention of hurting other people. Adam and his friends were never apprehended for setting fires, and were once praised by the fire service for extinguishing a grassland fire that they had been responsible for starting. Adam reported that he had no real interest in setting fires during this time.

His index offence was examined in more detail. Information was collected about events in the weeks, days and hours leading up to the fire, and about his thoughts and feelings around this time. His relationships at home and school were also explored. This particular offence occurred several weeks after the builder's yard fire described earlier. Shortly after this fire it occurred to Adam that, had he been apprehended and convicted for the fire, he would have been removed from home and placed either in custody or in residential care, an idea that appealed to him. He was becoming more desperate to escape the sexual abuse that he continued to suffer. He also wanted to disclose the abuse, in the hope that the perpetrator would be convicted and detained in custody, thereby protecting his brother from further abuse. Adam decided that a conviction for firesetting was the ideal solution to his problems: nobody would get hurt; he would be able to escape his abuser and disclose the abuse in the safety of security; and the perpetrator would be arrested, so protecting his brother.

His first attempt at getting himself arrested failed. He set fire to a derelict car. This was the first fire that he had set by himself. Unfortunately, nobody took any notice! Several days later, he set fire to a derelict warehouse. The fire service and the police soon arrived, who arrested Adam after being tipped-off by a passer-by who had seen Adam leaving the building. Unfortunately, Adam had not known that a vagrant had been sleeping in the building at the time of the fire. Although the vagrant was not seriously injured, it resulted in Adam being convicted of arson rather than criminal damage, and receiving a longer sentence than he had anticipated. Adam reported that he did not regret setting the fire, having achieved his original aims, but realized that he should have first checked that the building was unoccupied before setting fire to it.

Adam's father was also interviewed and administered the parent version of the two Firesetting History Screening Questionnaires. Adam's mother had committed suicide when he was aged 6 years and his father could give only scant details about his development before this time. He was able to provide some useful information about Adam's later childhood. It appears that Adam had no particular or unusual interest in fire during his childhood and had never set fires in the house. However, he did have a history of severe emotional and behavioural problems, some of which extended back to early childhood. His father reported that Adam had been overly aggressive and destructive to property, necessitating referral to a Child Guidance Clinic, records from which confirmed the father's account of events. These problems were exacerbated following the death of his mother, resulting in Adam attempting to kill himself at age 7 years by throwing himself under a moving car. His father later remarried, such that Adam became one of a family of 12 children. Adam and several of his siblings had also spent brief periods of time in residential care shortly after the death of their mother.

Direct behavioural observation

Daily observations were made of Adam's behaviour during the weeks following his admission to secure accommodation. Adam settled quickly into the daily routine, abided by the house rules and, on the whole, interacted appropriately with peers and staff. There was no evidence of firesetting behaviour, and regular room and body searches failed to find fire-raising materials. Further, Adam expressed no obvious interest in fire. He did not talk about setting fires and did not become overtly excited or animated when other young people discussed fire. Further, he showed no particular interest when the fire service were called to the Centre on several occasions to deal with false alarms, despite the sirens and flashing lights.

Residential staff did note, however, that Adam quickly became frustrated and agitated when denied access to certain activities. On two occasions he lost his temper, becoming verbally threatening and destroying personal possessions. This type of behaviour was targeted for further assessment by means of more detailed observation and psychometric assessment.

Psychometric testing

Routine testing on the Wechsler Intelligence Scale for Children—Revised (1974) showed Adam to have a full-scale IQ score of 83, with verbal and performance scores of 85, all in the 'low average' range of the Wechsler scale. Educational testing on the Schonell Graded Word Reading Test (Schonell, 1955) indicated a reading age equivalent of 12 years and a spelling age equivalent of 11 years. Adam also completed the Spielberger State-Trait Anger Expression Inventory (STAXI; Spielberger, 1991). Adam's responses on this indicated that he experienced frequent feelings of intense anger, sometimes for no apparent reason. Often he felt that he had been treated unfairly by others, and used certain situations to vent his anger.

Clinical Formulation

A functional analysis was carried out of Adam's index offence, as shown in Table 10.1. Adam appeared to have no particular interest in fire, using it as means to an end. The index offence can be construed as a form of negative reinforcement, helping Adam to escape from an aversive set of circumstances. The risk of Adam setting fires in secure conditions was considered to be minimal, allowing the additional precautionary

Table 10.1   Functional analysis of Adam's index offence

Antecedents
    Delinquent peer group
    Boredom
    Anger, especially resulting from sexual abuse
    Anxiety and frustration at feeling trapped by perpetrator
    Established knowledge of firesetting, both accidental and deliberate
Behaviour
    Arson
Reinforcing consequences
    Excitement
    Removal from home to a safe haven
    Ability to disclose abuse, resulting in feelings of revenge against perpetrator
    Protection of brother from perpetrator

security and supervision restrictions to be phased-out. An intervention programme was devised, targeting areas identified in the functional analysis. It was hypothesized that behavioural and cognitive change in these areas should further reduce the risk of firesetting and facilitate Adam's successful return to the community.

Intervention Programme

The programme developed is shown in Table 10.2. The first two stages of the programme were delivered over a 12-month period whilst Adam was detained in secure conditions. Stage 3 was carried out on an open unit on the same campus, over a period of about 4 months. Adam was then released into the community to serve the rest of his sentence on licence, under supervision from the probation service.

Some elements of the programme, such as sexual abuse counselling, relaxation training, and offence counselling, were delivered at an individual level by experienced practitioners. The sexual abuse work was carried out by a social worker specializing in this field. Relaxation training consisted of four one-hour sessions with a clinical psychologist, followed by self-practice using a relaxation tape. The offence counselling continued intermittently throughout the intervention programme and was carried out by Adam's residential key-worker. This work followed on from the assessment interviews,

Table 10.2   Intervention programme

Stage 1 : Secure conditions
    Sexual abuse counselling
    Offence counselling
    Anger control programme
    Problem-solving programme
    Relaxation training
Stage 2 : Secure conditions
    Fire-safety and awareness educational programme
Stage 3 : Open conditions
    Anger control refresher course
    Relaxation training refresher course
    Life-skills programme
    Family work

serving to help Adam identify areas in which he had made progress and to relate this to his offending behaviour.

Other aspects of the intervention, such as the anger control and problem-solving programmes, were carried out in small groups, consisting of four or five young people identified as having difficulties in these areas. Both group programmes consisted of structured, cognitive-behavioural packages. The anger control programme comprised eight one-hour groups held over successive weeks, employing techniques developed by Novaco (1978), Deffenbacher and colleagues (Deffenbacher, 1988; Deffenbacher et al., 1988) and Feindler and Ecton (1986). The problem-solving programme consisted of 10 one-hour groups, adapting techniques developed by Hains (1984). Participants were encouraged to examine the costs and benefits of various courses of action and to generate more effective solutions to interpersonal problems. Some group sessions involved rehearsal and group feedback in the form of role-play. Both group programmes were run by experienced residential staff with training in cognitive-behavioural work, with supervision from a clinical psychologist.

The fire safety and awareness educational programme took place over a period of 8 weeks, shortly before Adam's transfer to open conditions. The programme consisted of eight groups each lasting between one and two hours, carried out in conjunction with the regional fire service. Each group consisted of between six and 10 young people, most of whom had a history of fire-setting. The groups were a mixture of didactic teaching and discussion. Pictures and videos of real fires and fire damage were used to facilitate discussion. The course covered a variety of topics including the dangers of fire; the damage caused by arson to people and property; fire prevention and safety; human behaviour and fire; personal beliefs about fire; and attitude to offences. Participants were encouraged to discuss their personal experience of fire-setting and how they intended to avoid setting further fires.

Adam's time on the open unit was used to consolidate work carried out in security and prepare him for a return to the community. Emphasis was given to the development of life-skills and vocational training. Adam wished to live in semi-independent accommodation, designed for young people leaving Local Authority care. Whilst he wished to remain in close contact with his family he did not want to live at home. Adam had remained in contact with his family throughout his stay in security. Family sessions were held to explore family relationships and reinforce Adam's need for continuing support.

Outcome

Since leaving secure accommodation just over one year ago, Adam has not set further fires, and has not offended in other ways. Currently, he attends college full-time and holds down a part-time job. He hopes to find a job as an instructor in a leisure centre. He also has a long-term girlfriend, with whom he shares a small flat.

CONCLUSIONS

Adolescent firesetting is a complex behaviour, with potentially serious consequences for all concerned. While the literature on aetiology and classification is at a reasonably advanced stage, there is little sign that this knowledge is systematically being put to a practical use. On the basis of the evidence to hand, it is difficult to resist the conclusion that a great deal more outcome research is necessary to determine the effectiveness of intervention programmes with young firesetters.

REFERENCES

Adler, R. G., Nunn, R. J., Lebnan, V. M. & Northam, E. A. (1992). *Can firefighters stop children lighting fires?* Paper presented at the IVth World Congress on Behaviour Therapy, Gold Coast, Queensland, Australia.

Barnett, W. & Spitzer, M. (1994). Pathological fire-setting 1951–1991: A review. *Medicine, Science, and Law*, **34**, 4–20.

Bradford, J. & Dimock, J. (1986). A comparative study of adolescents and adults who wilfully set fires. *Psychiatric Journal of the University of Ottawa*, **11**, 228–34.

Bullock, R., Hosie, K., Little, M. & Millham, S. (1990). Secure accommodation for very difficult adolescents: Some recent research findings. *Journal of Adolescence*, **13**, 205–16.

Deffenbacher, J. L. (1988). Cognitive-relaxation and social skills treatments of anger: A year later. *Journal of Counselling Psychology*, **35**, 234–6.

Deffenbacher, J. L., Story, D. A., Brandon, A. D., Hogg, J. A. & Hazaleus, S. L. (1988). Cognitive and cognitive-relaxation treatments of anger. *Cognitive Therapy and Research*, **12**, 167–84.

DeSalvatore, G. & Hornstein, R. (1991). Juvenile firesetting: Assessment and treatment in psychiatric hospitalization and residential placement. *Child and Youth Care Forum*, **20**, 103–14.

Federal Emergency Management Agency. (1983). *Juvenile Firesetter Handbook: Dealing with Children Ages 7 to 14*. Washington, DC: US Government Printing Office.

Feindler, E. L. & Ecton, R. B. (1986). *Adolescent Anger Control: Cognitive-behavioural Techniques*. Oxford: Pergamon.

Geller, J. L. (1992). Pathological firesetting in adults. *International Journal of Law and Psychiatry*, **15**, 283–302.

Hains, A. A. (1984). A preliminary attempt to teach the use of social problem-solving skills to delinquents. *Child Study Journal*, **14**, 271–85.

Harris, G. T. & Rice, M. E. (1984). Mentally disordered firesetters: Psychodynamic versus empirical approaches. *International Journal of Law and Psychiatry*, **7**, 19–34.

Heath, G. A., Hardesty, V. A., Goldfine, P. E. & Walker, A. M. (1983). Childhood firesetting: An empirical study. *Journal of the American Academy of Child Psychiatry*, **22**, 370–4.

Hollin, C. R., Epps, K. J. & Kendrick, D. J. (1995). *Managing Behavioural Treatment: Policy and Practice with Delinquent Adolescents*. London: Routledge.

Home Office. (1988). *Report of the Working Group on the Prevention of Arson*. London: Home Office.

Jackson, H. F. (1994). Assessment of fire-setters. In M. McMurran & J. Hodge (eds), *The Assessment of Criminal Behaviours of Clients in Secure Settings*. London: Jessica Kingsley.

Jackson, H. F., Glass, C. & Hope, S. (1987). A functional analysis of recidivistic arson. *British Journal of Clinical Psychology*, **26**, 175–85.

Jacobson, R. R. (1985). The subclassification of child firesetters. *Journal of Child Psychology and Psychiatry*, **26**, 769–75.

Kazdin, A. E. & Kolko, D. J. (1986). Parent psychopathology and family functioning among childhood firesetters. *Journal of Abnormal Child Psychology*, **14**, 315–29.

Kolko, D. J. (1985). Juvenile firesetting: A review and methodological critique. *Clinical Psychology Review*, **5**, 345–76.

Kolko, D. J. (1988). Community interventions for juvenile firesetters: A survey of two national programs. *Hospital and Community Psychiatry*, **39**, 973–9.

Kolko, D. J. & Kazdin, A. E. (1986). A conceptualisation of firesetting in children and adolescents. *Journal of Abnormal Child Psychology*, **14**, 49–61.

Kolko, D. J. & Kazdin, A. E. (1988). Prevalence of firesetting and related behaviours among child psychiatric patients. *Journal of Consulting and Clinical Psychology*, **56**, 628–30.

Kolko, D. J. & Kazdin, A. E. (1989a). The children's firesetting interview with psychiatrically referred and nonreferred children. *Journal of Abnormal Child Psychology*, **17**, 609–24.

Kolko, D. J. & Kazdin, A. E. (1989b). Assessment of dimensions of childhood firesetting among patients and nonpatients: The firesetting risk interview. *Journal of Abnormal Child Psychology*, **17**, 157–76.

Kolko, D. J. & Kazdin, A. E. (1990). Matchplay and firesetting in children: Relationship to parent, marital, and family dysfunction. *Journal of Clinical Child Psychology*, **19**, 229–38.

Kolko, D. J. & Kazdin, A. E. (1992). The emergence and recurrence of child firesetting: A one year prospective study. *Journal of Abnormal Child Psychology*, **20**, 17–37.

Kolko, D. J., Kazdin, A. E. & Meyer, E. C. (1985). Aggression and psychopathology in childhood firesetters: Parent and child reports. *Journal of Consulting and Clinical Psychology*, **53**, 377–85.

Novaco, R. W. (1978). Anger and coping with stress. In J. P. Foreyt & D. P. Rathjen (eds), *Cognitive Behaviour Therapy*. Lexington, MA: Heath.

Prins, H. (1994). *Fire-raising: Its Motivation and Management*. London: Routledge.

Rice, M. E. & Chaplin, T. C. (1979). Social skills training for hospitalized male arsonists. *Journal of Behaviour Therapy and Experimental Psychology*, **10**, 105–8.

Schonell, F. J. (1955). *Reading and Spelling Tests*. Edinburgh: Oliver & Boyd.

Soothill, K. (1990). Arson. In R. Bluglass & P. Bowden (eds), *Principles and Practice of Forensic Psychiatry*. Edinburgh: Churchill Livingstone.

Spielberger, C. D. (1991). *State-Trait Anger Expression Inventory: Revised Research Edition*. Odessa, FL: PAR.

Stewart, L. A. (1993). Profile of female firesetters: Implications for treatment. *British Journal of Psychiatry*, **163**, 248–56.

Strachan, J. G. (1981). Conspicuous firesetting in children. *British Journal of Psychiatry*, **138**, 26–9.

Swaffer, T. & Hollin, C. R. (1995). Adolescent firesetting: Why do they say they do it? *Journal of Adolescence*, **18**, 619–623

Wechsler, D. (1974). *Wechsler Intelligence Scale for Children—Revised*. New York: The Psychological Corporation.

Yarnell, H. (1940). Firesetting in children. *American Journal of Orthopsychiatry*, **10**, 272–86.

11

Substance Use and Delinquency

MARY MCMURRAN
Arnold Lodge, Leicester, UK

The principal aim in working with offenders is to reduce the likelihood of further offending, and professional practice may be viewed in terms of risk assessment and risk management. Monahan (1993) suggests that adequate *risk assessment* depends upon the professional knowing what information is relevant, how to gather this information, and how to integrate the information to identify specific areas of risk. The point of risk assessment is to plan strategies for *risk management*, which includes a range of interventions designed to modify the offender's behaviour in order to reduce risk. The first part of this chapter will be devoted to examining the development of substance use and delinquency, leading up to an assessment procedure based upon this knowledge. In the second part of the chapter, risk management will be addressed by examining therapeutic interventions appropriate for reducing the risk of alcohol- and drug-related crime in young offenders.

THE DEVELOPMENTAL APPROACH

In studying the development of substance use and delinquency, it is clear that there is no single developmental pathway for either of these behaviours, that is, a young person may become involved in drinking, drug use or delinquency for a number of different reasons. Indeed, these behaviours are not unusual in adolescence. For example, Farrington and Hawkins (1991), in their study of 411 London males from age 8 years through to adulthood, recorded that 31% of this sample had acquired a criminal conviction by the age of 21 years. They note that

Clinical Approaches to Working with Young Offenders. Edited by C. R. Hollin and K. Howells.
© 1996 John Wiley & Sons Ltd.

this figure represents only officially recorded crime, and that the prevalence of delinquency is undoubtedly much higher when those who have not been detected or convicted are included. In a general sample of adolescent males, Tolan (1988) found that 84% of 16-year-olds reported committing one or more delinquent acts in the previous year. With regard to drinking and drug use, a degree of involvement in these behaviours is quite common amongst adolescents in the western world. Surveys of the UK population show that by the age of 13 years around 80% of young people drink at least occasionally, and by 18 years of age around 80% are regular drinkers (Goddard, 1992; Marsh, Dobbs & White, 1986). Around 50% of young people will have at least tried cannabis and solvents, although experimentation with hard drugs is relatively uncommon (Swadi, 1988).

The prevalence of delinquency peaks at around 17 years of age, and declines thereafter (Farrington, 1994). Many of those who do offend commit few and relatively trivial acts and most will grow out of crime as they enter adulthood. There appears, however, to be a core group which displays a continuity of disruptive and problematic behaviours from childhood through to adolescence and beyond (Farrington & Hawkins, 1991; Loeber, 1990). Even though the worst offenders at an early age are likely still to be the worst offenders later on, reductions in absolute levels of offending are likely to occur. Similarly, for most people, drinking typically increases between the ages of 17 and 22 years, and declines thereafter (Grant, Harford & Grigson, 1988). The age of onset of drug use varies by drug type, but decline in drug use begins in the mid-20s (Kandel & Raveis, 1989). That is, many young adults grow out of heavy substance use, with only relatively few continuing to problematic levels. This information gives rise to questions about why many young people engage in substance use and delinquency, and why some young people continue with these behaviours, in some cases developing more serious problems, while others grow out of them.

Drinking, drug use and delinquency emerge as part of a cluster of co-occurring problem behaviours in adolescence (Farrington & Hawkins, 1991; Jessor & Jessor, 1977). The types of behaviour which co-occur in adolescence are shown in Table 11.1. Involvement in one disapproved behaviour predicts involvement in the others. In a longitudinal study of 301 delinquents from age 16 years through to age 31 years, Temple and Ladouceur (1986) observed that drinking rose steadily from age 16 years to a peak at age 23 years, continued at a steady level until age 28 years, then began gradually to decline. In this same group, offending was highest between ages 16 and 21 years, with the peak at age 18, and declined thereafter until by the age of 31 years most had stopped offending. Where illicit drug use is concerned, a longitudinal study by Elliott, Huizinga and Ageton (1985) revealed that prior delinquency and involvement with delinquent peer groups predicted both later delinquency and drug use. These studies indicate that whilst substance use and delinquency are correlated, there is no evidence that substance use *causes* crime, at least in the early stages of development, in that delinquency peaks before substance use. Furthermore, some studies have shown that early alcohol use predicts later non-drug delinquency, whereas illicit drug use does not (Dembo et al., 1991), suggesting that attention to early alcohol use is highly important.

Table 11.1   Problem behaviours that occur in a cluster

Drinking
Smoking
Illicit drug use
Rebelliousness
Delinquency
Dangerous driving
Aggression
Poor academic achievement
Less church attendance
Less orientation to work
Early sexual intercourse
Unprotected sex

The nature of the relationship between substance use and delinquency requires further examination. Various types of relationship between the two sets of behaviours are possible, as listed in Table 11.2. These relationships may be placed in four categories: (1) substance-specific crimes: (2) substance use leads to crime; (3) substance use and crime are indirectly associated; and (4) crime leads to substance use. These categories are important when targets for prevention and intervention need to be identified. Where the intention is to reduce the likelihood of crime, targeting substance use is not always logical.

It is evident from research that similar factors in early childhood predict substance use, antisocial behaviour (i.e. problem behaviours which are not necessarily defined as crimes) and delinquency (i.e. criminal offending) in adolescents (Hawkins, Catalano & Miller, 1992). This is not surprising, given that substance use is frequently used as part of the definitions of both antisocial behaviour and delinquency. Since the relationship between the two classes of behaviour needs to be clarified, it is instructive to examine how substance use and delinquency interrelate across the developmental span.

Information is provided by studies of factors which are implicated in the onset, seriousness, duration of and desistance from both substance use and delinquency.

Table 11.2   Relationships between substance use and crime

1. Substance use is the crime:
2. Substance use leads to crime:
   - Crime committed to support substance use
   - Substance use changes behaviour
   - Substance use causes problems which lead to crime.
3. Substance use and crime are indirectly associated:
   - Common factors lead independently to substance use and crime
   - Context of substance use presents opportunities for crime
   - Substance use increases chance of arrest
   - Substance use used as an excuse for crime.
4. Crime leads to substance use
   - Crime provides money for substance use
   - Crime causes problems which lead to substance use.

Factors associated with an increased likelihood of these behaviours are known as *risk factors*, whereas those associated with a decreased likelihood of these problem behaviours are known as *protective factors*. These factors generally fall into two major domains: *individual factors*, including characteristics and behaviours of the person, and *socialization factors*, including family management, peer associations, and school and vocational performance. Risk and protective factors may be opposite ends of the same continuum (e.g. poor school performance—good school performance), but there is also evidence that some factors are exclusively risk factors and that their absence is not necessarily protective (e.g. hyperactivity; Stouthamer-Loeber et al., 1993). Although distinct protective factors have not yet been identified, the existence of some positive features has been shown to buffer against the effects of risk factors, for example Brook et al. (1989) found that academic achievement in adolescence offset the risk for substance use in young people with an angry temperament. The study of risk and protective factors may help explain the development of substance use and delinquency, and the relationship between the two sets of behaviours. With a view to prevention and intervention, it is important to pay specific attention to those factors—both risk and protective—which can be changed in order to reduce the likelihood of problem behaviours.

Looking across the developmental time span, from early childhood through to adolescence, it becomes clear that the relationships between these factors and the behaviours of interest change over time. Thus, whilst there may be one set of factors which explain the onset of substance use or delinquency, different factors explain the maintenance and escalation of these behaviours once they are established, and yet other factors explain desistance. One way of organizing information about the factors that influence the course and nature of substance use and delinquency is within a psychosocial development model (Farrington & Hawkins, 1991; Jessor, 1992; Oetting, 1992). Although various models exist, these generally describe and explain behaviours in terms of reciprocal person–environment interactions which evolve over time. The child may have personal characteristics which predispose him or her to the development of problem behaviours; however, other factors will influence the developmental course. Conditions within the family, school and peer relationships can promote or protect against the development of problem behaviours. These socialization contexts will exert their influence differentially at various stages in the child's development, with the family being most important in early childhood, and school and peers growing more important as the child grows older. Of course, the direction of influence is not only from the social context upon the child; the child also influences how the social environment responds towards him or her.

DEVELOPMENTAL PATHWAYS

In his review of the development of antisocial behaviour and delinquency, Loeber (1988; 1990) describes the temporal order in which different manifestations of disruptive behaviours emerge from early childhood through to adolescence, for three different types of offender. The *aggressive/versatile* offender is one who engages in violence, and sometimes also property-offences. The route to this end point typically starts with difficult temperament, progressing through hyperactivity and conduct problems, to the emergence of problem behaviours, and ending with delinquency. The *non-aggressive* offender offends against property only. The pathway to this shows less early hyperactivity and aggression, beginning with conduct problems in later childhood and progressing to delinquency. Substance use is common in both types, with the aggressive/versatile more likely to show a higher degree of involvement. The *exclusive substance user* does not usually display early conduct problems and may have an early history of internalizing problems (e.g. anxiety) as opposed to externalizing problems (e.g. hyperactivity). These pathways are represented diagrammatically in Figure 11.1. The aim in the rest of this section is to attempt to clarify how substance use may fit into this progression of events, by identifying the processes that may occur at the points noted in the figure: 1, early childhood; 2, late childhood/early adolescence; and 3, adolescence.

Before moving on, however, gender issues must be acknowledged. More boys engage in delinquency than girls, and, whilst both sexes show increasingly similar prevalence rates for substance use, boys are more likely to be heavy users. There is evidence that developmental pathways are similar for boys and girls, but also that there are significant differences which require attention (Farrell, 1993). Research has been concentrated on boys and insufficient attention has been paid to gender differences.

Early Childhood

Research into the precursors of both substance abuse and serious antisocial behaviour in adulthood shows difficult temperament and hyperactivity in infancy

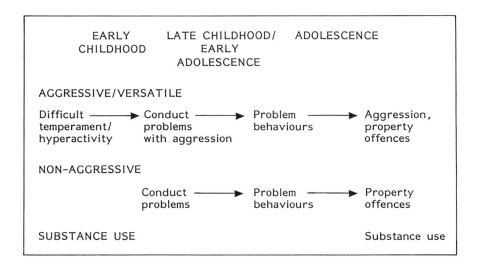

Figure 11.1   Development of problem behaviours (after Loeber, 1990)

and early childhood to be one starting point. A 'difficult temperament', a rather vague concept, is characterized by irregularities in eating and sleeping, inflexibility to changes in the environment, and frequent negative moods. Loeber (1990) suggests that difficult temperament is the earliest postnatal manifestation of what later becomes hyperactivity, the latter becoming evident only when the child becomes mobile. Hyperactivity is characterized by overactivity, impulsivity, short attention span and frequent negative moods. There is variation in the use of the term hyperactivity, some researchers referring to the hyperactivity, impulsivity, attention-problem constellation (HIA), whereas others use the diagnostic classification of attention-deficit/hyperactivity disorder (ADHD; DSM-IV; American Psychiatric Association, 1994).

Loeber, Stouthamer-Loeber and Green (1991) studied 205 boys for five years, starting when they were between 10 and 16 years old, collecting data about problem behaviours, offending and parenting from official records, parents and the boys themselves. Retrospective data on temperament and early behaviour problems were also collected for ages 1 to 5 years. Thirty-one boys were classified as 'not easy' in early childhood, whilst the remaining 174 were classified as 'easy' children. Those who were 'not easy' offended at a rate that was twice as high as the 'easy' boys, significantly more committed multiple offences, and significantly more showed criminal versatility (i.e. both aggressive and acquisitive offences). Delinquent lifestyle was also measured, this being a composite of self-reported delinquency and substance abuse. 'Not easy' boys were significantly more likely to score high on delinquent lifestyle. In a longitudinal study of 133 children from 5 years old through to adulthood, Lerner and Vicary (1984) found that a difficult temperament at age 5 years was associated with a continued difficult temperament in adolescence, as well as tobacco, alcohol and marijuana use.

Children with attention deficit problems appear to be at risk of developing in two different directions; there is evidence that attention deficit problems may persist with or without the development of hyperactivity (Wheeler & Carlson, 1994). Both sub-groups are likely to develop inadequate problem-solving strategies, those with hyperactivity being inattentive and impulsive, and those without being inattentive and disorganized.

Those who show both attention deficit and hyperactivity are more overtly troublesome and are more aggressive. Early aggression has been shown to predict later aggressive/versatile offending (Loeber, 1988; 1990). Klinteberg et al. (1993) report on a prospective study of 540 boys, who were rated at the age of 13 years for hyperactivity by their teachers and followed through to the age of 26 years, collecting information about alcohol problems and violent offending. Of the non-hyperactive boys ($n = 284$), 10% were registered for alcohol problems before the age of 25 years, compared with 33% of the hyperactive group ($n = 142$), that is, the hyperactive group were three times more likely to develop alcohol problems. Where violent offending was concerned, 2% of the non-hyperactive group and 16% of the hyperactive group had committed violent offences, that is, the risk of violence was eight times higher for the hyperactive group. Of the 95 subjects known to have alcohol problems, 25% ($n = 24$) had committed violent offences, compared with only 2.5% ($n = 11$) of those without alcohol problems, showing that the presence of alcohol problems increases the risk of violent offending by a factor of 10. Conversely, alcohol problems without violent offending and without hyperactivity in childhood, and violence without alcohol problems and hyperactivity in childhood were highly atypical. This is strong evidence for a relationship between childhood hyperactivity and later alcohol problems and violent offending in the same people; hyperactivity is a risk factor for both outcomes.

Those who show attention deficit without hyperactivity engage less in disruptive behaviours and are more anxious, shy and socially withdrawn. It has been suggested that this group lacks social skills, in contrast to the hyperactive/ conduct problem group who have the ability to interact positively with others but frequently do not do so because of poor behavioural control (Wheeler & Carlson, 1994). Social withdrawal protects against the development of delinquency (Farrington, 1994). This may be because in later life there is little association with delinquent peers; however, in this group there may be little association with non-delinquent peers either. This predicament may present a risk factor for later substance use, which develops as a strategy for coping with unpleasant feelings such as anxiety and the boredom or loneliness deriving from social isolation.

To complicate the picture, some aggressive children may also be shy and socially withdrawn. Farrington (1994) observes that shyness acts as a protective factor for delinquency in non-aggressive boys, and as an aggravating factor in aggressive boys. Research into adolescent substance use shows that high arousability (i.e. impulsivity and disinhibition) and high negative affectivity (i.e. anxiety, depression and low self-esteem) are independent risk factors for both initiation to substance use and heavier levels of use. A combination of the two factors exacerbates the risk for substance use and also leads to more problematic consequences, including aggression (Johnson & Pandina, 1993; Pandina, Johnson & Labouvie, 1991).

Personal characteristics such as difficult temperament, attention deficit, impulsivity and hyperactivity, may present a direct risk for substance use and delinquency in that these activities serve to regulate physiological or emotional states. However, not every child who displays these characteristics goes on to develop problem behaviours and so other factors must come into play. We must look more closely at how these personal characteristics impact upon the child's social environment—family, school and peers. To examine these factors requires that we move on to later childhood and early adolescence.

Late Childhood and Early Adolescence

A review of the precursors of adult substance use disorders by Wilens and Biederman (1993) indicates that attention-deficit/hyperactivity disorder (ADHD) places children at greater risk for developing later substance use problems. Maughan (1993), in a review of the precursors of adult aggressive offending, concludes that the most serious antisocial outcomes occur in those groups where there has been an early onset (i.e. before the age of 6 years) of ADHD. However, for both substance use and delinquency the development of ADHD into a conduct disorder in later childhood substantially increases the likelihood of persistent problem behaviours (Maughan, 1993; Wilens & Biederman, 1993). Conduct problems are variously defined, meaning anything from a general antisocial disruptiveness to the diagnostic classification of conduct disorder (DSM-IV; American Psychiatric Association, 1994), which may be diagnosed when any three of a range of problem behaviours have recently been evident, these problem behaviours including: bullying, stealing, running away, lying, firesetting, truancy, destroying property and fighting. How might conduct problems develop, and how might they be related to substance use?

Pelham and Lang (1993) review a number of laboratory studies designed to examine how ADHD in children influences parental alcohol consumption. In these studies, they trained children to help in experiments where they had to behave as 'normal' children or 'deviant' children in their interactions with adults. The normal child role was to be active, attentive, well-behaved, compliant and friendly. The deviant child role was to be overactive, inattentive, bossy, interruptive, non-compliant and defiant; the deviant child made a mess of the experiment room, never did what he was told straight away, and eventual compliance was accompanied by whining and complaining. The tasks set were for the adult and child to work together on an Etch-A-Sketch; the child to complete an arithmetic task alone whilst the adult did a cheque-book balancing task; and a joint play session. There was a break at this point, after which the adults were led to believe there would be another session of tasks, although this did not actually take place. During the break, adults were allowed access to alcohol. The measures taken were the adults' mood and their perceptions of the child's behaviour, as well as the amount of alcohol consumed.

One study involved parents whose own children were not hyperactive. Pelham and Lang found that interaction with a deviant child had a negative effect on adults' mood and upon their perceptions of the pleasantness of the interaction. As a group, those interacting with the deviant child drank more than those interacting with the normal child. The same experiment conducted with parents whose own children were hyperactive showed that their responses to the interaction with the deviant child were similarly perceived as stressful, yet they did *not* drink more than parents who interacted with the normal child. This may be because they have learned from their own experience that alcohol actually reduces the ability to cope, and they have given this up as a stress-reducing strategy. Further analysis of the data, however, showed that there were differences when adults' family history of alcohol problems was examined. Adults who had one or both parents with an alcohol problem consumed *more* alcohol after the interaction with the deviant child compared with those whose parents did not have an alcohol problem.

A further study by Pelham and Lang looked at the effects of alcohol consumption on adults' interactions with children. The experimental set-up was the same as before, except that half the parents in the study were given alcohol to drink before the interaction. Behavioural observations showed that alcohol had a substantial effect on these interactions, specifically that appropriate attending to the child was reduced, commands were increased, and levels of indulgence in the child were increased. In their review of risk factors for substance use, Hawkins, Catalano and Miller (1992) point out that family management practices which increase risk are 'characterised by unclear expectations for behavior, poor monitoring of behavior, few and inconsistent rewards for positive behavior, and excessively severe and inconsistent punishment for unwanted behavior' (p. 83). Similarly, Farrington and Hawkins (1991) say that 'poor parenting practices of lax supervision or monitoring, and harsh or erratic discipline' increase the likelihood of later delinquency.

These results show that interaction with a hyperactive child is stressful for parents, and that alcohol may be used to help adults cope, at least in the initial stages of experiencing this stress. Experience over the long term may reveal drinking to be an ineffective coping strategy in that it actually reduces one's ability to solve problems. However, adults whose own parents are heavy drinkers are likely to continue to drink to cope with difficult children. Parents who drink are likely to influence their children by presenting a model that drinking alcohol is acceptable, and more specifically they model alcohol use as a method of coping with problems, and alcohol use may lead to family management practices which are conducive to the development of substance use and delinquency.

Whilst hyperactivity in the child may affect parenting practices, it is worth reiterating that personal characteristics, such as difficult temperament/ hyperactivity, may present a direct risk for the later development of problem behaviours, irrespective of parenting practices. In the aforementioned longitudinal study of problem behaviours and offending, Loeber, Stouthamer-Loeber and Green (1991) analysed data for the 57 boys in their sample who had been arrested for offences, finding that the relationship between 'not easy' and rate of offending remained evident, even when parenting practices were partialled out. In addition, parenting practices conducive to the development of substance use and offending may occur without the influence of hyperactivity in the child, for example through parents having had poor parenting models in their own childhood, or currently living under circumstances of poverty, unemployment and lack of support which militate against good parenting. Also, a family norm of substance use may exist without being based upon the stresses of dealing with problematic children.

The development of conduct disorder does not present a certain risk for the development of persistent delinquency. Farrington and Hawkins (1991) report upon the risk factors for delinquency from a longitudinal study of males from the age of 8 years onwards. Factors which predicted having any criminal convictions, having criminal convictions at an early age, and persistence with or desistance from offending were studied separately. They found that early antisocial behaviour (i.e. troublesomeness at the age of 8 years) was a strong predictor of both participation in crime and having criminal convictions at an early age. However, troublesome behaviour in childhood was not strongly predictive of persistence of criminal behaviour into early adulthood. We shall move on to adolescence to look at issues relating to school and peers.

Adolescence

Where a child has problems with self-control and is not encouraged to control his or her behaviour, academic and social problems may ensue. The child may be unable to concentrate on school work and consequently fail to achieve academic success. School failure is, in turn, posited to lead to association with substance using and delinquent peers (Sher & Trull, 1994). Young people both *select* peer groups who are similar to themselves, and are *socialized* into the norms of their peer group (Kandel, 1985). All of these conditions serve to reduce opportunities for conventional involvement and increase opportunities for antisocial involvement.

In the study by Farrington and Hawkins (1991), low levels of family bonding were seen to be related to the likelihood of offending, but not to persistence of offending into adulthood. Low commitment to school, on the other hand, was strongly related to persistence in crime into early adulthood. Le Blanc (1994), in a longitudinal study of 309 males from around 14 years of age into adulthood, found that adult offending was significantly related to school performance during adolescence. Le Blanc (1994) suggests that poor performance at school is predictive of poor job stability in adulthood, and that this takes over as the main risk factor later in life. In their review, Hawkins, Catalano and Miller (1992) found the role of poor school performance in the development of later substance abuse to be equivocal. There is evidence to suggest that peer influence is a mediating factor in the progression to substance use.

Peer influence is widely assumed to affect substance use and delinquency amongst adolescents. In their longitudinal study of boys and girls from age 11–17 years through to age 13–19 years, Elliott, Huizinga and Ageton (1985) found that bonding with delinquent peers was strongly associated with both delinquency and drug use. Of those who bonded with delinquent peers, those with low conventional bonding (i.e. with family, school and community) showed increased levels of delinquency and drug use over time, whereas those who bonded with delinquent peers but also had strong conventional bonds showed no increase over time. This suggests that conventional bonding protects against the effects of bonding to delinquent peers.

Jessor (1992) makes the point that different problem behaviours may serve the same function for adolescents, for example illicit drug use and precocious sexual activity may both be ways of asserting independence from parental authority. It is worth remembering here that substance use and delinquency are not statistically abnormal behaviours in adolescence. Many young people will take up these behaviours in adolescence without having a history of earlier problems, simply because this is the social norm for that age group. Jessor (1992) also points out that any one problem behaviour may serve different functions across the developmental time span. For example, drinking and drug use may begin in order to fit in with a peer group but may later come to help the individual cope with personal problems. For some young people substance use may have had this function from the outset and they develop into substance use without showing much in the way of early antisocial behaviours.

With regard to behaviours that are against the law (including illicit substance use), many adolescents will grow out of them in time. The situation with regard to permitted behaviours, such as drinking alcohol, is that most young people grow out of problematic levels of use and settle into moderation. Why do some people moderate or stop substance use over time whereas others increase their consumption? Midanik, Klatsky and Armstrong (1990) studied drinkers over a five-year period, comparing those who became heavier drinkers with those who remained light drinkers. Those who increased their consumption were more likely to be younger, male, unmarried and smokers, and experienced more nervousness, depression and emotional trouble. Drinking to cope with personal problems appears to be particularly important in explaining the escalation of drinking. Thompson (1989), in a longitudinal study of adolescents, noticed that heavy drinking created disharmony with peer groups, particularly amongst those who drank for non-social purposes, suggesting that those who have personal problems may drink to alleviate them, but that drinking may serve to exacerbate these problems by alienating friends. Where drug use is concerned, Kandel and Raveis (1989), in their longitudinal study, found that those who gave up drugs were more likely to have married and become parents, and to have ceased delinquent activities and disengaged from drug-using friends. Quitters were more likely to have been social drug users, whereas those who continued drug use were more likely to cite personal reasons for drug use. Brook et al. (1989) found, in their longitudinal study of adolescents, that using drugs to manage psychological distress was associated with continuing drug use.

Farrington and Hawkins (1991) suggest that involvement in conventional society (i.e. commitment to family, school, work and non-offending peers) can facilitate a return to conventionality, that is, young people can grow out of crime. It may be that the responsibilities associated with a conventional lifestyle are incompatible with substance use and delinquency. For some people, however, prior substance use and delinquency may present an obstacle to conventional involvement in that they are rejected by conventional society. The study by Farrington and Hawkins (1991) shows that heavy drinking at the age of 18 years predicts persistence of crime into adulthood, although the same was not found for illicit drug use. This suggests that alcohol and drugs play different roles in the genesis of crime, and that heavy drinking may be the greater cause for concern.

Progression to serious substance use and/or delinquency is never inevitable and many young people will grow out of substance use and delinquency as they become more involved in conventional activities, such as starting work, having relationships and becoming parents. Whatever the route to delinquency, however, once substance use has begun the functions of this behaviour may change, and crime is likely to become more evident as substance use increases. How may substance use and delinquency be related to each other once both sets of behaviours have become established in adolescence?

RELATIONSHIPS BETWEEN SUBSTANCE USE AND DELINQUENCY

There are a number of possible relationships between substance use and crime, listed in Table 11.2. First of all, it must be stated that the two sets of behaviours may be connected through a common variable, for example both substance use and crime may serve to regulate arousal in those who were hyperactive children, or both substance use and crime may have been family norms, or normative peer group behaviours. Even so, a young person may get into trouble with the law in a number of ways, with a possible reciprocal developmental sequence emerging.

At any stage there is the possibility of alcohol- and drug-specific offences, where by virtue of substance use *per se* the individual is breaking the law. Some of these offences are age-specific, for example underage drinking on licensed premises, whereas others are not age-specific, such as unauthorized use of restricted drugs.

In the early stages of substance use, a young person is unlikely to have the financial resources to purchase alcohol or drugs and so drinking and drug use may be supported by acquisitive offences. If substance use develops to heavier levels, then this kind of relationship is likely to persist.

It is also the case that substance use may change behaviour, through impairing judgement or reducing self-control. As we have seen, some young people may have deficits in problem-solving skills and self-control which are further impaired by substance use.

Substance use may also lead to delinquency through the social context in which it occurs. First, groups of young people who are drinking or using drugs may together plan to commit offences. Second, the probability of violence may be elevated in social contexts regardless of the occurrence of substance use. Violence in association with alcohol use may be a function of the gathering together of predominantly young people looking for fun and excitement, and the relationship between drinking and crimes of violence may be correlational, describing only when and where the violence occurs (Lang & Sibrel, 1989; Murdoch, Pihl & Ross, 1990). McBride (1981), in his review of drugs and violence, also suggests that the context creates a situation in which violence is likely. The dealer aims to sell the lowest quality drugs at the highest price, whereas the buyer wants to buy the best quality at the lowest price, and so there is an atmosphere of mutual suspicion in which violence is likely. Third, the venues where drinking and drug use occur are usually the focus of police attention, and so the likelihood of arrest is increased in and around these venues.

With increasing involvement in crime, the offender may simply have a greater disposable income to spend on substance use. However, increasing involvement in both substance use and crime may lead to personal, social and financial problems which increase the likelihood of further involvement in both substance use and crime.

Of course, at any stage an offender may blame substance use for the commission of crime to minimize personal responsibility for behaviour or to achieve the best possible outcome—a lesser sentence, entry into a treatment programme, or whatever else that person values. In individual cases, the specific circumstances should be examined to determine what issues might affect validity of self-report.

As substance use and crime develop, they become part of the young person's general life-style. Where substance use and delinquency frequently co-occur, the relationship between the two may become more firmly entrenched through association; if young people drink or use drugs frequently, then most of their activities will occur in association with substance use, and if delinquency is part of the range of activities, then substance use becomes associated with delinquency. This may be internalized by the young person as the expectancy that substance use causes crime, with this expectancy developing into a self-fulfilling prophecy.

The challenge at this stage is to intervene to reduce the likelihood of alcohol- and drug-related crime. Methods of assessment and intervention will be covered in the remainder of this chapter.

ASSESSMENT

Assessment should address (1) the development of substance use and delinquency; (2) the current status of the behaviour, including type of substances used, quantity and frequency of use, and the contingencies which operate to maintain the behaviour; and (3) the relationship with criminal events. Interviews with the offender, and other relevant persons (e.g. parents) should investigate risk factors, paying attention to the interrelationships among relevant behaviours over time. Self-monitoring diaries, which ask the client to record what triggers substance use, what substances are used, in what quantities, when, where, with whom, and with what consequences, give information about the current status of the behaviour. Analysis of specific criminal events, using official records and interviews, can specify the role of substance use in the commission of crime. Direct observation, analogue assessments (e.g. role play), and psychometric tests can augment the information collected from interview and records, and these are particularly useful for monitoring change over time. Discussion of these methods is beyond the scope of this chapter, and readers are referred elsewhere for further information (Allen & Litten, 1993; Donovan & Marlatt, 1988; McMurran & Hollin, 1993).

A wealth of information will be collected in assessment, and this requires integration. One method of integration has been suggested by Gresswell and Hollin (1992), whereby information is arranged in developmental sequences, identifying antecedents, behaviour, consequences, and learning points in a dynamic progression (See Table 11.3). This is best illustrated by example.

MICHAEL

According to his mother, Michael was a difficult child who was disobedient, damaged his toys and books, and threw temper tantrums. At school he did not concentrate on his lessons and was often in trouble for running wild in the classroom and fighting with other children. Michael's mother was extremely stressed by his behaviour, and used alcohol and tranquillizers to help her cope. At times, she simply gave up trying to control him, since nothing seemed to work. His behaviour problems continued through primary school, and became worse when he moved up to secondary school at the age of 12 years.

Michael was behind the rest of the class in reading and writing, and he reported feeling 'thick'. He had a few friends at secondary school, mostly other boys who were also poor at school work and did not like school. Together they began to truant. Hanging around was rather boring, and so they began shoplifting, stealing small items such as magazines, which they used first for their own amusement and then sold on at school. Their illicit trading grew in scope, and they began to spend the proceeds on cigarettes and alcohol. They also regularly sniffed glue and other solvents. Michael found drinking and solvent use helped him enjoy his times with the other boys, since they would 'act daft' and get up to pranks. These pranks included vandalism and car theft, but he was never caught for these. Michael was apprehended for shoplifting on one occasion and received a police caution. His behaviour continued to cause friction between himself and his mother.

Michael formally left school at the age of 16 years, and he was then in and out of a number of unskilled jobs. He began to drink in pubs, where he met with people who drank more than he did, and found he needed more money to keep up with their alcohol consumption. When he was out of work he continued to shoplift, taking more valuable merchandise, and in addition he began to break into houses during the day. When drunk, he often got into fights and on one occasion he demanded money from another youth using threats of violence. He was charged with robbery and received a probation order. Michael says that going to the pub was his main social activity, and without this he would have 'gone insane with boredom'.

By the age of 17 years, Michael was drinking approximately four nights per week, and getting drunk on each occasion. He drank strong lager, and would usually consume around five or six pints in the evening. At weekends, he would usually go on to a nightclub, where he would drink four or five shots of spirits. Occasionally he would use poppers (amyl nitrate). When he was drunk, he was argumentative and belligerent, and frequently got into fights. Michael acquired convictions for several offences, including drunk and disorderly, criminal damage, and assault. He spent a period of four months in custody. By this time, he had also acquired a reputation for being 'mad' and his friends began to avoid him.

The index offence occurred on a Saturday night in a club. Michael was drunk and becoming argumentative with another patron when the bouncer spotted trouble brewing and removed Michael from the club. Michael was aggrieved at being dealt with in this way and attempted to fight the bouncer, who was able to fend him off. Michael turned away shouting angry obscenities, only to meet with a young man who was standing watching the incident. Michael enquired in a somewhat less than polite manner what the young man was looking at, and then seriously assaulted him. He was later charged with assault occasioning grievous bodily harm.

INTEGRATION OF INFORMATION

Stage 1. Childhood

Antecedents:	Difficult temperament; attention problems; hyperactivity; inconsistent parenting; mother models drinking and drug use as a response to stress.
Behaviour:	Poor control over behaviour; conduct problems.
Consequences:	Gets into trouble at school; poor school performance.
Key learning:	Dislikes school; not good at academic work.

Stage 2. Early adolescence

Antecedents: Sequence in stage 1, plus move to secondary school.
Behaviour: Truancy; shoplifting; smoking; drinking; solvent use; vandalism; car theft.
Consequences: Avoid school; gains money; relief of boredom.
Key learning: Delinquency and substance use both relieve boredom; theft facilitates substance use.

Stage 3. Late adolescence

Antecedents: Sequence in stage 2, plus drinking in pubs.
Behaviour: Heavy drinking; fighting; crime to support substance use.
Consequences: Reputation for fighting; trouble with the law.
Key learning: Heavy drinking causes violence and trouble with the law.

At this point, one can predict a number of possible progressions. It may be that this serious assault is sufficient to bring about a change in drinking and delinquency. It has been shown that some young offenders do respond to adverse events, particularly violence and crime, by reducing their drinking (McMurran & Whitman, 1990) Alternatively, there may be little to be gained by Michael in staying out of trouble in that he has no strong conventional role in society, therefore substance use and delinquency may continue. It is interesting to note that changes in drinking among young offenders also occur for positive reasons, such as finding a job and becoming a father (McMurran & Whitman, 1990). Ironically, in Michael's case the problems created by aiming to stay out of trouble, find a regular job, and rid himself of his reputation for violence may actually present a risk for even heavier drinking and drug use; these ambitions may be stressful, and his early parental model showed that substance use is a means of coping with problems.

INTERVENTIONS

It is clear from the risk factors implicated in the development of substance use and delinquency that different types of intervention may be appropriate across the developmental span. In the early years, prevention programmes aimed at providing support to parents and helping them to manage their children effectively are clearly important, as are interventions aimed at improving bonding with school through changes in school organization, classroom management, and teaching practices (Hawkins, Catalano & Miller, 1992; Mulvey, Arthur & Reppucci, 1993). Prevention programmes in later childhood aim to teach the individual the skills necessary for surviving adolescence without recourse to substance use or delinquency (Oetting, 1992; Rhodes & Jason, 1988). Prevention approaches will not be covered in this chapter, the aim here being to concentrate on interventions that focus on the individual who is already involved in substance use and delinquency. However, it is worth pointing out that whilst the opportunity for early prevention is past for those who are already involved in problem behaviours, many offenders will eventually have children of their own and parent training for offenders may impact upon the next generation.

Meta-analyses of rehabilitation programmes for young offenders have shown that structured cognitive-behavioural programmes are most effective (Izzo & Ross, 1990; Lipsey, 1992). Relevant components of intervention for substance users include motivational interviewing, behavioural self-control training, problem-solving skills training, expectancy challenge, emotion control training, social skills training, relapse prevention, and general life-style modification. These will be described briefly here; a fuller description may be found elsewhere (McMurran, 1994; McMurran & Hollin, 1993). Matching these components with offenders' specific needs is important. A programme for 'Michael' in the example presented earlier, might include behavioural self-control training to reduce alcohol consumption, expectancy challenge to modify the link between drinking and violence, and life-style modification to engage him in a more prosocial life-style.

Motivation to Change

Farabee, Nelson and Spence (1993) found that clients referred for substance abuse interventions through the criminal justice system showed less desire to change than did voluntary clients. They suggest that motivational issues should be viewed as important needs to address, rather than selection criteria for programmes. Prochaska, DiClemente and Norcross (1992) describe a model of change in addictive behaviours, where there is a predictable motivational route from the position of not recognizing a problem (precontemplation), through recognition (contemplation), preparation for change, to action and maintenance of change. Different strategies are relevant at various stages, with cognitive interventions (e.g. consciousness raising) being more useful during the early stages, and behavioural techniques (e.g. behavioural self-control training) being more useful during later stages. Miller and Rollnick (1991) describe motivational interviewing techniques for enhancing motivation to change.

Behavioural Self-control Training (BSCT)

As we have seen, some young offenders have a history of poor control over their behaviour. BSCT aims to teach the individual to become a 'personal scientist' by collecting and analysing personal data, testing techniques for change, and monitoring outcome (Mahoney & Thoresen, 1974). First, the target behaviour must be specified and examined, along with other relevant factors. Information about substance use, the circumstances in which it occurs, and the consequences is usually collected in a daily diary. With this information the relationships between antecedents and outcomes can be examined and goals for change can be set. *Goals* may be to moderate or cease substance use, but a goal of reducing crime without changing substance use may also be valid as a type of criminological harm reduction. *Personal rule-setting* aims to alter the antecedents to the behaviour and may include limiting time spent using substances and the amount of money spent on substance use. Rules may also address the context of substance use to minimize the likelihood of crime, for example avoidance of certain people or places. *Rate control* aims at moderating the behaviour where this is the goal choice and includes changing the type of substance used and the rate at which it is consumed in a using situation. *Self-monitoring* and *self-reward* are aimed at maintaining awareness of the behaviour to check that goals are being met and rewarding oneself for success.

BSCT has been shown to be effective in reducing alcohol consumption under a number of conditions: where the intervention has been conducted individually, in groups, or using a self-help manual (Miller, 1978; Miller & Baca, 1983; Miller & Taylor, 1980).

Problem-solving Skills Training

Problem-solving skills training has two major contributions to make with young offenders who are attempting to reduce substance use. First, impulsivity is one risk factor for delinquency and 'stop and think' interventions have had considerable impact in reducing delinquency. Ross, Fabiano and Ross (1986) included a problem-solving component in their offender rehabilitation programme, finding that, in comparison with a control group, scores on an impulsivity measure were lower and there was a lower rate of readmission to prison with new convictions. Second, changing substance use can reveal a range of problems with which the individual has to deal, for example finding other leisure pursuits and other ways of coping with emotions. Providing young people with the skills to address life's problems has greater long-term potential than providing a ready-made solution to each problem as it arises. Chaney, O'Leary and Marlatt (1978) found that drinkers in a problem-solving intervention significantly improved on a number of measures of drinking.

Problem-solving skills training is based on the work of D'Zurilla and Goldfried (1971) and aims to teach people to identify and analyse their problems, consider a range of possible solutions, and implement an action plan. D'Zurilla and Nezu (1982) describe the process in five stages:

- *Orientation*, where there is recognition of a problem, cueing the problem-solving process
- *Problem definition and goal setting*, where the problem is clearly specified and realistic goals are set
- *Generation of alternatives*, where a list of potential options is creatively generated
- *Decision making and action*, where each option is assessed and the best are selected into an action plan
- *Evaluation*, where progress is reviewed.

Problem solving is terminated at this point if the goal has been achieved, or repeated if it has not.

Expectancy Challenge

Outcome expectancies are cognitive representations of the 'if–then' relationship between events. A person may be at risk for continued substance use when the expectation is that good effects will be experienced. In addition, the outcomes that a person expects after substance use may be risk factors for crime. For example, a study comparing a group of adult rapists whose offences were alcohol-related with a group whose offences were not alcohol-related found that the former believed that they were more likely to do something sexually risky after drinking (McMurran & Bellfield, 1993). Whilst this belief is clearly a representation of past experience, it is also a risk factor for further offending after drinking.

Outcome analysis, which is simply listing the positive and negative effects of substance use, is one method of challenging expectancies of positive effects from substance use. This component has been rated by offenders in an alcohol programme as highly useful (McMurran & Thomas, 1991). Also, exposure to substance-using situations in which the client does not drink can prompt contemplation of the effects of substances. Criminogenic expectancies need to be identified and replaced by non-criminogenic expectancies. There are a number of questionnaires that identify general outcome expectancies for alcohol (Young & Oei, 1993), some of which contain criminogenic items (e.g. alcohol makes me violent), but no measure of purely criminogenic expectancies exists. Beck et al. (1993) recommend identifying beliefs through open-ended questioning and challenging beliefs through the 'Socratic method', which is asking probing questions regarding the client's evidence for their beliefs.

Emotion Control Training

There are two principal emotions that are relevant to substance use in adolescents: anger and anxiety. We have seen that early aggression is a risk factor for both later substance use and delinquency, and that anxiety is a risk factor for substance use. Anger management programmes, based on the work of Novaco (1975), have been designed for young offenders (McDougall et al., 1987). These include self-monitoring, education, self-instruction training and relaxation training, and are relevant where aggression is the result of anger or tension, as opposed to instrumental aggression (McDougall & Boddis, 1991). Anxiety management techniques include progressive muscle relaxation, the use of calming imagery, self-instructional training and cognitive restructuring (Hallam, 1992).

Social Skills Training (SST)

The purpose of SST is to enable the individual to interact effectively with others. Social skill involves the perception of relevant cues from the environment, processing the information in order to come to a decision about how to respond, and then making the appropriate response. One particularly relevant area to address is refusal skills, that is, saying 'no' to peers who encourage substance use.

Hollin (1990) points out that SST with young offenders, as with others, has typically focused upon the response part of the process, using the training techniques of *instruction* in the required behaviour, *modelling* (i.e. demonstration) the required behaviour by another person, *rehearsal*, and *feedback* about performance. Whilst this aspect is important, problem-solving skills training, addressing social issues, should also be included.

Relapse Prevention

Relapse prevention, based on the work of Marlatt and Gordon (1985), aims to prepare people to anticipate and cope with high-risk situations that may precipitate a relapse to substance use. First, high-risk situations are identified by examining past relapses, drinking diaries, and fears for the future, then coping skills are taught for each type of situation. Clients are also informed that they may experience craving for substances, and are taught to withstand these cravings by making positive self-statements (e.g. 'I can cope'), reviewing the reasons they decided to change their behaviour, and distracting themselves with other activities. Cravings may also be reduced by cue exposure and response prevention, where alcohol or drug paraphernalia are presented to the client without allowing substance use to occur (Rohsenow et al., 1991). In case a lapse should occur, clients are taught to prevent a lapse becoming a full-blown lapse (the goal violation effect) by understanding that lapses can be limited and by devising a set of procedures to deal with lapses. Once relapse prevention strategies have been taught, a programme of graded practice in real-life situations is instituted.

Life-style Modification

Since problem behaviours occur in a cluster in adolescence, Jessor (1992) recommends that attention be paid to the adolescent life-style as a whole in attempts to prevent or correct problem behaviours. This may hold more promise than focusing upon specific problem behaviours independently, which Jessor (1992) says leads to 'the "problem-of-the-week" approach, in which efforts are mobilized to fight teenage pregnancy one week, drunk driving the next, illicit drug use the next, crime after that, and so on' (p. 379). The individual's circumstances should be changed to support a non-delinquent, non-substance-abusing life-style. Attention should be paid to work, leisure activities and relationships. Prosocial activities and association with prosocial peers should be encouraged.

One example of a broad-based life-style modification programme is the community reinforcement approach of Sisson and Azrin (1989), which includes employment counselling, social skills training, leisure advice and relationship counselling. This has been shown to reduce drinking days and increase working days better than hospital treatment for drinkers.

SPECIFIC ISSUES

When working with young offenders, there are a number of additional issues to take into account regarding style, intensity and special needs.

Style of Intervention

First, McMurran (1991) points out that adolescent offenders are independent and typically not academically inclined. This suggests that didactic, classroom-based education will not suit this group. Indeed, traditional education conveying the facts about alcohol and drugs has consistently been shown to be ineffective with adolescents generally (Hopkins et al., 1988; Kinder, Pape & Walfish, 1980). Interventions should be active and skills-based, and possibly even conducted in the natural environment. Second, since adolescents are disinclined to listen to what adults have to tell them, but are apparently open to the persuasion of their peers, the possibility of interventions conducted by peers holds merit (Swadi & Zeitlin, 1988). Finally, Andrews and colleagues (1990) caution against group work with offenders, since this may actually be criminogenic for some. A clearer idea of who will benefit from group work should be a topic for future research.

Intensity of Intervention

Lipsey's (1992) meta-analysis of juvenile delinquency treatment programmes shows that those that are more frequent and of longer duration are associated with better outcome. There is, however, evidence to suggest that brief interventions can be effective for some substance users, particularly those with less severe problems (Bien, Miller & Tonigan, 1993). Matching clients to the most appropriate intensity maximizes cost-effectiveness. In addition, some offenders are available for intervention for only a short period, owing to the length of probation, imprisonment or licence, and so interventions must necessarily be brief. McMurran and Hollin (1993) describe a modular approach, whereby clients may enter and leave the modular sequence at any point, thus allowing clients to be matched with appropriate components of intervention. A modular programme containing the components of intervention described in this chapter is presented in Figure 11.2.

Special Needs

At present, little attention has been paid to designing programmes for those with special needs, for example minority ethnic groups, young women and people with learning disabilities. A survey of probation officers, along with other health professionals, suggested that minority ethnic groups do not have equal access to substance use programmes because services do not cater for their needs (Chrysanthou, 1993). There may be as many similarities as differences in the aetiology of both substance use and offending for both females and males, and the intervention strategies described in this chapter are as relevant for young women as for young men. Young women may, however, have special needs

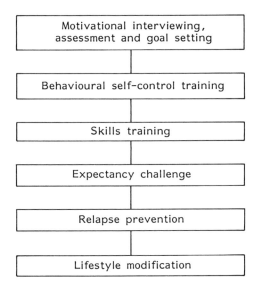

Figure 11.2   Modular programme (after McMurran & Hollin, 1993)

which should be addressed. Working with mixed-sex groups may not benefit the women in that their needs can be subordinated to those of the men (Mistry, 1993). People with learning disabilities may benefit from learning highly specific strategies. One intervention with adult learning disabled offenders used a video of a putative client to whom the offenders gave advice on how to reduce drinking, showing that this method enhanced the learning of self-control strategies (McMurran & Lismore, 1993).

EVALUATION STUDIES

It is appropriate to point out that much of the research evidence for the interventions presented in this chapter comes from programmes for problem drinkers, and it has been commented by Mattick and Heather (1993) that there is a 'disappointing lack of attention being paid to drug classes other than alcohol' (p. 424). Much of the literature on interventions for adolescents comes from work with college students. Brenna (1992) has remarked that 'there is a limited literature that adequately describes treatment approaches or outcomes with a juvenile offender client population', although there is evidence that cognitive-behavioural approaches work with adult substance-using offenders. Peters and May (1992), for example, evaluated a six-week programme for adult male and female prisoners, showing that those who completed the programme evidenced better coping strategies in both knowledge and role play tests, and that programme completers reoffended at a lower rate one year post-release compared with programme drop-outs.

Various cognitive-behavioural approaches have been used effectively in reducing delinquency generally (Andrews, 1995; Hollin, 1990) although there is evidence to suggest that substance use is not changed in general programmes. Braukmann and colleagues (1985) studied male juvenile offenders in two types of group home: those homes operating a teaching-family approach, which includes motivation, skills training, and relationship development, and other homes using counselling. Young people in the former produced a greater reduction in substance use and a greater increase in prosocial behaviours during the programme, but the only sustained effect at one-year follow-up was an increase in prosocial behaviour. The authors conclude that there is a need for specific drug and alcohol prevention and treatment components in delinquency treatment programmes.

Interventions with substance-using young offenders are often evaluated using indirect measures of change of both substance use and delinquency. Day, Maddicks and McMahon (1993) conducted a brief cognitive-behavioural intervention with imprisoned young male offenders who presented with alcohol-related problems. This intervention included self-monitoring and contingency management skills, along with identifying and challenging maladaptive cognitions. Those completing the programme showed reduced anxiety and depression and increased internality of control. Based on the premise that behavioural and cognitive skills deficits contribute to both substance use and delinquency, Hawkins et al. (1991) conducted a skills training programme with detained young offenders, both male and female. Their programme included consequential thinking, self-control, social networking, problem solving, negotiation, and drug and alcohol refusal skills. Role-play measures of drug and alcohol avoidance, social problem solving, and self-control skills improved post-intervention in comparison with a control group. Indirect clinical measures of change in the target problem are not wholly satisfactory, yet they indicate that intervention may be successful.

Few researchers have measured substance use and delinquency at follow-up. Baldwin et al. (1991) evaluated alcohol education courses for young offenders diverted from the criminal justice system. Those who completed a skills-based course, including self-monitoring, goal-setting, and assertiveness training, showed greater reductions in alcohol consumption and self-reported life problems compared with those in a talk-based course, which comprised non-directive counselling. Both groups showed a reduction in reoffending. Platt, Perry and Metzger (1980) described a programme for imprisoned young male heroin users, which included behavioural groupwork, problem solving skills training, and community reintegration. Those who completed the programme showed lower conviction rates and better adjustment at follow-up, compared with a matched control group. Fewer reported using heroin, although the difference was not statistically significant.

The indications are that cognitive-behavioural interventions aimed at reducing substance use and crime show promise, but more work is needed in developing and evaluating interventions with young offenders.

CONCLUSION

Substance use and delinquency are issues of considerable public concern. Interventions aimed at managing risk in those already involved in these problem behaviours should be designed and implemented according to those principles which are known to be associated with effective outcomes (McMurran, 1995). Currently, there is enthusiasm for the 'war on drugs', yet problems associated with alcohol use should not be forgotten. Alcohol use and related problems are undoubtedly more prevalent. Clearly, intervention programmes require adequate resources if they are to be conducted to high quality standards. Prevention programmes should not, however, be neglected. Societal changes towards providing young people with opportunities for prosocial involvement, including family support, adequate education, and the prospect of employment, remain a priority.

ACKNOWLEDGEMENT

Thanks are due to Professor David Farrington for his advice on the preparation of this chapter.

REFERENCES

Allen, J. P., & Litten, R. Z. (1993). Psychometric and laboratory measures to assist in the treatment of alcoholism. *Clinical Psychology Review*, **13**, 223–39.

American Psychiatric Association. (1994). *Diagnostic and Statistical Manual of Mental Disorders (Fourth Edition)*. Washington DC: American Psychiatric Association.

Andrews, D. A. (1995). The psychology of criminal conduct and effective treatment. In J. McGuire (ed.). *What Works: Reducing Reoffending*. Chichester: Wiley.

Andrews, D. A., Zinger, I., Hoge, R. D., Bonta, J., Gendreau, P. & Cullen, F. T. (1990). Does correctional treatment work? A clinically relevant and psychologically informed meta-analysis. *Criminology*, **28**, 369–404.

Baldwin, S., Heather, N., Lawson, A., Robertson, I., Mooney, J. & Braggins, F. (1991). Comparison of effectiveness: Behavioural and talk-based courses for court-referred young offenders. *Behavioural Psychotherapy*, **19**, 157–72.

Beck, A. T., Wright, F. D., Newman, C. F. & Liese, B. S. (1993). *Cognitive Therapy of Substance Abuse*. New York: Guilford Press.

Bien, T. H., Miller, W. R. & Tonigan, J. S. (1993). Brief interventions for alcohol problems: A review. *Addiction*, **88**, 315–36.

Braukmann, C. J., Bedlington, M. M., Belden, B. D., Braukmann, P. D., Husted, J. J., Ramp, K. K. & Wolf, M. M. (1985). Effects of community-based group-home treatment programs on male juvenile offenders' use and abuse of drugs and alcohol. *American Journal of Drug and Alcohol Abuse*, **11**, 249–78.

Brenna, D. (1992). Substance abuse services in juvenile justice: The Washington experience. In C. G. Leukefeld & F. M. Tims (eds), *Drug Abuse Treatment in Prisons and Jails*. Rockville, MD: US Department of Public Health and Human Services: NIDA Monograph 118.

Brook, J. S., Whiteman, M., Gordon, A. S. & Cohen, P. (1989). Changes in drug involvement: A longitudinal study of childhood and adolescent determinants. *Psychological Reports*, **65**, 707–26.

Chaney, E. F., O'Leary, M. R. & Marlatt, G. A. (1978). Skill training with alcoholics. *Journal of Consulting and Clinical Psychology*, **46**, 1092–104.

Chrysanthou, M. (1993). The curious case of the missing ethnic minority drinkers (unpublished report). Manchester: Central Manchester Health Promotion.

Day, A., Maddicks, R. & McMahon, D. (1993). Brief psychotherapy in two-plus-one sessions with a young offender population. *Behavioural and Cognitive Psychotherapy*, **21**, 357–69.

Dembo, R., Williams, L., Getreu, A., Genung, L., Schmeidler, J., Berry, E., Wish, E. D. & La Voie, L. (1991). A longitudinal study of the relationships among marijuana/hashish use, cocaine use and delinquency in a cohort of high risk youths. *Journal of Drug Issues*, **21**, 271–312.

Donovan, D. M. & Marlatt, G. A. (1988). *Assessment of Addictive Behaviors*. London: Hutchinson.

D'Zurilla, T. J. & Goldfried, M. R. (1971). Problem solving and behavior modification. *Journal of Abnormal Psychology*, **78**, 107–26.

D'Zurilla, T.J. & Nezu, A. (1982). Social problem solving in adults. *Advances in Cognitive-Behavioral Research and Therapy*, Vol. 1. New York: Academic Press.

Elliott, D. S., Huizinga, D. & Ageton, S. S. (1985). *Explaining Delinquency and Drug Use*. Newbury Park, CA: Sage.

Farabee, D., Nelson, R. & Spence, R. (1993). Psychosocial profiles of criminal justice- and noncriminal justice-referred substance abusers in treatment. *Criminal Justice and Behavior*, **20**, 336–46.

Farrell, A. D. (1993). Risk factors for drug use in urban adolescents: A three-wave longitudinal study. *Journal of Drug Issues*, **23**, 443–62.

Farrington, D. P. (1994). The nature and origins of delinquency. Paper presented at the Second European Conference of the Association for Child Psychology and Psychiatry, Winchester, UK, September 1994.

Farrington, D. P. & Hawkins, J. D. (1991). Predicting participation, early onset, and later persistence in officially recorded offending. *Criminal Behaviour and Mental Health*, **1**, 1–33.

Goddard, E. (1992). Young people's drinking. In D. Cameron and M. A. Plant (eds), *Alcohol and Young People: Learning to Cope*. London: The Portman Group.

Grant, B. F., Harford, T. C. & Grigson, M. B. (1988). Stability of alcohol consumption among youth: A national longitudinal survey. *Journal of Studies on Alcohol*, **49**, 253–60.

Gresswell, M. & Hollin, C. R. (1992). Towards a new methodology for making sense of case material: An illustrative case involving attempted multiple murder. *Criminal Behaviour and Mental Health*, **2**, 329–41.

Hallam, R. (1992). *Counselling for Anxiety Problems*. London: Sage.

Hawkins, J. D., Catalano, R. F. & Miller, J. Y. (1992). Risk and protective factors for alcohol and other drug problems in adolescence and early adulthood: Implications for substance abuse prevention. *Psychological Bulletin*, **112**, 64–105.

Hawkins, J. D., Jenson, J. M., Catalano, R. F. & Wells, E. A. (1991). *Research on Social Work Practice*, **1**, 107–21.

Hollin, C. R. (1990). *Cognitive-Behavioural Interventions with Young Offenders*. New York: Pergamon Press.

Hopkins, R. H., Mauss, A. L., Kearney, K. A. & Weissheit, R. A. (1988). Comprehensive evaluation of a model alcohol education curriculum. *Journal of Studies on Alcohol*, **49**, 38–50.

Izzo, R. L. & Ross, R. R. (1990). Meta-analysis of rehabilitation programs for juvenile delinquents. *Criminal Justice and Behavior*, **17**, 134–42.

Jessor, R. (1992). Risk behavior in adolescence: A psychosocial framework for understanding and action. *Developmental Review*, **12**, 374–90

Jessor, R. & Jessor, S. L. (1977). *Problem Behavior and Psychosocial Development: A Longitudinal Study of Youth*. New York: Academic Press.

Johnson, V. & Pandina, R. J. (1993). Affectivity, family drinking history, and the development of problem drinking: A longitudinal analysis. *Journal of Applied Social Psychology*, **23**, 2055–73.

Kandel, D. B. (1985). On processes of peer influence in adolescent: drug use: A developmental perspective. *Advances in Alcohol and Substance Use*, **4**, 139–63.

Kandel, D. B. & Raveis, V. H. (1989). Cessation of illicit drug use in young adulthood. *Archives of General Psychiatry*, **46**, 109–16.

Kinder, B. N., Pape, N. E. & Walfish, S. (1980). Drug and alcohol eclucation programs: A review of outcome studies. *International Journal of the Addictions*, **15**, 1035–54.

Klinteberg, B. A., Andersson, T., Magnusson, D. & Stattin, H. (1993). Hyperactive behavior in childhood as related to subsequent alcohol problems and violent offending: A longitudinal study of male subjects. *Personality and Individual Differences*, **15**, 381–8.

Lang, A. R. & Sibrel, P. A. (1989). Psychological perspectives on alcohol consumption and interpersonal aggression. *Criminal Justice and Behavior*, **16**, 299–324.

Le Blanc, M. (1994). Family, school, delinquency, and criminality: The predictive power of an elaborated social control theory for males. *Criminal Behaviour and Mental Health*, **4**, 101–17.

Lerner, J. V. & Vicary, J. R. (1984). Difficult temperament and drug use: Analyses from the New York longitudinal study. *Journal of Drug Education*, **14**, 1–8.

Lipsey, M. W. (1992). Juvenile delinquency treatment: A meta-analytic inquiry into the variability of effects. In T. D. Cook, H. Cooper, D. S. Cordray, H. Hartman, L. V. Hedges, R. J. Light, T. A. Louis & F. Mosteller (eds), *Meta-Analysis for Explanation: A Casebook*. New York: Russell Sage Foundation.

Loeber, R. (1988). Natural histories of conduct problems, delinquency, and associated substance use. In B. B. Lahey & A. E. Kazdin (eds), *Advances in Clinical Child Psychology*, Vol. 11. New York: Plenum Press.

Loeber, R. (1990). Development and risk factors of juvenile antisocial behavior and delinquency. *Clinical Psychology Review*, **10**, 1–41.

Loeber, R., Stouthamer-Loeber, M. & Green, S. M. (1991). Age at onset of problem behaviour in boys, and later disruptive and delinquent behaviours. *Criminal Behaviour and Mental Health*, **1**, 229–46.

Mahoney, M. J. & Thoresen, C. E. (1974). *Self-Control: Power to the Person*. Monterey, CA: Brookes/Cole.

Marlatt, G. A. & Gordon, J. R. (eds). (1985). *Relapse Prevention*. New York: The Guilford Press.

Marsh, A., Dobbs, J. & White, A. (1986). *Adolescent Drinking*. London: HMSO.

Mattick, R. P. & Heather, N. (1993). Developments in cognitive and behavioural approaches to substance misuse. *Current Opinion in Psychiatry*, **6**, 424–9.

Maughan, B. (1993). Childhood precursors of aggressive offending in personality disordered adults. In S. Hodgins (ed.), *Mental Disorder and Crime*. Newbury Park, CA: Sage.

McBride, D. C. (1981). Drugs and violence. In J. A. Inciardi (ed.), *The Drugs–Crime Connection*. Beverly Hills, CA: Sage.

McDougall, C., Barnett, R. M., Ashurst, B. & Willis, B. (1987). Anger control. In B. McGurk, D. Thornton & M. Williams (eds), *Applying Psychology to Imprisonment*. London: HMSO.

McDougall, C. & Boddis, S. (1991). Discrimination between anger and aggression. In M. McMurran & C. McDougall (eds), *Proceedings of the First DCLP Annual Conference*, Issues in Criminological and Legal Psychology, No. 17. Leicester: The British Psychological Society.

McMurran, M. (1995). Alcohol interventions in prisons: Towards guiding principles for effective intervention. *Psychology, Crime and Law*, **1**, 215–226.

McMurran, M. (1994). *The Psychology of Addiction*. London: Taylor and Francis.

McMurran, M. (1991). Young offenders and alcohol-related crime: What interventions will address the issues? *Journal of Adolescence*, **14**, 245–53.

McMurran, M. & Bellfield, H. (1993). Sex-related alcohol expectancies in rapists. *Criminal Behaviour and Mental Health*, **3**, 76–84.

McMurran, M. & Hollin, C. R. (1993). *Young Offenders and Alcohol: A Practitioner's Guidebook*. Chichester: Wiley.

McMurran, M. & Lismore, K. (1993). Using video-tapes in alcohol interventions for people with learning disabilities. *Mental Handicap*, **21**, 29–31.

McMurran, M. & Thomas, G. (1991). An intervention for alcohol-related offending. *Senior Nurse*, **11**, 33–6.

McMurran, M. & Whitman, J. (1990). Strategies of self-control in young offenders who have controlled their alcohol consumption without formal intervention. *Journal of Adolescence*, **13**, 115–28.

Midanik, L. T., Klatsky, A. L. & Armstrong, M. A. (1990). Changes in drinking behavior: Demographic, psychosocial, and biomedical factors. *International Journal of the Addictions*, **25**, 599–619.

Miller, W. R. (1978). Behavioral treatment of problem drinkers: A comparative outcome study of three controlled drinking therapies. *Journal of Consulting and Clinical Psychology*, **46**, 74–86.

Miller, W. R. & Baca, L. M. (1983). Two-year follow-up of bibliotherapy and therapist directed controlled drinking training for problem drinkers. *Behavior Therapy*, **14**, 441–8.

Miller, W. R. & Rollnick, S. (1991). *Motivational Interviewing: Preparing People to Change*. Addictive Behaviors. New York: The Guilford Press.

Miller, W. R. & Taylor, C. A. (1980). Relative effectiveness of bibliotherapy, individual, and group self-control training in the treatment of problem drinkers. *Addictive Behaviors*, **5**, 13–24.

Mistry, T. (1393). Establishing a feminist model of groupwork in the Probation Service. In A. Brown & B. Caddick (eds), *Groupwork with Offenders*. London: Whiting and Birch.

Monahan, J. (1993). Limiting exposure to Tarasoff liability: Guidelines for risk containment. *American Psychologist*, **48**, 242–50.

Mulvey, E. P., Arthur, M. W. & Reppucci, N. D. (1993). The prevention and treatment of juvenile delinquency: A review of the research. *Clinical Psychology Review*, **13**, 133–67.

Murdoch, D., Pihl, R. O. & Ross, D. (1990). Alcohol and crimes of violence: Present issues. *International Journal of the Addictions*, **25**, 1065–81.

Novaco, R. W. (1975). *Anger Control*. Lexington, MA: Lexington Books.

Oetting, E. R. (1992). Planning programmes for prevention of deviant behaviour: A psychosocial model. In J. Trimble, C. Bolek & S. Miemncryk (eds), *Ethnic and Multicultural Drug Abuse*. Binghamton, NY: Harrington Park Press.

Pandina, R. J., Johnson, V. & Labouvie, E. W. (1991). Affectivity: A central mechanism in the development of drug dependence. In M. Glantz & R. Pickens (eds), *Vulnerability to Drug Use*. Washington, DC: American Psychological Association.

Pelham, W. E. & Lang, A. R. (1993). Parental alcohol consumption and deviant child behavior: Laboratory studies of reciprocal effects. *Clinical Psychology Review*, **13**, 763–84.

Peters, R. H. & May, R. (1992). Drug treatment services in jails. In C. G. Leukefeld & F. M. Tims (eds), *Drug Abuse Treatment in Prisons and Jails*. Rockville, MD: US Department of Health and Human Services: NIDA Research Monograph 118.

Platt, J. J., Perry, G. M. & Metzger, D. S. (1980). The evaluation of a heroin addiction treatment program within a correctional environment. In R. R. Ross & P. Gendreau (eds), *Effective Correctional Treatment*. Toronto: Butterworths.

Prochaska, J. O., DiClemente, C. C. & Norcross, J. C. (1992). In search of how people change: Applications to addictive behaviors. *American Psychologist*, **47**, 1102–14.

Rhodes, J. E. & Jason, L. A. (1988). *Preventing Substance Abuse Among Children and Adolescents*. New York: Pergamon Press.

Rohsenow, D. J., Niaura, R. S., Childress, A. R., Abrams, D. B. & Monti, P. M. (1991). Cue reactivity in addictive behaviors: Theoretical and treatment implications. *International Journal of the Addictions*, **25**, 957–93.

Ross, R. R., Fabiano, E. A. & Ross, R. D. (1986). *Reasoning and Rehabilitation*. Ottawa: University of Ottawa.

Sher, K. J. & Trull, T. J. (1994). Personality and disinhibitory psychopathology: Alcoholism and antisocial personality disorder. *Journal of Abnormal Psychology*, **103**, 92–102.

Sisson, R. W. & Azrin, N. H. (1989). The community reinforcement approach. In R. K. Hester & W. R. Miller (eds), *Handbook of Alcoholism Treatment Approaches*. New York: Pergamon Press.

Stouthamer-Loeber, M., Loeber, R., Farrington, D. P., Zhang, Q. van Kammen, W. & Maguin, E. (1993). The double edge of protective and risk factors for delinquency: Interrelations and developmental patterns. *Development and Psychopathology*, **5**, 683–701.

Swadi, H. (1988). Drug and substance use among 3333 London adolescents. *British Journal of Addiction*, **83**, 935–42.

Swadi, H. & Zeitlin, H. (1988). Peer influence and adolescent substance abuse: A promising side? *British Journal of Addiction*, **83**, 153–7.

Temple, M. & Ladouceur, P. (1986). The alcohol–crime relationship as an age-specific phenomenon: A longitudinal study. *Contemporary Drug Problems*, **13**, 89–115.

Thompson, K. M. (1989). Effects of alcohol use on adolescents' relationships with peers and self-esteem: Patterns over time. *Adolescence*, **24**, 837–49.

Tolan, P. H. (1988). Delinquent behaviours and male adolescent development: A preliminary study. *Journal of Youth and Adolescence*, **17**, 413–26.

Wheeler, J. & Carlson, C. L. (1994). The social functioning of children with ADD with hyperactivity and ADD without hyperactivity: A comparison of their peer relations and social deficits. *Journal of Emotional and Behavioral Disorders*, **2**, 2–12.

Wilens, T. E. & Biederman, J. (1993). Psychopathology in preadolescent children at high risk for substance abuse: A review of the literature. *Harvard Review of Psychiatry*, **1**, 207–18.

Young, R. McD. & Oei, T. P. S. (1993). Grape expectations: The role of alcohol expectancies in the understanding and treatment of problem drinking. *International Journal of Psychology*, **28**, 337–64.

Concluding Comments

CLIVE R. HOLLIN
School of Psychology, The University of Birmingham, UK

KEVIN HOWELLS
Department of Psychology, Edith Cowan University, Australia

The force of this book, we believe, is to reinforce the message that there is clear evidence that when practitioners get it right, they can be highly effective in lowering rates of offending and, in the process, prevent victimization and save public money. Further, with the allocation of sufficient resources, even more could be achieved. It would be naïve, however, to assume that the argument in favour of a clinical approach to working with offenders is won. It must be acknowledged that there will always be critics, but the case for working with young offenders is becoming increasingly strong on grounds of both empirical support and questions of effectiveness.

However, the force of this position is perhaps secondary to the debate on the basic philosophy for criminal justice policy that is currently beginning to take shape. As we write, there is an ideological struggle taking place around the issue of the best policy for managing juvenile crime. There are signs emerging from official *communiqués* that effectiveness in preventing offending is waning in value as a touchstone by which to judge the effectiveness of the criminal justice system. The position appears increasingly to be taken that the criminal justice system should be a vehicle for retribution, so that society can see that offenders are made to suffer for their transgressions. This move is most clearly seen in the 'get tough' rhetoric, which talks about opening boot camps for young offenders with no other aim than to make them suffer for their crimes. This rhetoric even goes as far as, in the news today, a public figure calling for the televised flogging of offenders.

In the face of these developments it seems likely that there will be new battles to be fought, battles in which the traditional weapons of outcome data and

---

Clinical Approaches to Working with Young Offenders. Edited by C. R. Hollin and K. Howells.
© 1996 John Wiley & Sons Ltd.

effectiveness may be outmoded. Alongside the defence and development of a clinical approach to working with offenders, it may be time for Volume 5 to start discussing the philosophy of punishment and associated moral issues.

Author Index

Subject Index

Indexes compiled by Liz Granger.

Related titles of interest from Wiley...

Working with Offenders
Psychological Practice in Offender Rehabilitation
Edited by **Clive R. Hollin**

Leading experts in their fields give an introduction to the theory and practice of criminological and legal psychology and discuss ways of assessing and treating the varying types of offender.

0-471-95776-3   288pp   December 1995   Hardback
0-471-95349-0   288pp   December 1995   Paperback

What Works: Reducing Re-Offending
Guidelines from Research and Practice
Edited by **James McGuire**

Offers a critical review of research and practice with the focus on identifying interventions and models of offender treatment that really do work and are practical, and ways of evaluating treatment and offender services.

0-471-95053-X   264pp   1995   Hardback
0-471-95686-4   264pp   1995   Paperback

Handbook of Psychology in Legal Contexts
Edited by **Ray H.C. Bull** and **David Carson**

Highlights and emphasises both the extent to which psychologists are already assisting and informing the legal system and the potential that exists for collaboration between lawyers and psychologists.

0-471-94182-4   694pp   1995   Hardback

Young Offenders and Alcohol-Related Crime
A Practitioner's Guidebook
Mary McMurran and **Clive R. Hollin**

"The book definitely lives up to its claim to be a "Practitioner's Guidebook"... it contains some of the clearest, most user-friendly accounts of cognitive and behaviour theory and of motivational interviewing that I have come across..."   *- Probation Journal*

0-471-93839-4   208pp   1993   Paperback